Praise for *The Healthy Workplace Nudge*

"*The Healthy Workplace Nudge* is not your standard wellness-for-business book. In fact, Rex Miller directly challenges most of the ways companies deliver wellness programs to their employees. His team of researchers addresses why we need wellness programs in the first place: a lack of care.

"More than that, this book provides new pathways and practical approaches. Most importantly, it calls for a new kind of leadership. A leadership of care."

—**Bob Chapman**, CEO, Barry-Wehmiller; coauthor, *Everybody Matters: The Extraordinary Power of Caring for Your People Like Family*

"Workplaces are killing people, costing economies and business fortunes in the process, and no one seems to care—or believes that anything can change. *The Healthy Workplace Nudge* shows what it would take to enhance employee well-being and provides compelling examples of the change that is possible."

—**Jeffrey Pfeffer**, author, *Dying for a Paycheck*; professor, Stanford Graduate School of Business

"The 'wellness' industry is complex, siloed, and confusing. Miller has engaged a group of top health professionals, researchers, wellness program specialists, building designers, and forward-thinking business leaders to chronicle the current state of the wellness industry and carefully lay out some frightening challenges ahead. This book will help leaders to step back and focus on what is most important and impactful when it comes to the health, engagement, and performance of their employees. Spoiler alert: Culture eats wellness for breakfast."

—**Leigh Stringer**, workplace strategy expert; author, *The Healthy Workplace: How to Improve the Well-Being of Your Employees—and Boost Your Company's Bottom Line*

"Creating environments that allow people to be their best selves every day is not just a nice to have; it's a business imperative. While everyone agrees philosophically that healthy, happy employees are tantamount to innovative and successful business, rapid change in the wellness industry demands a clearer definition of the hows and whys of employee health. This book masterfully cuts through the noise to shed light on to what works and what doesn't. Rex has truly helped carve the way to the future of the workplace."

—**Ryan Picarella**, president, Wellness Council of America, WELCOA

"Combining the world's largest asset class (Real Estate) with the world's fastest-growing industry (Health and Wellness) represents the most significant economic and societal opportunity of our time. It's not someone else's responsibility or even opportunity. This is about all of us breaking our industry silos of real estate, HR, healthcare and financial performance. Rex Miller's team and their research describe not only the full potential but the threat to business and our economy, if we don't take advantage of this historic tipping point."

—**Paul Scialla**, founder/CEO, Delos; founder, International WELL Building Institute

"Rex has done a wonderful job blending employee welfare results with the heart. He provides the data to confirm that companies that focus on the 'people model' have an impact on their related health investments. The heart is the center of all goodness, emotionally and financially!"

—**Tom Carmazzi**, CEO, Tuthill

"In our hearts, we know that we should genuinely care for all people, everywhere. At home, on the street, and at work, we should care for others and be cared for. However, our minds have been fooled to believe that profit is king, at the expense of care. In *The Healthy Workplace Nudge*, Rex Miller connects what we know in our hearts to be true with concrete methodologies that will transform our minds regarding wellness in the workplace."

—**Wade Lewis**, VP, Business Services, ISS

"It is not only possible for organizations to be communities of human flourishing, but this is also the natural state when people exert themselves in a common, meaningful purpose. If this sounds overly idealistic, it is indicative of the pressing need to win the battle for well-being. But it requires leaders who understand and embrace that, like all living things, humans desire to flourish. For such leaders, *The Healthy Workplace Nudge* will be a clarion call to lead the humanizing of our workplaces."

—**Steven E. Carter**, PhD, author, *Good Leader*; president/CEO, Carter, Inc.

"I've always believed that the number one responsibility for a business leader is to create an environment in which people can excel—but that requires creating an environment that aligns the body, soul, spirit, and mind. Most corporate efforts have focused on improving the physical environment of work, but Rex's book "nudges" us to address the spiritual and mental elements of well-being by creating a culture of care that recognizes that energy, not time, is our most valuable asset."

—**Barbara Jackson**, director, Burns School of Real Estate and Construction Management, University of Denver

"Rex takes a chainsaw to the oft-marketed idea that wellness is achieved by implementing health testing, free gym memberships, and, oh yes, fewer snacks in the lunchroom. In its place, he presents the far more powerful concept of health and happiness, and then proceeds to weave inspirational stories of success."

—**Craig Janssen**, managing director, Idibri

"Memorable characters, humane CEOs, caring physicians, and a cast of other fascinating characters have inspired Rex Miller to tell one of the best argued, entertaining, and factually solid stories about the connective tissue between the wellness movement and the built environment. *The Healthy Workplace Nudge* will inspire you. It inspired me!"

—**Susan S. Szenasy**, director of design innovation, Metropolis

THE
HEALTHY
WORKPLACE
NUDGE

THE
HEALTHY WORKPLACE NUDGE

HOW HEALTHY PEOPLE, CULTURE, AND BUILDINGS LEAD TO HIGH PERFORMANCE

REX MILLER

PHILLIP WILLIAMS, AND

DR. MICHAEL O'NEILL

WILEY

Library of Congress Cataloging-in-Publication Data:

Names: Miller, M. Rex, 1955- author. | Williams, Phillip, 1957- author. | O'Neill, Michael, 1959- author.
Title: The healthy workplace nudge : how healthy people, culture and buildings lead to high performance / Rex Miller, Phillip Williams, Michael O'Neill.
Description: Hoboken : Wiley, 2018. | Includes bibliographical references and index. |
Identifiers: LCCN 2018006249 (print) | LCCN 2018008038 (ebook) | ISBN 9781119480235 (pdf) | ISBN 9781119480167 (epub) | ISBN 9781119480129 (hardback) | ISBN 9781119480235 (ePDF)
Subjects: LCSH: Work environment. | Employee health promotion. | Corporate culture. | BISAC: BUSINESS & ECONOMICS / General. | BUSINESS & ECONOMICS / Human Resources & Personnel Management. | BODY, MIND & SPIRIT / Inspiration & Personal Growth.
Classification: LCC HD7261 (ebook) | LCC HD7261 .M544 2018 (print) | DDC 658.3/82–dc23
LC record available at https://lccn.loc.gov/2018006249

Printed in the United States of America

10 9 8 7 6 5 4 3 2 1

Inspired by and in memory of my mom, Lisa's mom, and my brother Britt.
In gratitude to my lifelong mentors Charles Simpson and Clifford Christians.
—Rex Miller

For all of us who have worked in, and work to create, places for people,
young and old, rich and poor . . . ipsum attollere (raise your game).
—Phil Williams

To my wife and best friend Danelle O'Neill, whose interest in the health
and well-being of others, inspired my contribution to this book.
—Mike O'Neill

CONTENTS

FOREWORD

It has become clear that work is the number one cause of stress; that stress is a big driver of chronic disease, and that the rise of chronic disease and associated costs are a direct threat to the survival of businesses. This book hammers this point. Businesses have no more room to fight with insurance companies or shift costs to employees. We must begin to reduce stress, and health-related costs, by creating cultures of care. This book will show you how.

The Healthy Workplace Nudge is not your standard wellness-for-business book. In fact, Rex Miller directly challenges most of the ways companies deliver wellness programs to their employees. His team of researchers addresses why we need wellness programs in the first place: a lack of care.

The Healthy Workplace Nudge also explains the limitations of ROI thinking when it comes to employee health. The book describes a model of people in harmony with profit. It begins with the lives entrusted to us. With them, we create lasting value. Together. We don't chase ROI when it comes to wellness. I tell our frontline leaders, "Let's do the right thing; it's our job to make it work for the business." The marriage of profits and people makes us a better and more competitive company.

When we visited with Rex, we saw that his research confirmed our view of business: creating a workplace where people feel safe, giving them genuine appreciation, and providing well-trained supervisors all come together to produce happy people and a thriving organization.

This book confirms that we as leaders can and must rehumanize why and how we deliver wellness. As you read it, make it personal. Think about the people who work around you, especially the ones in your span of care. Where do they come from? What are their hopes? Do they go home at the end of the day energized and inspired by their time at work?

Is work fulfilling? Or do they return home drained and stressed by their time with us? *The Healthy Workplace Nudge* takes a serious look at why so many wellness efforts fail to improve the lives of employees.

More than that, this book provides new pathways and practical approaches. Most importantly, it calls for a new kind of leadership. A leadership of care.

—Bob Chapman,
CEO, Barry-Wehmiller;
coauthor, *Everybody Matters:
The Extraordinary Power of Caring
for Your People Like Family*

ACKNOWLEDGMENTS

For some, writing is a solitary affair. This book was a barn raising. I found myself in constant communication with about 30 of our inner circle. I needed their expertise and help to validate stories and details, poke holes in my reasoning, and to give an oft-needed kick-start. I traveled several times just to sit with some of my guides. Meeting face-to-face was so much better than connecting by phone or Skype. In many cases, I only wanted them to tell their story one more time, like my kids wanted to hear their favorite stories just before bedtime. I already knew the details; I knew the punchlines. I wanted a way to give those words the life and resonance I felt sitting with them. For some reason, the atmosphere, breathing room, and friendship provided that boost I needed.

It took a while to find a voice for this book. It was a chorus of about 100 contributors. Every chapter is an ensemble on its own. Together they turned into a harmonized four-act symphony. It is our most serious work to date, but it also touches the emotions more than any previous projects. Health and well-being quickly turned from research into something very personal for all of us. We began as a collection of the curious and became a cohort of the committed.

Richard Narramore, Wiley's senior editor, led the previous three projects and helped guide us to our unifying theme. He has continuously challenged my thinking, asking, "What book do you want to write? You have three here." This project was no different. My editor, Ed Chinn, and I created an "Editing Floor" section. The strategy was simple: let's frame it up and start writing. Then we can step back and see what book this really is. That strategy asked more from Ed than in past books. His fine-tuned editing eye often found hidden treasure, but also kept an eye out for that common thread. We left another full book on the editing floor. For various reasons – space, style, coherence, consistency – several interviews and companies had to be removed. Seeing them excised was very difficult.

The idea for this project was first birthed at the CBRE headquarters. Lew Horne hosted the session; it was the first time I met Paul Scialla. It was clear there that we were touching a new, vital, and compelling story. We had to dig deeper. Shortly after that meeting, Haworth, Delos, DPR, and The Carter Group enthusiastically came together and said they would fund the effort to explore a new frontier. I am profoundly grateful for their faith and support to launch this mission.

I want to thank Phil Williams and Dr. Mike O'Neill for their willingness to coauthor this book. They both served as guides, interpreters, and scouts. I relied on their expertise and their encouragement. I also enjoyed the many trips that allowed us to piece this story together.

I'd like to especially thank Haworth and Mabel Casey. Without their support 10 years ago we would have never had the opportunity to test the idea that leaders could come together, without permission, and solve common complex challenges. It seems to be working. On a practical note, Michelle Kleyla with Haworth provided the ear of reason and common sense. I have come to call her my handler.

I had several guides and protectors along this journey. Paul Scialla treated me like a nephew and understudy. He opened doors and pulled me back from rabbit trails. I met Leigh Stringer through her book, *The Healthy Workplace*. It was my first compass into the wilds of wellness. She was also generous with support and introduced me to Mem Senft, who joined early. She was skeptical and had good reason. We had no bona fide wellness experts on our team until we found Mem; she brought others along. She became our guide, conscience, and incredible door opener. Kate Lister and Scott Muldavin were our truth-with-numbers squad. I met and talked with both several times to make sure I was doing the math.

Patrick Donnelly and Drew Suszko were my two closest summit collaborators. They gave time and BHDP's resources to help me better choreograph many of the exercises. Our events became incredible learning and creative labs.

I leaned on other past MindShift graduates, like Bob Fox and Craig Janssen, who challenged my direction for different summits, but also filtered what we produced through their lens as business owners. Randy Thompson, with Cushman Wakefield, generously read and critiqued our first draft.

Part of what makes our experiences so essential is the ability to spend time onsite with some of the most advanced thinkers on the topic. They host and participate. Haworth held our inaugural summit in Chicago. Janelle Weber and PQM brought us into an incredible dining experience and conversation around the issue of hospitality.

Barbara Spurrier and Dana Pillai hosted our immersion into health and well-being at the Mayo Clinic and the WELL Living Lab. Google has been a partner on a few of our projects. Josh Glynn and his work services (REWS) team hosted us in San Francisco and brought Bill Duane to share their new research on well-being. DPR opened their San Francisco offices, providing an ideal environment for our project-based learning. They also gave us behind-the-scenes access to their unique open culture. One of my favorite locations was Denver's Four Winds Interactive. They provide embedded interactive displays that feel a bit like those futuristic touch displays in the movie *Minority Report*. This summit provided a window into the future of building sensors, personal wellness technology, and interactive media. Rich Blakeman gave us access to their facility. It was an incredible playground to explore the technology of wellness. Our final summit was hosted by Calvin Crowder and Wade Lewis at GoDaddy. That was our book's barn raising summit, and our most creative session as we watched two years of work come together in four different book concepts.

I was able to meet directly with many more leaders and fascinating personalities than in previous projects. I owe that to our members inviting us into their relationships and networks. I met five best-selling authors, leaders of some of the most admired companies on the planet, medical experts and academics who opened worlds I never imagined existed. You will meet and read about them in the book.

Because there are so many people to thank, I've created an addendum to list the participants and contributors.

The roles of some were so vital that we could not have completed this project without them. Michael Lagocki has worked with me on the last three MindShift efforts. His role has grown from event facilitator and live scribe to codesigning events and taking on the role of the ears and emotions of the participants or reader. His advice continues to elevate our events and the quality of our work.

I owe the deepest gratitude on this project to Ed Chinn, my editor. He's much more than that. Ed traveled and participated in each of the summits and was, in many ways, an understudy, stepping in and keeping the process on track while I was pulled away to wrestle with life. At times, I felt like Rocky Balboa with my eye swollen shut and gasping for air in the corner. Ed stepped in, like Mickey, and kept saying, "Dig deeper, you can do it, kid." Creators know the magic in movies and books happens in the editing room. That was Ed's study in Spring Hill, Tennessee.

I want to express my love and appreciation to my family, especially Lisa. It was a hard year for our family, and she shouldered most of that. Lisa stayed positive and always encouraging. Lisa is our guardian of health and has become a gifted caretaker. I've come to see that role as a combination of gentle angel and fierce drill sergeant in giving care. And she can be a lawyer when dealing with the health-care world. She attended several of the summits and insisted we practice what we learned along the way. The hardest new rule she gave me was saying goodbye to bacon.

When I look back, this project feels like one of the wilderness high adventure treks I've taken with my oldest son. They all start with naïve optimism. That disappears with the reality that most of this trip is a three-mile-an hour trudge with a 50-pound pack on my shoulders. It doesn't matter how beautiful the world is around me, I'm still carrying this pack. Every trip gives incredible high points, but most of the time it's one foot in front of the other and finding creative ways to make that feel fun. The finish, however, is hard to describe. Deep satisfaction and a desire for a shower, a steak, something. When I sent my last chapter to Ed for editing, I ran some chores. I was in that happy relief state. The Kwik Lube attendant told me it would take a while to get my car serviced. I was bored with the outdated magazines in the waiting area, and my phone was on 2% battery life when I saw McDonald's next door. "I haven't had a cheeseburger and fries in years. I wonder . . . ." So, after a few feeble attempts to talk myself out of it, I succumbed to temptation and walked over. I was "Homered." You'll learn about that in Chapter 9. I ordered a cheeseburger and small fries. They were good, no lie.

When I returned home, I shared the story with Lisa. All she could say is, "What?" Then she laughed. "Darling, you've been cooped up way too long." So, I guess the moral is, wellness is a journey. The good news, I've taken our lessons seriously, and today I am measurably healthier than I was a year ago and the year before that. I wish the same for you. I hope you embrace wellness as a journey and keep your sense of humor in the process.

ABOUT THE AUTHORS

Rex Miller is a five-time Wiley author. *The Commercial Real Estate Revolution* and *Change Your Space, Change Your Culture* won international awards for innovation and excellence. He is a respected futurist, frequent keynote speaker, and an elite leadership coach. His MindShift process applies a unique crowdsourced approach to tackling complex leadership challenges. Mr. Miller was named a Texas A&M Professional Fellow for his work in leading edge leadership processes.

The MindShift model invites diverse participants into a creative and collaborative process. This makes each book deeply researched, easy to read, and practical to apply.

The previous book, *Humanizing the Education Machine*, collaborated with over 100 leaders and experts to break the vicious cycle of reform efforts without change and shows communities, schools, and leaders how to lead transformation on a local basis.

More than half of MindShift's work is guiding organizations through change and improving project, team, and organizational culture. Recent clients include Google, Disney, Microsoft, GoDaddy, Intel, FAA, Delos, Haworth, Turner Construction, Balfour Beatty Construction, DPR Construction, Seattle Children's Hospital, MD Anderson Hospital, Universal Health Systems, Oregon Health Science University, University of Illinois, Texas A&M, University of Denver, and many others.

Mr. Miller is also a USPTA certified tennis professional, a member of the National Speaker's Association, and actively mentors young leaders. He believes leaders come from anywhere in an organization or community and hopes his work helps empower hidden leaders to step up and step forward to create positive change.

Phillip Williams is the president of Commercial Business Development at Delos and directs the business development of health and well-being services and solutions for the commercial real estate market sector. Delos is a real estate technology and research company focused on helping to create healthier, higher-performance places for people.

He has spent his career in the commercial design, engineering, and construction industry and prior to Delos served as a vice president with Webcor Builders, where he initiated and lead the Systems Engineering, Sustainability, and International Consulting groups. Prior to Webcor he held senior leadership and management positions with Southland Industries and Carrier/United Technologies Corporation.

Phil has a BS in engineering, and his research and industry affiliations have allowed him to stay at the forefront of leading ideas that have consistently been focused on people in the built environment.

As the industry chair for the Center for the Built Environment (CBE) through the University of California, Berkeley, and a founding executive board member for Eco-Districts (a nonprofit focused on the economy, ecology, and equity of development and redevelopment of urban centers), he has been able to help transition theoretical research for the commercial private and public markets for scalable adoption.

Through service on the Joint Steering Committee for the Well Living Laboratory (WLL) a Mayo Clinic research collaborative, his industry experience has contributed to the understanding and inclusion of health science for the benefit of people through the improved design, construction, and operations of buildings and communities.

Phil is a founding member of the Industry Technical Advisory Group for Lawrence Berkeley National Laboratory FLEXLAB. He is a representative from San Francisco to the United Nations Global Compact and served as the chairman of the San Francisco Mayor's Task Force on Private Sector Green Buildings. He is a member on technical advisory boards for several Silicon Valley emerging technology companies, venture capital, and research organizations.

Dr. Michael O'Neill is currently director of the Global Workplace Research, Workplace Strategy and Market Insights teams for Haworth, Inc. At the start of his career, he worked at BOSTI, a firm that pioneered the use of analytics to show how workspace design affects employee performance. Later, he was a professor of interior design and industrial engineering at the University of Wisconsin.

Mike has a BA in cognitive psychology, and MA and PhD in architecture and human behavior. For his doctoral work, he developed software that models peoples' decision making during way-finding tasks within buildings, based on the biological properties of neural networks. He has authored over 50 articles, two books on workplace research and design, is a coauthor of an upcoming book on well-being (2018 release).

Mike developed HumanSpace^{TM}, software that estimates the impact of workspace design on the financial value of human capital and identifies the most important features. He believes that predictive analytics "made easy" can help organizations make better decisions about how they allocate investment in their office space – based on improving the economic value of their people. He is also on the advisory board of TableAir, a European tech startup (space sensors and user experience software).

Other areas of interests include cars and planes. Mike is a Porsche Club of America national driving instructor and holds a competition racing license through Midwest Council of Sports Car Clubs, racing a vintage Porsche 911. He also holds a Private Pilot license.

INTRODUCTION: THE ELEPHANT WHISPERER

In his book, *The Righteous Mind* [1] Jonathan Haidt suggests that we are all like a rider on an elephant. The rider is our conscious mind. It is intelligent, rational, and intentional; it thinks, decides, and acts.

But, here's the problem: We lumber along, atop an enormous beast of culture, subconscious desires, assumptions, genetic predispositions, and complex webs of fears, biases, and subjective experiences and feelings. The elephant is going to go where the elephant is going to go. Our conscious mind can choose and announce all it wants, but the elephant is larger.

The Healthy Workplace Nudge tells the story of good intentions, rationality, and high levels of intelligence, all riding an impenetrable, unresponsive, and resistant leviathan. That brute has been around a very long time and is not threatened by anything the rider could imagine.

Ten years ago, I and some associates created an approach to solving unresponsive and resistant dilemmas, known as "wicked problems." They're not wicked in a moral implication, but in the sense that they cannot be solved, only navigated. But first, we had to change conversations that were stuck. We called that process MindShift. And a MindShift has to first become an elephant whisperer.

To whisper to the elephant is to build certain triggers, chutes, and ramps into the elephant's thinking. For example, Richard Thaler, the 2017 Nobel Prize winner in economics, has captured the behavioral economics idea of "nudge." A nudge is a subtle design in buildings, policies, strategy, marketing, food choices and sizes, and other nuances in society that make the good choices easier. A nudge also flips the narrative; for example, from "Quit killing yourself" to "Start living younger." Reframing the narrative is the fresh start nudge. For our purposes, a nudge is anything that makes it easy for the elephant to pick a better path.

You will meet several intelligent riders, lumbering elephants, and nudges in the pages to follow.

This journey started several years ago when I saw the powerful and transforming result of an office working together to explore what wellness and well-being meant to them. CBRE is the largest real estate company on planet Earth. Their Los Angeles office, rebuilding after the Great Recession, worked with wellness and design professionals to translate their vision into a new kind of workplace. That resulted in the first corporate space to bring medical and building science together. It revolutionized their business and their own people. Furthermore, it attracted thousands of curious leaders and professionals to come, see, and learn.

I was one of those who made the pilgrimage. And I came away fascinated. But, to some degree, touring that space was like watching a well-staged magic trick. The workspace was impressive, but something of an illusion. The real magic came from the unseen journey the leader and his people took to create that space. The outcomes weren't predicted (or even likely). So, I asked them what I've asked others with comparably enchanted workplaces:

"How did you pull it off?"
"How did you survive the politics and pushback?"
"Why did you think you could do it?"
"What stories describe how you lost your naïveté?"
"Where did it almost fly off the tracks?
"How did it turn around?"
"How did it change you and your people?"

In most cases, their answers did not present a scripted list of lessons learned, but rather a chronicle of the journey's insights.

The process as a journey is the key to taming the elephant. Each organization raises and rides a different one. Unlike what is described in many business books, we found patterns not formulas. Simply plucking the lessons from an expert rider and applying them to your elephant typically fails.[2]

Elephants are also social animals. The same thing is true for great projects and work. The environments we create to facilitate work become proxies for how well we work and live together. CBRE did not direct their employees to swallow something new. They engaged their people and their culture and created a highly social process that resulted in the by-product, a magical environment.

They had to let go of previous assumptions about how they once accomplished work, what a "normal" office might look like, design, and wellness. They had to wake up in a new world every morning, literally making it up as they traveled. To do that required them to whisper new directions to the elephant. Trust me – that is a gut-wrenching, exhausting, stressful, and humbling process. But it produces something of immense value.

They created something new, a place that truly embodied health and well-being by introducing medical science into design. You've heard the old adage that the process of making a great sum of money is more valuable than the money itself. In that sense, CBRE's process was worth far more than what the eye could see. The process of creating their new home provided the context to learn a new way to work together. I went back several times, trying to understand what was in the process to produce such transforming power.

Figure I.1 The elephant is going to behave as it wishes.

But, before I figured it out, I fell under the same spell. I concluded that they had simply found a way to do wellness better. And that naïve assumption is where our work really started. We started by believing the wellness elephant was not only large, but wise, sensitive, and caring. In time, we began to realize we fell into an illusion. So, we had to dig down through the strata of illusion to the bedrock of reality.

In the lost craft of barn raising, not only was the barn built much faster, but the deepened intimacy, trust, reciprocity, sense of purpose, satisfaction, celebration, and learning also made priceless contributions to the community. Our collective journeys to wellness carry the same potential of barn raising. The barn didn't cause the performance boost; it was a catalyst for what happened.

The Heathy Workplace Nudge explores the journey of, and relationship between, the rider and the elephant.

The Things We See and the Things We Miss

The Healthy Workplace Nudge describes our search to explain how some companies have created healthy, happy, and resilient organizations, while most have not. This book examines why there are so many emphases and promotions for wellness and well-being, with so little to show for it.

Leaders of industry and business clearly must, and many do, understand they face the constant threat of disruptive innovation. Despite knowing that, too many fail to see or respond to the warning signs. Kodak knew about digital photography. They invented it. Before Amazon created ubiquitous distribution, Sears stores and catalogs covered the land. Whole Foods was king of the organic food world; now it is just part the Amazon universe. Many saw the truth; many missed it.

Our brains are designed to come to clear and rational conclusions. But only in hindsight. If we knew *then* what we know *now*, Kodak, Sears, and Whole Foods would still be giants. And the 2008 crash wouldn't have happened, and I would still have my 401(k) intact and be able to retire. Inside each collapse is a beguiling narrative (the elephant) to ignore contradictory evidence (the rider). And it usually works: the best and the brightest minds in the financial industry closed their eyes and simply rode the lumbering beasts off the path to destruction.

Chronic disease is a massive and growing bull elephant, and the wellness industry and corporate leaders have been unable to slow it down. The ride, however, is taking us all down the same destructive path. If we don't slow this beast down, we will reach the end of the road, a sheer cliff, by 2025. The collective effort to slow and reverse its path will require the kind of creative and courageous leadership we saw after the Great Depression, in the rebuilding of Europe after World War II, and landing men on the moon.

Because American companies employ more than 160 million people, they have the largest platform and greatest leverage for accomplishing this mission. We will introduce you to leaders who understand that. Furthermore, they recognize the positive ripple effect that happy, productive, and healthy employees carry back home and to their soccer coaching, book clubs, community groups, places of worship, and families each day.

I make this promise: If you take your office and colleagues toward health and well-being, it will transform your life, your work, your relationships, and your work space. *The Healthy Workplace Nudge* explains why taking this journey is urgent.

Promises, Promises

The promises we have heard from "reputable sources" for decades have, until now, cancelled out the warnings from critics and prophets. After all, this small choir is comprised of nut jobs, screwballs, and iconoclasts. Banished voices. However, they know and won't let anyone forget that the $3.7 trillion wellness industrial complex made convincing promises:

- To reduce health costs by improving health
- To attract and retain employees
- To improve engagement
- To return $3 for every $1 invested in wellness

Those promises turned out to be the loud ranting of riders bouncing along dusty roads on top of the elephant. They meant nothing. In fact, health costs keep rising at an average of 7% per year.[3] And we have no evidence that wellness efforts improve employee attraction and retention. Workplace engagement has remained under 30% since Gallup first started conducting its Global Engagement Survey.[4] And, if wellness generated a

300% return on investment, companies would be looking for ways to increase the investment, not ways to cut it.[5]

Our Well MindShift project, including more than 100 industry experts and business leaders, concluded that wellness efforts, as they are today, cannot deliver any of its promises.

But we did find hope for the future of the workplace and the country. You will find that hope detailed in vivid stories from all across the country. In most cases, these are not "brilliant" leaders running complex sophisticated programs. Rather, you will meet serious, down-to-earth, tenacious, and healthy leaders who are easy to talk to and continually curious, courageous, and caring. The question is, if it is that simple, why isn't everyone doing it? That is what our MindShift team worked hardest to understand. I think the answers will drive you to devour, underline, highlight, and dog-ear the pages. Regardless if you're in charge, in a support role, or stuck in an organization that doesn't get it, you will pause several times and think, "If they can do it, we can too!".

The View from the Ridge

Several years ago, my older son and I joined a 10-person expedition backpacking through a 140,000-acre preserve in New Mexico's Sangre de Cristo Mountains. We hiked 110 miles in 10 days, including eight mountain ascents.

Our expedition required eight months of preparation. We learned how to pack light, how to set up camp in the dark, meticulously clean our campsite, and protect our food from bears. And then, after three days with our guide, we were suddenly on our own. We suffered a few injuries and weathered a lightning storm on a mountain ridge. We saw bears and rattlesnakes, but we also saw pure mountain streams and breathtaking sunsets. We tripped, stumbled, bled, and cursed like sailors in front of our sons. But we also discovered the quiet and sublime joy of sitting around an evening fire, just listening to the lazy pops of the crackling fire. It took me three days to unplug from my digital dependence and frantic pace; I finally slipped into a new rhythm and found deep joy in our grand adventure.

We spent our last night atop the preserve's most recognizable landmark, Tooth of Time. The 500-foot granite monolith tops the

9,000-foot peak providing a panoramic view of the 140,000 acres. From that vantage point, we could see the great sweep of our trail. From that magnificent overlook, as we "mountain men" relived the expedition, the trail took on a new dimension. We connected the dots we missed when we were down there. We saw the seamlessness of that gorgeous habitat as we had not seen it before.

As I listened to the boys touching the bonds of their shared experiences and stories, I felt wistful that the journey would end tomorrow. We sat on the ridge at sunset and watched the valley slowly darken. Some of the boys slept on the ridge in order to be awakened by the sunrise. Tracing the 10 days and seeing the finish several miles below generated the energy for a final push. Our descent took several hours hiking along the switchbacks, but eventually, we arrived at the finish line. I just wanted to cross the line and get to the camp for a shower. But one of the boys was thinking like a leader: "Hey, let's cross this together at the same time." He captured the magic our journey produced. We started as a collection of naïve and dissimilar individuals; we finished as a closely bonded and seasoned team.

When we finally arrived into camp, we saw the next wave of crews coming in. Our boys eagerly told the "newbies" of the mountain sights, thrills, and challenges to come. They had the right: they earned the patch.

Our MindShift group has now come down from our patrol in search of wellness. I think we earned the patch. Like the trek with my son, this exploration of new territory took us to unimagined discoveries (about the territory, but perhaps more about ourselves). We are forever changed.

This section is a practical guide to the book. Let it give you a lay of the land and whisper some guidance for what you will see, hear, taste, touch, and smell. Just as I could not have made the mountain trek alone, I couldn't have completed this project alone. We have crossed over into uncharted territory for business, our society, and our personal lives. One big lesson to take from this book is the *journey itself* is the point: it's the solution far more than the artifacts we discovered along the way. You will find no manuals, recipes, formulas, or best practices in these pages. That's because finding health and happiness are highly human endeavors. Just follow the maps and listen to the guides ahead.

Figure I.2 A nudge encourages the elephant to pick a better path.

Part I, Slow-Moving Storm: A History of Warnings and Apathy

This section reveals that business is in the direct path of a slow-moving, deadly storm. This is an emergency warning for leaders to take immediate action. The looming health crisis and its destruction of business and the economy is a probable but still avoidable forecast. This section also highlights the storm shelters being built by some very forward-thinking leaders and companies. By doing so, they have retooled their cultures and developed readiness for future uncertainty.

America is now entering a catastrophic collision with a slow-moving storm of health-care costs. If the current "storm tracking" is accurate, within the next decade those costs will devour our GDP and double federal income taxes. Alzheimer's spending will hit over $1 trillion by 2050. The same pattern is true of Type 2 diabetes. According to the

Cleveland Clinic's Dr. Michael Roizen, by 2025 we will hit that point which is "undoable."[6]

At that point, the storm will produce profound societal disruption.

And, tragically, this has been one of the most predictable crises in history.

Part II, Is There Shelter from the Storm? A Search for Wellness

These chapters present the critical need for shelters from the storm. But, it first examines what wholeness looks like. In the process, we expose the flawed foundations and the false hopes of too many wellness efforts. We also strip away the false promises, expose the self-interest of the wellness industrial complex, and rehumanize the conversation. You will see that the search for wellness is both a very personal issue and a very personal journey.

Let me be more specific.

Our search for the truth took us to many wellness events. But we only heard stories about the pot of health at the end of the rainbow. As I wandered the corridors and green rooms of the events, I saw that the experts and speakers had far more clarity and certainty on stage than one-on-one facing tough questions. They exhibited no curiosity in considering the issues I raised or in the data that contradicted their story. They were just defensive. Someone had to have some answers!

Then I met a small cadre of other voices. And I learned that a dark pub provided a more conducive atmosphere for straight talk. I heard a voice just over my right shoulder: "Look at the numbers," he whispered. Then another voice spoke into my left ear: "Follow the money."

When I did as they instructed, our presence in this world quickly became a threat. What had we stepped into? Why did we provoke such strong reaction?

Those questions launched the next phase in our journey of discovery.

Part III, Magical Nudges: The Road to Health and Well-Being

This section provides alternatives to ineffective wellness programs. According to experts like Dr. Roizen, Dr. Goetzel, and Soeren Matkke,

that includes about 95% of wellness programs. This section also takes a
new look at human nature; it explains why our best efforts to instruct,
inspire, push, bribe, threaten, poke, or bully turn out to be expensive,
frustrating, and ultimately ineffective. That's because people are not
rational beings.

We thought they were; they're not.

Traditional corporate wellness programs have usually assumed if
employees only had information about healthy choices and received

Figure I.3   There's a better way to achieving wellness.

an incentive discount on their health insurance premium, that would be enough to persuade them to change. That hasn't worked and won't. Remember? Humans are not rational decision makers.

And that is why *nudges* (from behavioral economics) have become such an emergent force. They can influence policy, programs, work design, workplace strategy, purchasing decisions, physical environments, social network effects, etc. A nudge is often all it takes to make a good choice easier and a bad choice difficult.

Finally, they benefit *everyone* who steps into the building. Since we spend 90% of our lives inside built environments, it makes sense to, in Paul Scialla's words, "use real estate as a healthcare intervention tool to deliver preventative medical intentions to building occupants."[7]

This section takes a highly pragmatic approach. Based on our interviews and other research, we start with nudge thinking, how to change behavior by changing the environment. The second rung, and highest ROI, provides a healthy building. The third level reduces the friction, the stress, in the workplace. The fourth rung ties budgets and outcomes together. David Radcliffe, vice president of real estate and workplace services at Google, asked one our summits, "Are we squeezing pennies in our facilities but losing dollars of engagement?" We finish this section with a personal nudge toward becoming your best self.

Part IV, Haven in a Heartless World: The Need for Safe Places

People have always needed safe places. For most of human history, that place was called "family." By the middle of the twentieth century, that safe zone began to crack up. Author, historian, and social critic Christopher Lasch noted the erosion of the family in his 1977 book, *Haven in a Heartless World: The Family Besieged*. Lasch didn't miss a detail of the collapse; deteriorating schools, crime, drugs, greater sexual freedom, divorce, television, the economic pressures that drove both parents into full-time jobs, the migration of production away from the family, and other stress factors.

As meager and inadequate as it was, corporate America's creation and expansion of wellness programs demonstrated a need to help build safe places for one another.

Even the emergence of the wellness-industrial complex validates the societal reach for safe havens. That same reach motivates the voices that challenge the complex. Regardless of the vast disparities in what we see, we all give cohesive witness to the need for a human touch in all our relationships, institutions, policies, technologies, and habits.

Part IV describes how companies are creating safe havens through healthy cultures and engaged leadership. It provides a leadership roadmap for first chair and second chair leaders. It reinforces the promise and potential of creating workplaces that are human-centered enterprises in harmony with performance and profits.

This section reveals the new havens in a heartless world, the companies that surpassed simple concern about health-care costs and saw the historical opportunity to do the right thing. They built better

Figure I.4 Happy elephants make for a harmonious workforce.

environments, reduced stress, and properly handled those who show up every day in their factories, plants, farms, offices, and social service institutions. Several of these leaders see an even larger picture than a vital and engaged workforce. They see the domino effect of sending happy employees home who feel safe, appreciated, strengthened, and cared for. The reader will meet leaders and organizations that have successfully built cultures of care.

Finally, this section will help you, the reader, understand how to do that within your own sphere of influence.

You too can become an elephant whisperer.

PART I

Slow-Moving Storm: A History of Warnings and Apathy

CHAPTER 1

A Slow-Moving Storm

The Existential Threat to Business and the Economy

> *Sound managerial decisions are at the very root of their impending fall from industry leadership.*
> —Clayton Christensen, *The Innovator's Dilemma*

In the beginning, I thought our team came together to write a book. But, in fact, we were like those once described in a Cormac McCarthy novel: "They grouped in the road at the top of a rise and looked back. The storm front towered above them and the wind was cool on their sweating faces. They slumped bleary-eyed in their saddles and looked at one another. Shrouded in the black thunderheads the distant lightning glowed mutely like welding seen through foundry smoke."[1]

Like that band of cowboys, our troupe stopped in the road when we saw the distant storm. We knew what it meant; our original purpose and destination no longer mattered. I saw the first flashes of lightning and heard the faraway muffled thunder when I met Dr. Michael Roizen at the Cleveland Clinic. Although it was distant, I could tell the storm carried deadly ferocity. For the first time in my life, I saw a true existential crisis. Before I give you a peek into that slow-moving storm, let me explain why and how we came to write this book.

A writer friend of mine was once embedded with a gaggle of reporters for a seven-day papal visit to a Middle Eastern country. In his first experience of being one of "the boys on the bus," my friend's biggest surprise was what seemed like a total absence of press curiosity. He told me, "I expected to meet people who assumed nothing and probed everything. Surely, they would listen and ask questions thoughtfully and carefully. Instead, I saw journalists ignoring the subject of their coverage. They conducted loud cell phone calls, talked, ate, spilled drinks, swore, and stepped on people to get better positions, often as the pope was speaking!"

Let me assure you, that does not describe our approach. Curiosity drives MindShift.

We distrust the scripts and official announcements. We prefer to excavate the who, what, when, where, why, and how without the help of the authorities and their jackhammers. We agree with Steve Jobs: "It's more fun to be a pirate than to join the Navy."[2]

That approach took us through three books; you hold the fourth. Our battle plan gathers 50 to 100 dissimilar, knowledgeable, strong, and gifted thought leaders. Then we move around the United States together, visiting innovative and sometimes radical outliers. We call those gatherings "summits," but they're more like scavenger hunts. We grab relics, stories, honest research, and other artifacts and rush back to the cave for further analysis. Then we do it all over again a few weeks later.

We lead with our weakness.

Inexperience is our strongest asset. Because we know nothing, we *have to be curious.* So, we wear camo, distract the gatekeepers, build illusions, slip cash to the night security people, "borrow" reports, and hang out with insiders as well as outsiders. Think of us as the guys in *Oceans 11.* We embrace audacious goals, build daring plans, have a grand time, and knock over the Bellagio. Or something like that.

In the beginning, we called this project "Wellness." That word meant something then; it means something totally different now. At its core, this book is really about a set of problems: the systems, ideas, habits, and walls that prevent people from attaining what they do best and enjoy most in America's workplaces.

Others saw that problem long before we did. Since they carried credentials and presented official authorizations at the guard shacks, they entered America's offices and factories and built an industry around their solutions. They issued lots of scripts, press releases, programs, and marketing plans. The problem was, their bold brilliance made the problem worse.

Then we arrived with nothing. Except curiosity and another great (my second and final) quote from Steve Jobs:

> *When you first start off trying to solve a problem, the first solutions you come up with are very complex, and most people stop there. But if you keep going, and live with the problem and peel more layers of the onion off, you can often times arrive at some very elegant and simple solutions.*[3]

That's where our story began.

Looking back, my unfamiliarity with workplace wellness was a benefit. Because I was a novice about the subject, I had to get educated quickly. That meant digging deep. So, I immersed myself in the relevant areas of architecture, design, medicine, psychology, human resources, and health. It seemed like I read every book, watched every video, scoured every website, and interviewed every authority within the various realms of applicable knowledge.

> *My unfamiliarity with workplace wellness was a benefit. Because I was a novice about the subject, I had to get educated quickly.*

I knew that Delos had started new collaborations, connecting building science with medical science, with the Cleveland Clinic and the Mayo Clinic. So, I thought a few conversations on the medical side of the wellness topic would help connect some dots and clarify how buildings influence the mind and body. I reached out to Paul Scialla, founder and chief executive officer of Delos. And he built a bridge to Dr. Michael Roizen, chief wellness officer for the Cleveland Clinic.

Dr. Roizen, the first chief wellness officer for any medical institution, holds numerous patents, has written several best-selling books, appeared multiple times on *Oprah* and is a partner, colleague, and co-columnist with Dr. Mehmet Oz. Roizen is a very young 71. In fact, his "RealAge"[4] score is 51.2 years old. His dark hair, impeccable dress, and commanding voice help him to fill any room. He moves and talks quickly, drawing from his encyclopedic knowledge in conversation, interviews, and

Figure 1.1   Meeting Dr. Roizen.

speeches. He doesn't stand before audiences; he prowls like a cat. Roizen
is the pragmatic fanatic of wellness.

He and the Cleveland Clinic have many critics. That is true of every
outlier we met. They attract sharpshooters from the ridges. But our
MindShift approach likes projects that provoke critics. We like them for
the same reason that musicians create tension with chord progressions
that feel incomplete or chords that clash. That dynamic stimulates
interest, engagement, and a sense of motion.

When I first entered Dr. Roizen's office, he was walking on a
treadmill, talking on his cell phone, and shuffling papers on his standing
desk. He waved me to a chair at a table piled with reports. My quick
glance around the office took in stacks of paper, boxes of reports, awards,
photos, and books. His corner office gave a sweeping view of the grounds
of the Cleveland Clinic's Wellness Institute.

The interview started with his brief history of the deadly perils
encountered on the road to career prosperity and convenience. It seemed
that he too was once a cowboy, stopped dead in the road by a gathering
storm.

Figure 1.2   Dr. Michael Roizen, chief wellness officer for the Cleveland Clinic.

"We know exactly when this rise of chronic disease started, 1983. We (adults) ate 2,340 calories, plus or minus 60 calories, per day from 1858 to 1983. Then we started increasing 2% per year. We reached 400 extra calories per person per day by 2000. The problem now is compounded by a concurrent drop in physical activity. Fifty percent of Americans—woman, man, employed, unemployed, Hispanic, Asian, whatever—do less than 10 minutes of physical activity any day of the week. The average 65-year-old person is five-foot-seven and weighs 33 pounds more than the same average 65-year-old did in 1991. Our norms are screwed up. Obesity is now a norm.

> *We ate 2,300 calories, plus or minus 60 calories, per day from 1858 to 1983. Then we started increasing 2% per year. We reached 400 extra calories per person per day by 2000.*

If you look at Kaiser's data, individual out-of-pocket expenses have increased threefold and employer expenses have also increased. In the

*last 20 years, we looked at what medical costs did to productivity gains.
Every dollar, every penny of productivity gains since 1994 has been used up
by medical costs.*

Dr. Roizen's data should be chilling to every business leader. It means
that, as medical costs have eaten away profitability, businesses have been
forced to run faster to simply stay even. That reality drains dollars away
from development and innovation and quietly shifts management's focus.
The $18,000,[5] on average, companies pay per employee in 2018 for
health coverage will, by 2023, increase to $25,245 per employee! And
that is to cover a nonproductive cost. That is over $25 million for a
company of 1,000 employees. At that point, companies must resort to
draconian cost cutting just to cover lost ground.

Storm Details: The Mother of Wake-Up Calls

Dr. Roizen was, for me, the mother of all wake-up calls. That's because
he so clearly sees and explains the most epic burning platform of all time.
Until that meeting, I had never seen a true threat to the very existence of
a business or our nation. We've all become numb to frequent hurricanes
or droughts "of the century" and other catastrophic crises: climate
change, terrorism, the Middle East, North Korea, Russia, etc. But, in
our first three-hour meeting, Dr. Roizen clearly explained what the
slow-moving storm of chronic disease was doing—and will continue to
do—to people, companies, and nations. Three hours, one message with
multiple supports and visual aids. Stories, graphs, charts, videos, and
report after report. Listening to Dr. Roizen was like drinking from an
open fire hydrant.

He made a compelling presentation—no, that's not correct; he
scared the hell out of me with his description of federal spending on
health care. If the current rate keeps up, by 2050 almost 40% of GDP
will be required to cover our health costs, *plus* doubling federal income
taxes to pay for the government's portion of health costs. A 2000
RAND report projected that chronic illness would grow to reach 50%
of the population by 2025.[6] We soared past that metric in 2012.[7]

To get a sense of the power of Dr. Roizen's three-hour presentation
to me, please watch his message to the 2017 Global Wellness Summit.[8]
He gave them the short version of what he gave me.

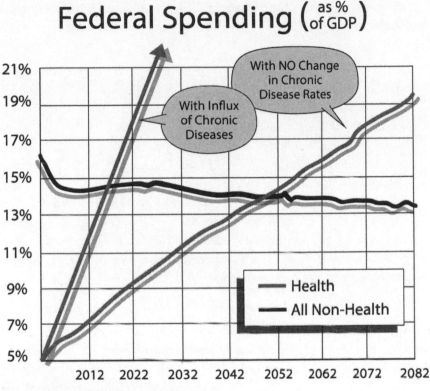

Figure 1.3   Influx of chronic disease.

The one-on-one presentation he gave me blew me back in my chair; a knot began growing in my stomach. I could not wrap my head around his doomsday scenario. Before I could ask the "Yes, but . . ." question, the fire hydrant opened again.

"That's actually not the real data," he continued. "It only takes into account the normal aging of the population. Notice it doesn't include any influx of chronic disease. When you add the rise of chronic disease, it means between 2023 and 2025 we will hit that point which is undoable. We will have to bend the curve with a worldwide effort on the scale of a Marshall Plan!"[9] The chart represented in Figure 1.3 was adapted from the slide deck he used at the Global Wellness summit.

He was clearly suggesting profound societal convulsions, the kind of economic instability never seen on a large scale in the United States.

> *. . . between 2023 and 2025 we will hit that point which is undoable. We will have to bend the curve with a worldwide effort on the scale of a Marshall Plan!*

He explained that chronic disease drives the logic for such a massive mobilization:

Look; hip and knee arthroplasty; 67,000 in 1974. We recently surpassed a million, and the prediction is going up sixfold with only a 30% increase in the population. Alzheimer's spending goes from $216 billion to a little over $1 trillion in today's dollars by 2050. Let's go back to the first curve I showed you and look deeper at the numbers for Type 2 diabetes. There were 2.2 million patients in 1974 when I started to practice. In 2015, it reached 30 million. You can see it will continue to rise more than 50% to close to 55 million people over the next 15 years. Our genes haven't changed. Our lifestyles have. Chronic disease causes 84% of all health costs; 67% occurs in the working population. *We used to say that 50% of medical costs come in last year of life. It isn't that way anymore because we're spending so much to get to the last years of life.*[10]

Finally, Dr. Roizen explained why business leaders must become their own chief wellness officers; they cannot relegate oversight of this to HR departments alone. Companies have a unique opportunity to reverse this trend because of the millions of people they directly touch daily and then indirectly touch when employees return home. However, using wellness programs to combat chronic disease doesn't work alone. He boiled it down to one mission on pursuit: "Our job is to develop healthy employees who bring energy to work. That's the only way the corporation can survive."

> *Our job is to develop healthy employees who bring energy to work. That's the only way the corporation can survive.*

When he finished (only because I had to catch a flight), my lens on the world was permanently altered. I felt like the kid in the movie *Sixth Sense,* seeing realities that remained invisible to others. Although I don't "see dead people," I do see them (as individuals, families, employees, whole workforces, and communities) on a conveyor belt passing through predictable medical crises and then moving into the inevitable jaws of death.

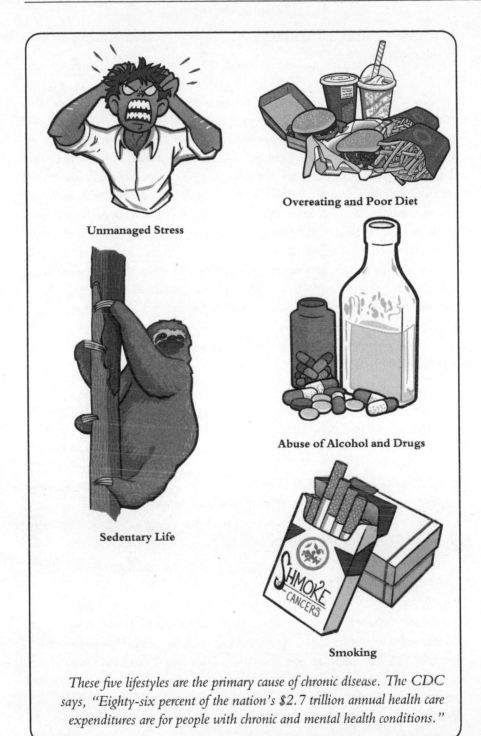

Unmanaged Stress

Overeating and Poor Diet

Abuse of Alcohol and Drugs

Sedentary Life

Smoking

These five lifestyles are the primary cause of chronic disease. The CDC says, "Eighty-six percent of the nation's $2.7 trillion annual health care expenditures are for people with chronic and mental health conditions."

Our Personal Python

Mark Benden, department head and director of the Ergonomics Center at Texas A&M, is on a mission to get you and me up out of our comfortable chairs and *move*. He understands another effect of the coming storm.

Mark told me that the average office worker can sit for 13 to 15 hours a day. Even going to the gym for 30 minutes a day won't offset the damage that prolonged sitting or inactivity imposes on our endocrine, immune, cardiovascular, and digestive systems. Simply standing up activates those systems and helps to rebalance blood sugar levels and triglycerides. At a bare minimum, we should sit no more than 50 minutes at a time before taking a 10-minute walking break.

One of Mark's studies found obese elementary students experienced greater fluctuations in blood sugar when seated. But standing desks helped them, and those with ADHD, to pay greater attention and perform at the same academic level as the rest of the class.

Employers face an immediate challenge with the Millennials in the workforce and Digital Natives entering the workforce. Mark explains:

You and I were 150 pounds when we graduated from college. We were in good shape, and good to go. After a few healthy (and low-cost) decades, our employers may have to deal with some of our health problems in our 60s.

But, with many college graduates today already coping with obesity, their companies will be hit with the employee health problems much earlier. They will have to deal with employees in their 40s facing 25 years of seriously declining health and rapidly increasing cost. If you come out of college at 220 pounds and throw another 40 pounds by retirement, 260 pounds is a whole different dimension.

Mark talked about medicine now reaching a point where we measure quality of life years (QALY). Like a Kelley Blue Book valuation for life, you look at the age and then discount it based on miles and damage. 1 QALY is equivalent to a year of perfect health. It is an economic tool to help compare the cost of medical intervention with the remaining years the intervention is projected to add. In light of

Figure 1.4   Sitting is killing us.

Dr. Roizen's doomsday scenario, we are surely headed for inevitable and severe health rationing. And, as chilling as it sounds, our economic survival will make life-and-death decisions, and make them quickly and efficiently.

Just Five Things

I asked Dr. Roizen, "Is there hope?"

Figure 1.5   Poor health choices become our personal pythons.

"The data are pretty clear. We need to achieve what I call five normals (these have recently been expanded to 6+2 and will be explained in Chapter 13). They include blood pressure less than 140 over 90, LDL cholesterol levels under 100, a waist less than half your height, blood sugar under 100, and zero nicotine! In the 28-year Nurse's Health Study, in the Swedish Men Study, and in the Medicare studies, just five things would reduce chronic disease by 80% and 90%: reduce toxins (drugs and alcohol), manage stress, increase physical activity, improve food choices and portion size, and improve sleep. But, only 2.7% of Americans do even four of the five!"

We're sleeping with a python.

Most people believe that pythons kill their prey by crushing them to death. They don't. They constrict their victims so that when the prey exhales to catch its next desperate breath, the python silently squeezes all the remaining space out of the lungs. Each breath pulls in less and less oxygen. It is slow, efficient, and terrifying suffocation. Pythons feel the heartbeat of their victims. When it stops, they know it's dinner time.

. . . five things would reduce chronic disease by 80% and 90%. Reduce toxins (drugs and alcohol), manage stress, increase physical activity, improve food choices and portion size, and improve sleep.

That same constricting process also applies to people, businesses, and nations. A Kaiser Family Foundation chart shows that National Health Expenditures have doubled every decade since 1960, more than double the rate of inflation. We cuddled up with this killer, not realizing it is in deadly sync with all our contractions in national productivity, innovation, and growth.[11]

In the 1970s, Dr. Roizen's economics professor projected health care costs would increase from 7% of GDP to 12% by the year 2000. And that additional cost burden would drive manufacturing out of the country. The United States hit that 12% a full decade earlier.

When productivity gains are continually nullified and health costs rise faster than profits, we will know, as surely as a gazelle being suffocated by a python knows, the full details of an unrelenting and lethal crisis.

So, what can we do in the face of that crisis? Think of the gathering storm as a hurricane. We live in its path. Will we buy sheets of plywood to board up the windows of the neighborhood houses? Will we join the brigade of volunteers filling bags of sand for the river banks? Or will we, as some always do, dance the night away out on the pier? Can we take the quick and sure steps necessary for survival, or are we doomed to be destroyed by that monster?

We believe we have time and the tools to avoid disaster. And we hope others will join us in that conviction and that quest. The remaining chapters of this book will give you the stories, tools, models, and vision that could galvanize a corporate and national response to this very real and epic collision.

Leadership Nudge

If your health costs double by 2025 how will that impact profits, growth, or employees?

Personal Nudge

Go to the ShareCare site and take the Real Age Assessment. Compare your chronological age to your biological age. Find out how you can live younger. https://www.sharecare.com/static/realage

CHAPTER 2

The Rainbow in the Storm

Medical Science Meets Building Science

I think the key question is, how do we construct movements that are integral to the purpose and mission of the company, but that require a lot more participants than just the people within the company itself?

—John Hagel

Lew Horne saw the end coming. Soon after commercial real estate hit its peak in the summer of 2007, rising defaults signaled that a major bubble would soon burst. Nearly 16 months before Lehman Brothers collapsed and world economies spiraled into chaos, Lew's company, CBRE, the largest real estate company in the world, was already gripped by its own journey into the abyss. By January 2008, their stock had dropped 50%. When the carnage ended in February 2009, 92% of its value had been erased.

By 2010, CBRE showed signs of sustainable growth. But the world in which they operated had changed profoundly. Life would never be the same again. One lesson was clear to Lew: the old business model, the "art of the deal" that made brokers so independent and wealthy in the past, would no longer work in the new world of highly interconnected, volatile markets. Lew could see that CBRE needed a new business model, one that would leverage the collective wisdom confined within the company's silos.

Above all, he knew that the market "correction" was not simply a storm that CBRE weathered, but a sea change. It required a total rethinking of the industry. That rethinking would also require a new CBRE. CBRE's reinvention would require dismantling the traditional broker-centered culture and replacing it with a team-based, egalitarian workplace. That meant they needed new office space. Lew and his workplace strategy team knew they had to get the new space right. The seriousness of their quest took them as far as Amsterdam to study new workplace designs.

They knew that instead of a traditional pecking-order office layout, all private offices would be eliminated. In fact, the new space would contain no assigned workspaces. They saw it as a totally open, "free-range" environment. Lew faced a steep uphill battle, starting with his boss who was resistant. Not because he didn't believe it was necessary, but because he feared the exodus of star brokers and an office uprising over the changes. Lew's green light came with warnings. They all knew they were dealing with the kind of decision that makes or breaks careers.

Lew thought deeply about the future. CBRE needed a dramatic new strategy to create greater value for clients. He could see the untapped value if he could come up with a way to integrate the different platforms of services they offered. Silos stood in the way, like they do in many companies. However, what made Lew's plan work was that he had a vision for how to create greater value.

But that vision for leveraging the power of teams had to win over a long tradition that rewarded individual stars.

Silos stood in the way, like they do in many companies.

Lew was deeply convinced it was the right thing to do. And he was willing to lead by example by being the first to work without an office. In the end, he won. The new headquarters turned out to be a great success. In the first six months, more than 4,000 clients and prospects toured the space. I was one of them. But I wasn't among the rubber-necked, selfie-shooting tourists. Lew gave me the grand tour. I told that story in our book, *Change Your Space, Change Your Culture.*[1]

. . . a new vision for built environments as places that increase and protect the health of those who occupy them every day.

But, I missed the larger story—a spark that flamed a revolution in buildings. *That* story revealed a new vision for built environments as places that increase and protect the health of those who occupy them every day. I also missed the story's backdrop, the inescapable need for businesses and our economy to mount a national movement toward wholeness. Rehumanizing the workplace had to be the first beachhead for reversing the clear and present threat of runaway health costs.

The Birth of Well Buildings

In 2007–2008, Paul Scialla stood in the eye of the financial meltdown storm. He had recently made partner at Goldman Sachs, along with his twin brother, Peter. But, within that same time frame, the Scialla brothers had also developed a side project, exploring the relationship between buildings and human health and happiness. In 2007, they cofounded Delos, the company to carry that vision.

In 2013, at the age of 39, both left Goldman for full-time commitments to Delos. Delos first focused

Figure 2.1   Paul Scialla.

on improving the conditions in the hospitality industry. MGM Grand Hotels gave them one of their first projects.

At that time, Lew Horne knew nothing about the Scialla brothers. And they had never heard of Lew. But the paths of their lives approached a fortuitous convergence. And it all happened because of the flu season in Los Angeles. In a minuscule-but-momentous event, someone sneezed in CBRE's new open office. Then he or she made a casual comment, "I wonder who will catch my flu?" And that question seemed to float throughout the building.

When the question reached Lew, he caught the significance; he knew the concern and hesitancy about a shared workplace and furniture.

He admitted, "I never thought of that, but immediately wondered how we should address it."

He knew he wanted to find an effective solution that avoided chemicals. CBRE's Onno Zwanefeld knew Paul Scialla and his work with Delos. Onno introduced Paul to Lew.

And that is how Lew and Paul came to work together on translating Delos' hospitality standards for the workplace. The CBRE headquarters became the first corporate workplace to receive the WELL Certification for a commercial office space through the WELL Building Standard™ (WELL) pilot program.[2] Visitors jumped from about 30 people per month (in the old office) to more than 1,000 a month. That pace continued for over a year. People came to

Was that transformation just lightning in a bottle or was it an idea whose time had come?

see more than leading-edge design. CBRE experienced a business and culture transformation with wellness at the core. Was that transformation just lightning in a bottle or was it an idea whose time had come?

The building came as a rainbow in the thunderhead that, although abating, was still darkening the economy.

At that time, I only knew about the astonishing response to CBRE's new workplace. I did not know about Lew and Paul's new venture. But because CBRE kept ordering copies of *Change Your Space, Change Your Culture*, I returned to California to meet with Lew; I wanted to hear about life after the project. He was still excited about it; he said the new space had sparked a radically new kind of conversation that was truly centered on the employee and their happiness and health.

He described the dramatic public and internal interest in the project. He said it had taken them all by surprise and had also become a catalyst for broader business change. Lew knew the topic had a big head of steam with both positive and dangerous potential. Even at that point, in 2014, some people saw wellness as the new bandwagon. And everyone knows that bandwagons are to be jumped on. That mass appeal made it difficult for business leaders who tried to take wellness seriously. Lew did not want to see their success and interest tainted, similar to the way early sustainable building efforts were labeled as "greenwashing."

Then we imagined: "Could we mobilize a group of corporate leaders and experts to look further into this trend and perhaps create some form of clearinghouse for workplace wellness?"

I agreed to spearhead the effort. After reaching out to and for the right people, we found 12 leaders who agreed to take a day to meet and discuss the implications of this interest in well buildings and the larger question of workplace wellness.

In the summer of 2015, I returned to CBRE, accompanied by Paul Scialla and Phil Williams from Delos. Our group included other recognized leaders within the overlapping worlds of design, construction, and wellness including Mabel Casey with Haworth, a longtime supporter for several MindShift projects. CBRE's Lew Horne and Dave Pogue hosted us.[3]

We tried to make sense of the incredible public response to the project and process. We explored how the new design for a healthy workplace changed CBRE's culture: it shifted behaviors, improved morale, and transformed their operations. What was different about that project? Why was there such an enormous response and what does it mean? Because the commercial real estate industry typically operates outside the corporate wellness conversation, we felt the need to learn more. What did wellness and well buildings mean for the future?

The Workplace Enters the Wellness Conversation

We all saw that the CBRE-Delos collaboration was historic. We believe it was the first time that the workplace, as an instrument of wellness, seriously entered the conversation. Workplace wellness was certainly not a new topic. The war against rising medical costs and, of course, the drive to attract and keep talent and improve low employee engagement had been on the minds of corporate leaders for several decades. But those efforts fell primarily into the HR world. With CBRE-Delos, the workplace, for the first time, burst on the scene as the potential game-changing weapon in that war.

Our gathering in LA shed light on another question. The wellness industry had not kept up with the growing size and complexity of the health cost and chronic disease crisis. It was all a confusing mash of programs, vendor business models, short-term strategies—little continuity and a lot of fragmentation. It seemed destined to produce a vicious cycle of fixes that would fail.

With CBRE-Delos, the workplace, for the first time, burst on the scene as the potential game-changing weapon in that war.

Humanizing the Workplace

Following the economic storms of 2007—2009, our group really caught sight of a shimmering rainbow of new possibilities.

The CBRE-Delos work also turned the various issues into a human conversation. We all had to look at wellness through the lens of (1) workplace environment, and (2), employee experience, health, and well-being. That would be a departure from a traditional focus on buildings, operations, costs, and amenities. The separate worlds of real estate and human resources had collided. Could we build a bridge with those in the land of wellness? If so it would dramatically change the calculus in the competition for talent and corporate responsibility.

The potential effect of environment on happiness and health seems intuitive. However, office buildings are seldom designed for humans. Most are viewed as economic units that compete against other buildings. Cost, speed to market, occupancy rates, rents, operations, and cash flow all drive the birth and life of such buildings. The shorthand for that calculus is called a *cap rate*. Few buildings escape that assembly line rationale. Unless a developer can link the cost of iconic design or an enhanced user experience to higher rents, the process reverts to buildings and the people who will work in them becoming mere commodities.

> *The potential effect of environment on happiness and health seems intuitive. However, office buildings are seldom designed for humans.*

In Paul Scialla's eureka moment, he imagined building values based on how they improve the lives of humans. As a Wall Street guy, he was not blind to the economic and market forces that drive commercial real estate. He saw buildings that improve human lives as the ultimate high-return investment.

Knowing that more than 80% of a company's exposure is the cost of its people, and people spend more than 90% of their lives in buildings, what would it take to turn any building into a platform that improves the health and well-being of its occupants? In other words, what kind of return on that 80% invested in people is plausible, possible, or feasible, based on a healthier building? What is it really worth to provide a friendly and supportive environment in which people can do their work?

1%, 5%, 10%, more?

What is it really worth to provide a friendly and supportive environment in which people can do their work?

Human performance and the business case for buildings is seldom a coherent and cohesive argument. David Radcliffe, vice president of real estate and workplace services for Google, asked one of our summit gatherings, "Are we squeezing pennies to reduce building cost and losing dollars of engagement?"

Good question.

I came out of the CBRE meeting in Los Angeles like a sparrow caught in the jet stream. I was moving very fast. Working with 12 prominent leaders excited about workplace wellness felt like being on the ground level for a new startup. It was a disruptive idea, moving our industry's focus from environmental sustainability to human health and happiness. I knew what to do: assemble the best and brightest from the wellness, architecture, construction, workplace, real estate, healthcare, and academic worlds; convene in quarterly summits across the country; research, synthesize, and write.

I thought research for a book on workplace wellness would be a simple extension of the work we did in *Change Your Space, Change Your Culture*. We had already addressed stress, health risks, and the emergence of well buildings. Our mission appeared straightforward— how do we bring corporate real estate and human resources together? How do we adopt the best of workplace strategy and design to enhance the best in workplace wellness? I wore my expert hat, and it felt good. Surely, we could move this conversation forward in significant ways.

Our first adventure would begin to learn the language and customs in this world of wellness. We assumed that world existed to solve a problem. Those inside the wellness world seemed to be clear about their mission and effectiveness. However, one rabbit trail led to lowering risk and cost. Another ran to attracting and retaining talent. Another wanted employee engagement. But none of them ever intersected or produced what they had promised. I assumed my questions and skepticism just reflected inexperience and lack of knowledge. My questions were like pulling a loose thread on a sweater. That unraveling began to attract the attention of an emerging band of iconoclasts, true believers, and reformers.

Exposing the Wellness Industrial Complex

From the beginning, our MindShift team agreed that our challenge was how to understand and articulate the wellness story and provide a roadmap through that territory. And we quickly, earnestly, and aggressively moved into that mission.

But, then I met Al Lewis.

The Harvard-trained guru of disease management, Al is the disruptive force, the enfant terrible, of the wellness world. With his rumpled khakis, navy blazer, and finger-combed brown hair, Al stands on platforms and flails his arms like the balloon man at a car wash opening. As the man with the facts, he is fearless, even delightfully provocative; "Please," he says to wellness vendors, "Sue me. I need the publicity!"

> *The Harvard-trained guru of disease management, Al is the disruptive force, the enfant terrible, of the wellness world.*

When I met him, he recounted his history and success, followed by his sudden repudiation of the very discipline he started. Like a character in a novel, Al had a crisis of conscience; he saw the clear and certain evidence that his own work produced no improvement in health or health costs. In fact, it created the opposite. In that interview, he identified all the major wellness voices; he bluntly called some liars and scam artists. I had already interviewed many of them for our project; other interviews were scheduled.

Our conversation threw me off balance, but I was intrigued. With Al's permission, I sent the recording and the transcript of our conversation to our Well MindShift team.

The first phone call hit within the hour. Our leading wellness expert and cheerleader was rattled and alarmed. She warned me that Al was poison to the wellness conversation. Within a day, I was uninvited to a wellness event sponsored by a leading wellness consulting firm. The reason? They heard I had interviewed Al. The level of intrigue increased. Cue the *Jaws* soundtrack.

Then Al introduced me to Tom Emerick, former head of benefits for Walmart, BP, and Burger King. I flew to Arkansas and stayed in Tom's guest home for two days. Tom, a former petty officer in the US Navy, stands in a military posture. His gray hair and Muskogee, Oklahoma, flat drawl lend an air of warmth and accessibility. But his command of facts can be intimidating.

Tom drove me through the countryside as he told me his story. He started his career as an actuary. That's important to know because he was the only person out of all the academics and health experts we interviewed who actually examined the health and mortality outcomes of different wellness approaches.

His left-brained, dispassionate, monotone, genius-level recall buried me in facts, studies, and decades of field experience. After all, he worked with an employee population of over 1 million for 11 years. I recorded our two-day session. That thread further unraveled the wellness garment.

In fact, it was beginning to look like this emperor had no clothes.

Then Tom introduced me to Soeren Mattke, author of the 10-year RAND study on the effectiveness of wellness programs. Mattke, a graduate of the University of Munich in his native Germany and Harvard, is a cardiologist and a leading global health policy authority. He sometimes speaks with the wide-eyed glee of a 12-year-old who has discovered a trunk of kryptonite in his basement.

Mattke's research shredded an entire industry's core narrative. Wellness programs don't work; the money invested is wasted.

Mattke's research shredded an entire industry's core narrative. Wellness programs don't work; the money invested is wasted. He opened the door to Jeffrey Pfeffer, who wrote the book *Leadership BS*. Naturally, his book makes the case that the positive management narratives are exactly as identified in his title.

Several organizations—including WELCOA, the largest nonprofit wellness education organization in the United States—reinforced the industry's need for change. These experts spun us 180 degrees from where we thought we were going. Very simply, no one else had yet connected these dots and distilled the information into a cohesive and comprehensive story and roadmap.

At that point, I didn't know what to do.

I was caught between two opposing and irreconcilable camps of equal depth and conviction. The new and irrefutable information threw me and the whole project into a crisis. If our mission was to no longer elevate and clarify the wellness industry's core narrative, doctrine, and dogma for improving health and well-being, then what was our new destination?

I was convinced that the answer was not some middle ground between these two opposing camps, but rather something altogether different. Our team plunged on ahead.

The Real War: Leadership Engagement

After several decades of various wellness strategies—at a cost of almost a trillion dollars—the various wellness approaches failed to slow the rate of medical costs or the rise in chronic disease. And the wellness industry acknowledges the lack of progress and low rates of engagement. Its solution? To shift their narrative away from outcomes and focus on participation and strategies to improve employee engagement.

It has been said that generals always fight the last (and, therefore, the wrong) war. We could see the wellness industry was also fighting the wrong (and a losing) war—trying to change individual behavior. Repackaging, upgrading, and adding the word "holistic" doesn't change the truth or increase the chances of success.

Our research located the real war.

The real objective is not trying to solve the health cost crisis. And it is not targeting individuals through programs that poke, prod, and pay them to change behavior. The real war is leadership engagement. It is fought to win the hearts and minds of employees. That is the strategy embraced by leaders like Bob Chapman, Tom Carmazzi, Blake Irving, Josh Glynn, Greg Kunkel, Dr. Roizen and others. And, it is working.

Those leaders are taking the offense. They know that separate and isolated efforts are ineffective. Only an integration of best efforts—walking the talk, creating a healthy environment, designing healthy nudges, truly caring about their employees, and helping them to own their health and well-being—into a seamless flow of full engagement and collaboration is effective. And they see the present cultural moment as the time to cultivate health and a true sense of well-being; they fully understand the ripple effect of happier employees. The United Nation's World Health Organization came to a similar conclusion; read their report—*Healthy Workplaces: A WHO Global Model for Action.*[4]

> *The real war is leadership engagement. It is fought to win the hearts and minds of employees.*

Fight to Win

Business faces a health crisis that requires a multidiscipline, unified app-roach. Yet, most companies use only one or two weapons. They also apply programmatic and conventional tactics to a stealthy and complex enemy. I don't think most leaders have full awareness of what they are up against. I certainly did not until several months into the research. We have been lulled into adopting a containment strategy, and not a very good one. Senior leaders must engage. We cannot begin until corporate commanders step back onto the battlefield and regain real-time "situational awareness."

I ask every senior leader I meet these questions:

- What is the percent of your *full* health cost to revenue?
- What is the biggest health issue your company faces?
- What have your cost trends been for the past three years?
- How much of your health costs have you shifted to employees over the past three years?

I've not yet met one leader who could answer any of those questions without calling their HR director or CFO. Guess what? They didn't know either.

Imagine you are in a battle, a fight for your business's life. Your HR forces are outnumbered and outmaneuvered. You are losing the war because costs are rising faster than profits. The quarterly health cost reports provide a number, a cost. If that cost doesn't raise your eyebrows, you go to the next report. The report offers no context, no story, and no connection to what you think drives the business. Just like the cost of the workplace is not linked to the 80% cost of employees, the cost of healthcare is simply another line item on the budget. Any number on a spreadsheet produces an immediate bias. Reduce that number. In fact, someone's bonus is probably tied to reducing those numbers.

Because it is a war of attrition, the real dangers and threats don't register.

Let's paint a different scenario. Imagine a sudden acute crisis: A cash crunch. A key supplier folds. A software crisis suddenly cripples the business. Any of those disasters would make your executive floor look like a field hospital in a war zone.

What kind of coordinated tactical response will equal the crisis?

Tom Emerick and the Cleveland Clinic's Dr. Michael Roizen have each said our nation needs something equivalent to a Marshall Plan mobilization to avoid disaster. That gives us a glimpse into the severity of the problem.

But it seems that the first and most urgent task is to change the narrative. We must have a new language and a new story.

A statement often attributed to Confucius is true and applicable here, regardless of who said it: "The beginning of wisdom is to call things by their proper names." Only proper names permit us to enter the real rather than the illusory world.

I keep going back to the three comments I heard early in our work.

> *Tom Emerick and the Cleveland Clinic's Dr. Michael Roizen have each said our nation needs something equivalent to a Marshall Plan mobilization to avoid disaster. That gives us a glimpse into the severity of the problem.*

These succinct pieces of wisdom order my thinking about these issues. I think of them every day:

Leaders have to care, and they can't care for people they don't know.

—Bob Chapman

It is easier to spread influence with people you know.

—Dr. Nickolas Christakis

People feel like wellness programs are done to them, not for them.

—Al Lewis

If corporate leaders read, lived, and implemented these three things every day, we could immediately impact all of America's employed citizens! Think of the effect of consistently doing those things; think of the ramifications that would ripple throughout the country.

Leadership Nudge

Is your company capable of measuring the return on an improved employee experience?

Personal Nudge

Does your place of work make the day go easier or add friction to your life?

CHAPTER 3

Storm Damage

The Cost of Forgetting

Acting like a manager of a high-end hotel, our "Experience Managers" are responsible for ensuring that employees (our VIP guests) have a meaningful experience in the workplace. Because work doesn't always start or stop at the door of the facility, the XM does more than oversee daily operations. They get to know the employees. They assist leaders, managers, and supervisors to plan and celebrate events, anniversaries, and achievements. Our XMs also recognize when an employee is dealing with life's difficult circumstances. They deliver flowers, cards, and notes of kindness and compassion. They are empowered and given direction to simply "do the right thing."

—Calvin Crowder, vice president for global
real estate, GoDaddy

The campaign and election of Donald Trump as the 45th president of the United States struck like an earthquake, and the aftershocks have continued to roll across the land. Six weeks after the election, I listened to NPR's Scott Simon interview Professor Shannon Monnat. She is the Associate Professor of Sociology and Lerner Chair for Public Health Promotion at Syracuse University.

Her explanation of how rural and small city America flipped the election mirrored the way earthquakes suddenly rise from invisibility to bring mammoth disruptions. As I listened to Professor Monnat, I realized that the disruptions were just beginning to ripple through our society. Five days later I interviewed her.

When I asked how she detected the role of despair in rural America's role in the election, she said, "I was working on a project examining county-level mortality rates from drugs, alcohol, and suicide, relative to economic conditions and social healthcare factors. I noticed counties with the highest rates of these 'deaths of despair' were also experiencing a lot of economic distress. These are towns once thriving and vibrant with a strong manufacturing or mining base. And those jobs just went away."

Counties with the highest rates of these "deaths of despair" were also experiencing a lot of economic distress.

The scale of Monnat's work shows a predictable pattern when sudden economic disruption slams into a collective sense of powerlessness. It takes on the pattern of a cold front colliding with a warm front, forcing the warm air of fading hope into the atmosphere. That hope turns to despair and plunges downward, creating a vortex capable of destroying individuals and families and ripping right through communities.

Monnat grew up in Lowville, New York, a town of less than 5,000 people between the foothills of the Adirondack Mountains and the Tug Hill Plateau. My mother grew up in the same area. So, I am familiar with the towns in that blue-collar region. I well remember Webster's Tannery in Malone. The old ramshackle wood-framed building carried the wondrous aroma of leather. I remember the bins filled with work gloves and the shelves of leather work boots. It's all gone now, along with the mill across the river. It's all been replaced by three prisons. Incarceration is a growth industry in the zones of despair.

Dr. Monnat knows the once-thriving small business terrain of that part of America: "These were the types of jobs that tended to employ manual laborers or other types of work not requiring a college degree. They paid decent wages and often came with benefits and retirement plans. Since the 1980s, those jobs have just disappeared. These are the places where the data show major upticks in opiate abuse, alcohol-related mortality, and suicides."

Washington, Indiana, is another old factory town that lost the factories. Meth addiction is a major problem. Knowing that just getting to school was an enormous challenge for some students, LeAnne Kelley,

What do you do when the jobs leave but the people stay?

the principal of Washington High School, developed an early warning system for teachers and staff. They found five factors that serve to flag a child at risk. Each factor escalates the risk and mobilizes action. I saw her "war room," listing every student and all the factors facing each. That system ranks the factors in order of digression. A student reaching a certain threshold activates an intervention.

The principal told me about Melinda (not her real name), a student who started missing school, getting poor grades, acting out, and developing a harsh personality. She measured as high risk of dropping out on the SOS ED.[1] When the teachers set up an "intervention journal," they learned that her parents' car had been repossessed. Melinda wanted to be at school but lack of transportation became a daily and often unsurmountable hurdle. Their attention to the problem got everyone on the same page, and developed a deeper appreciation of Melinda as a person and the challenges of her situation. Teachers banded together to make sure that she got rides to and from school. Melinda's behavior changed; her anger and passion were channeled to becoming a leader and helping other kids who were starting to disengage or veer toward bad behavior.[2]

Standing in LeAnne's war room, I realized I was watching a high school principal walking across a battlefield like a military commander. Yes, she was concerned about education. But, even more than that, she was trying to save a town from a slow and agonizing death. She summed up the reasons for the battle when she asked me, "What do you do when the jobs leave but the people stay?"

Since that day, I've wondered how many business leaders carry that kind of passion for the pain and dysfunctions of the city or the zip code where they work.

A Nation in Pain

When I asked Dr. Monnat about the relevance of the Trump election, she said:

> On election night, I was watching Trump performing better than polls predicted in places like Pennsylvania, Ohio, and even New Hampshire. And I thought, well, you know what? These places look like my map of despair zones.

Well, let me just test out this idea. I first looked at the county-level data for the election returns from Michigan. I ran some associations and found a positive relationship. Huh; I wonder if it's just Michigan. I expanded to the Rust Belt states, and I saw the same relationship. I looked at Appalachia and New England. I looked at the Mountain West, and it was the same pattern in all these different regions. Why? What was the message? What's going on in these places?

Part of what she saw was the unintended consequences of the way pain is evaluated and treated. Historically, "vital signs" included body temperature, blood pressure, heartbeat, and respiration rate. But some agencies now include pain as the fifth vital sign. That moves it into an elevated consideration as a life-threatening symptom.

And that transition also changed the way we treat pain. Opioids were once restricted to treat acute pain. That quickly devolved to using them to address *chronic* pain. Many health professionals see that as the tipping point. I quickly admit that anyone who has suffered chronic pain understands the nightmare of trying to find relief. I remember my dad, having suffered back injuries in World War II, going to heroic measures to alleviate pain—at least four surgeries, various back braces, heat rubs, heating pads, and eventually a neuro-stimulator. Finally, in the early 1990s the VA prescribed OxyContin to help him (and many others) manage the pain. When he prepared for a final back surgery, his new doctor was alarmed at the doses he had been prescribed. He needed to have the drugs out of his system before surgery. I watched my dad fight high fever and chills, vomit throughout the process, and curl up in excruciating pain in a fight between his body and the hold OxyContin had secured on him. He was fortunate. He broke free.

Professor Monnat told me: "Big Pharma and pain clinics targeted rural areas with large supplies of manual laborers. Workers would get hurt on the job or would just wear their bodies out. Mining companies employed doctors on staff to write OxyContin prescriptions for their miners so they could keep working to not lose productivity."

The heroin dealers knew exactly where they go. The demand was already in place, thanks to the pain killers.

Cheap heroin from Mexico followed. "The heroin dealers knew exactly where they go. The demand was already in place, thanks to the painkillers. If we hope to tackle this problem we need to understand its roots."

So, what does this have to do with your work? What Professor Monnat described does not exist in a sterile research lab. As you will see in more detail later, some of the people you work with every day struggle with the same kind of addictions and dysfunctions. I came face-to-face with it on our MindShift team. With that member's permission, let me tell you her story.

As the director of the Burns School of Real Estate and Construction Management at the University of Denver, Barbara Jackson is an eminent educator. Through our MindShift sessions, meal gatherings, and more casual times, we only knew her as a wise and valuable contributor to our work. But we did not know that when Barbara was an infant in upstate New York, her parents' divorce forced her to be relocated to an aunt's home. Even though her father remarried and lived near her, Barbara lived with her aunt until she was four. And that is when, one rainy night, her aunt simply told her, "Take your stuff to your father's house."

Barbara was terrified. Besides the cold and damp night, she didn't know how to navigate the streets to her father's house. But that seemed of little concern to her aunt. Somehow, the little girl found her father's home. But when she knocked, her new stepmother opened the door and told her to get away, "We don't want you here."

And that night marked the beginning of her homeless life. Although she passed in and out of various homes (including short and sporadic times at her father and stepmother's and with her mother), she lived primarily in the back of an old station wagon and other vehicles, boxes, and makeshift shelters.

When she entered school, she found a sanctuary. For the first time in her life, she discovered a true "safe place." Naturally, in the great symmetry of life, Barbara became an educator. Today, she holds a PhD, has directed great academic institutions, has been honored with special citations from the US State Department and the US Army Corps of Engineers, and has received numerous other awards and honors. The MindShift team knew some of those noble details, but we didn't know the story of her childhood.

We are all surrounded by people with stories of poverty, pain, illness, and other challenging life conditions. They work in your office, live next door, sit beside you on airplanes, and perform surgery on your children.

The stories don't disqualify anyone. Rather, they give depth and breadth to those who lived them.

Why Business Leaders Should Care

Every business includes at least one Barbara Jackson. Most have several. They have known places, humiliations, and desperations that most of their coworkers could not fathom. That's why it is critically important to know them. *We need them and their strengths and capacities!* The shape of their lives has produced wisdom, survival mechanisms, vulnerabilities, and discernment of situations that your business must know and factor into workplace policies and practices.

A recent article in the health blog Quizzify shoots to the bottom line of why this is a serious problem that businesses cannot ignore:

Here are five things you, as administrators, need to know:
1. Opioid abuse has jumped *500%* in the past 7 years.
2. The price per milligram of morphine-equivalent paid by employees has *declined about 75%* in the past 15 years. This is due to more generous coverage (by you!), more use of the formulary and most distressingly, more pills per prescription. There is virtually no other product whose use doesn't increase as the price falls. And there are very few products whose price falls that much.
3. The *$78-billion all-in cost* in the United States of opioid use, abuse, and treatment works out to about *$756 per employee per year.* To put that in perspective, that's about 10 times what you spend on heart attacks and diabetes events (not that those aren't important too!).

   15% of your workforce, probably more, are addicted to drugs, alcohol, or tobacco.
4. Workers compensation claims costs are *ten times higher* when long-acting opioids are involved.
5. Your ER visit claims coded to opioid issues have probably *increased threefold* since 2003.[3]

Stress is a root cause for many of these problems. In an NIH study, "Zillman and Bryan confirm that stress will cause people to engage in unhealthy behaviors, such as poor dietary practices or a lack of exercise as a means of emotion-focused coping."[4] And all of this reveals the substrata

> *And all of this reveals the substrata of a loss of care and control in our country and our workplaces, a feeling of not being good enough, and feeling that whatever an individual says, does, or believes just doesn't matter anymore.*

of a loss of care and control in our country and our workplaces, a feeling of not being good enough, and feeling that whatever an individual says, does, or believes just doesn't matter anymore.

I do understand that most companies do not see their business as one of saving society. However, they can begin to address these root issues by recognizing the problem does exist. Creating an environment that is ready and willing to deal with that reality is a better option than looking the other way or simply complying with the legal minimum. It requires hard work to develop clear policies that provide accountability, action, and care. Creating that kind of environment is a tangible way of giving a damn.

What Do You See?

Most people, companies, and institutions suffer some form of myopia. We tend to be nearsighted. While that is understandable, it is also dangerous: it ignores or misinterprets the larger landscapes of regional or national life. We all live within vast social, economic, and political ecologies. And they exert more influence on our factories, schools, offices, and other places of business than we might imagine.

For example, half of Americans feel financially insecure, and only 55% could replace half a month's income with liquid assets.[5] The stress of financial uncertainty, combined with the erosion of social capital, leave many without life mastery skills or even minimal coping mechanisms. So many feel so trapped that they resort to unhealthy escapes from their private despair. That is the birthing room for dependency and addiction.

How can we empathize with them; how can we help them, if we can't even see them?

Worrying about financial survival or the fear of losing a job drains humans of essential energy and creativity. Nine out of 10 adults say they would rather have work stability over growth opportunities. This is the hidden, and sometimes not-so-hidden, drama that walks in and out of your workplace every day.

Sometimes when I hear people talk about being "drained," I remember that Jean Houston, bestselling author and speaker, wrote about a nationwide poll in Japan asking people to identify the largest national challenge. More than 1 million people said that "spiritual aridity," or dryness, was the biggest threat. Such dryness, she suggested, is the inevitable result of living too long on the surface of life, of not allowing roots to dig deep into life's underground wells.[6] Here's how I described that in my first book: "The shallow pursuit of material success, the erosion of extended family and community, and the hard and rapid pace of life have left the culture and psychic landscape as dry and inhospitable as the desert."[7]

It seems that when we live too far, too long from the ancient fountains of classic wisdom, we begin to believe that we can find everything we need in fabricated culture, environments, relationships, and even virtues. We assume we can buy or build everything we need. But, in time, we realize that we've lost a certain sustainability and cohesion of community. We're just drained; the atmosphere has become too arid to support the ecosystems of trust, connection, human reliability, selflessness, and community.

Some companies are taking the offense and fighting against that human aridity. I've met with leaders who are deeply in touch and concerned about the real-life people who work for them and their challenges. Instead of reacting symptomatically with intervention programs, they are trying to make their workplaces safe havens of support, security, and satisfying work. And they all look different. The true leaders are not downloading their leadership patterns from scripted sources.

> *The true leaders are not downloading their leadership patterns from scripted sources.*

Their thinking is fresh, innovative, creative, and bold.

Dale Sowder is the CEO of Holland Hospital, in Holland, Michigan. It is a thriving organization that employs more than 2,000 people in a Rust Belt state. Four studies conclude that hospitals face unprecedented turnover. "This study confirmed what is the worst-case scenario for many hospitals, they are losing critical employees faster than they can replace them," said Bill Haylon, CEO of LFT.[8] However, with a pay scale that is 32% less than their competition, Holland Hospital has less than 5% job openings in an industry with an average of higher than 19% turnover.[9] With lower-than-market wages, I had to ask why.

And Dale told me: "Our people love to work here. Our pay scale allows us to hire additional staff and reduce the workload. We also discovered a wonderful unintended side benefit. The reduced load allows employees to plan and coordinate more. Our people keep learning and improving and so do our processes."

Craig Janssen, the owner of Idibri, a specialty engineering firm in Dallas, is not faced with burnout or turnover, but with competition for talent.

When we sat down to talk, I said: "Craig, your industry is extremely competitive. I know you just got hit with a 40% increase in healthcare costs on top of about 12% in 2016. You passed on 4% of that increase to your employees but you've haven't had any turnover in years. Why?" He replied:

We pay below our competition. That allows us to buffer some of the volatility. People who aren't feeling insecure about their position or personal financial stability. . . . In other words, they know they won't go backwards, don't feel the need to have a high income and come to work, to work. We provide great resources and autonomy but what helps them more than anything is a stable income.

My people are confident they will be protected from upcharges compared to being exposed to every upcharge we get hit with. They understand how our business works and how we work hard to find other ways to offset these increases.

The real point here is that leaders who really know their people are better able to develop strategies like Dale's and Craig's approaches. Each leader tailored work structures and environments around the specific shape of his workforce. Dale alleviated intense schedules and the stress of always working in a reactive mode. Peace of mind over job security and pay fluctuation produced harmony among Craig's employees. Furthermore, addressing those keystone issues took pressure off wages. Both companies built happy workplaces. Each organization is in a competitive market for talent. Yet, neither company has microkitchens, yoga rooms, or Zen gardens.

This research forced me and members of our MindShift team to talk to hundreds of people about life pressures. We heard the worries and frustration of parents as they battled schools just to get someone to care about their child. In our research, we discovered that 50% of our school kids are being left behind; 25% because of their learning differences and

25% because of their zip code. I heard stories about the financial and emotional stress of caring for elderly parents, caring for special needs children, struggles with chronic disease, and many other factors that create insecurity, worry, and stress. But I also heard stories about jobs, workplaces, and bosses that provided the only safe place in their lives.

. . . the whole person, not just the "employee," comes to work each day and goes home each night. And with them come and go all of their thoughts, worries, frustrations, aches, pains, ailments, and more.

In the book, *Work on the Move 2*,[10] Kate Lister (Well MindShift member) and Tom Harnish write, "the whole person, not just the 'employee,' comes to work each day and goes home each night. And with them come and go all of their thoughts, worries, frustrations, aches, pains, ailments, and more."

That's why I frequently ask leaders to go on a "listening tour." And now I ask *you*: Get out of your office. Get to know those who work for you. Discover "the whole person, not just the 'employee.'" Become acquainted with the lives they lead and the pressures they face inside and outside of work.

I found talking to so many people about their lives helped me to really *see*. And the main thing I see is the missing key element—the human side of these complicated workplace equations.

Zones of despair created (or revealed) a new era of imbalance. And leaders do not have the luxury of letting the employees just gut it out. We all have a stake in everyone's success and safety. The problems of our colleagues and coworkers belong to us too. We can carry that burden together or just try to cope when we lose someone or when our life or business is suddenly disrupted. The opioid epidemic exposes the thin membrane that keeps chaos from invading individual, familial, business, and national order. The owners and leaders I've met feel the burden of responsibility for the "mouths they feed." They also feel squeezed and can't continue to absorb costs that are rising faster than profits. The bridge between these competing pressures is personal engagement.

I will tell you the stories of more leaders like Dale and Craig. We will describe how they push the chaos back and establish buffers that provide safe havens for employees. That also helps to create highly productive and profitable enterprises. Everyone wins when we move beyond judgment and prejudice to see societal and personal damage more humanely. Those afflicted were simply caught in the storm's path. The sheer ability to *see* it that way enables us to build positive language, structures, and action for bringing them back into the community of happy and productive citizens.

Leadership Nudge

What policies does your company have in place to help those with personal and family struggles get help?

Personal Nudge

If you needed help with a personal or family struggle, where would you go? Would you get help?

CHAPTER 4

Stress

Portrait of a Killer

Sylvia was exhausted and ready to leave the office by 3 p.m. Another day of fire drills and meetings. And her day wouldn't be over for another three hours. Two more mind-numbing meetings, a dreaded confrontation with her boss about a project gone bad, and trying to find time to encourage a depressed team. She wanted them to feel like the company cares, even though she knows it doesn't. As she thought about home, she glanced at the stack of reports she must read by tomorrow, now four inches higher than when she came in this morning.

Sylvia was two employees short on her 12-person team. Robin, Steve, and Janet gave their best, almost every day. They pulled a lot of extra weight. But she had to babysit five good people who took no initiative. Two other team members were absolutely toxic. They made every task difficult and every meeting contentious. Both were easily offended and used any offense as a weapon with Human Resources.

Sylvia's hands were tied. She tried to restrain the toxic twins, or at least contain their damage, but "policy" got in the way. She knew she shouldn't, but sometimes the pressure caused her to complain to a trusted few of her peers. Naturally, Sylvia felt overwhelmed by her circumstances. To add to the stress, she felt like her job could be in jeopardy.

Sylvia lived 25 miles from the office, but traffic made the commute at least an hour, or even longer with weather or accidents. She got home at about 7:15 and then switched gears to prepare dinner for her and her son.

She worries about Roberto's learning differences. The school seems to put up more hurdles than help. After dinner, Sylvia worked with Roberto on his homework, not because she knew the material, but because she had to help him focus and manage his frustrations.

When Roberto went up to bed around 9:30, Sylvia opened her laptop at the kitchen table, poured a glass of Pinot Grigio, and released a long, groaning sigh. The firewall at work made the computer painfully slow, but she had to reduce the pile of e-mails.

No one at work understands the price they all pay for being always "on."

She went to bed around 11 and awakened at 6 a.m. to start it all over again. However, she wasn't rested. Sylvia's late-night e-mails, reading reports, worry about tomorrow, and a bit of television kept her brain switched on for a few hours. She took a couple of OTC sleeping meds to turn her brain off.

When she sought advice from HR, they recommended the stress management program their vendor was offering. She enrolled, but quickly saw it was a waste of time. The facilitator didn't listen. When Sylvia used the word "stress," the facilitator began to demonstrate "mindful breathing." She really couldn't take more time out of her day for a class; the primary stress relief she needed was two more reliable employees and freedom from the toxic ones.

Figure 4.1   Sylvia and Roberto.

Sylvia doesn't understand, and no one else at work understands, the price they all pay for being always "on"—pushing hard, doing more with less, sucking it up, and taking one more for the team. The python tightens when they exhale.

Stressed-Out Baboons

If work is so good, how come they have to pay us to do it?

—Mike Royko

Sylvia's conditions are increasing her mortality. Probably yours too, if you are getting six or fewer hours of sleep each night. The problem is in large part structural. She works for a pecking-order company and has little autonomy to fix the problems on her team. The pecking order also creates a stratified entitlement culture: stress collects in the middle and toward the bottom of the organization.

Robert Sapolsky, the American professor, neuroendocrinologist, and author, has studied the social habits of animals in the wild for over 30 years. His research on stress-related disease in baboon culture reveals similar parallels to the workplace:

The reason baboons are such good models is, like us, they don't have real stressors . . . If you live in a baboon troop in the Serengeti, you only have to work three hours a day for your calories, and predators don't mess with you much. What that means is you've got nine hours of free time every day to devote to generating psychological stress toward other animals in your troop. They're just like us: They're not getting done in by predators and famines, they're getting done in by each other.

They're just like us: They're not getting done in by predators and famines, they're getting done in by each other.

Up until 15 years ago, the most striking thing we found was that, if you're a baboon, you don't want to be low ranking, because your health is going to be lousy. But what has become far clearer, and probably took a decade's worth of data, is the recognition that protection from stress-related disease is most powerfully grounded in social connectedness, and that's far more important than rank.[1]

In the National Geographic documentary *Stress, Portrait of a Killer*,[2] Sapolsky tells the story of a baboon tribe that followed the model. The lower-ranking baboons carrying stress-induced obesity (belly fat), were more susceptible to all the symptoms of metabolic syndrome. When the tribe found rotted meat in a garbage dump, the alpha males took the prize while the females and lower-ranking males sat at the perimeter.

The toxic meat killed the entire clan of alpha males. That placed the females in charge. When the females took over, the tribe morphed away from a hierarchical command into a grooming culture. The tribal time that was once spent intimidating, defending, or staying on alert changed over to caring, connection, and nurturing.

Primates in the Workplace

The Whitehall studies, conducted over several decades beginning in 1967, tracked 18,000 male employees in the British civil service, and over 10,000 civil servants, both male and female. The studies asked how the workplace affected health and mortality. The results represent the human version of Sapolsky's work.

The first Whitehall study found that those at the lower end of the pecking orders experienced more severe adverse symptoms of metabolic syndrome. "After controlling for these risk factors, the lowest grade still had a relative risk of 2.1 for cardiovascular disease mortality compared to the highest grade."[3]

Please Help Me!

"My body hurts. I feel exhausted. I feel emotionally numb. I can't move as fast as I want to. Please help me." Mina Mori, 26, left this note just before she committed suicide in 2008. The investigation revealed that she worked "in excess of 140 overtime hours a month." The Japanese have a specific word for death from overwork—*karōshi*.[4]

According to Jeffrey Pfeffer, "It's even worse than that." In the research for his new book,[5] he discovered that deaths related to overwork are the fifth leading cause of death in the United States. He also told me: "We understand that people's minds affect their bodies. Why are we surprised at the numbers? Life's demands, financial insecurity, lack of control, overwork and stress—it's killing us." Using the epidemiological studies that have been around for decades and aggregating them to develop cost projections and business implications, his team estimates that deaths due to overwork in America conservatively total 130,000 a year.

He also wrote in *Fortune* magazine:

> *According to Jeffrey Pfeffer, deaths related to overwork are the fifth leading cause of death in the United States. His team estimates that deaths due to overwork in America conservatively total 130,000 a year.*

The 10 workplace conditions included some that affected people's level of stress, such as work–family conflict, economic insecurity (fearing for one's job and income), shift work, long working hours, low levels of

Figure 4.2   Workplace stress is linked to death.

organizational justice (fairness), an absence of control over one's work, and high job demands—and one factor, whether the employer-provided health insurance, that, particularly prior to the passage of the Affordable Care Act, affected people's access to health care.[6]

Your Body Under Chronic Stress

Cortisol is the gas pedal that accelerates your heart and releases energy (glucose). It gets us up in the morning, energizes us for peak needs, and is then supposed to turn off at night. But stress pushes the same pedal. If your body is not in survival mode (like fighting a tiger), but stress insists that it *is* fighting to survive, serious complications become dangerous to your health:

Blood sugar falls out of balance.

Arteries produce a waxy substance to cushion the vessels from increased pressure. The wax hardens into plaque, which narrows artery walls and raises blood pressure.

The brain also instructs the body, "Hold on to those calories." Guess where they go? Right to the abdomen.

Suddenly, we must cope with cascading factors of chronic stress: weight gain, high blood pressure, diabetes, immune system suppression, and cardiovascular disease. It also shuts off your parasympathetic nervous system (your recovery mechanism).

These symptoms are called metabolic syndrome. It is the number one cause of chronic disease.[7]

Loneliness also contributes to stress. Most people are friendly and have friends. The problem is energy or time. Research reveals a growing number of depleted and lonely people. The more people are exhausted, the lonelier they feel. "Research by Sarah Pressman, of the University of California, Irvine . . . demonstrates that while obesity reduces longevity by 20%, drinking by 30%, and smoking by 50%, loneliness reduces it by a whopping 70%."[8]

. . . while obesity reduces longevity by 20%, drinking by 30%, and smoking by 50%, loneliness reduces it by a whopping 70%.

Well-Being Before Wellness

I am the amateur in every group and with everyone I interview. However, all this evidence about the primacy of stress seemed overwhelming, obvious, and intuitive to me. So, I just kept asking, "Why is the focus of wellness aimed at physical health when stress is clearly the driver behind most of the problems that wellness efforts are trying to solve?"

I learned from Dr. Roizen and others that in the beginning of the wellness surge, no one saw stress as a factor. But then, like a fluorescent light turning on, the role of stress began to slowly dawn on everyone. So, in many ways, it was all backward. Wellness leaders started with physical health and then finally discovered stress as the largest driver of *un*wellness.

> *The real cost of poor employee health and well-being is not medical or pharmaceutical costs. It's not even the associated absenteeism. It's the toll that poor health takes on a person's productivity while they are at work—something that researchers and managers have labeled* presenteeism.[9]
>
> —Kate Lister

In other words, well-being comes before wellness (we explore that in more detail in Chapter 10).

That one perspective—well-being before wellness—changed everything for me. And it should change the details and direction of wellness efforts. It should send every human resource manager, corporate executive, policy expert, wellness program designer, and architect back to the drawing board. It seems that everyone leaned the ladder against the wrong wall. An entire industry has spent billions trying to solve symptoms—obesity, heart disease, diabetes, strokes, and other physical breakdowns. But stress is the serial killer behind all those mortal afflictions.

An entire industry has spent billions trying to solve symptoms—obesity, heart disease, diabetes, strokes, and other physical breakdowns. But stress is the serial killer behind all those mortal afflictions.

Well-Being Requires a Mind Shift—Not a New Program

A recent article in a prominent HR journal announced that employers are taking wellness to a higher level. Well, let's hear the drum roll, trumpets, and popping champagne corks. It seems, according to the article, that after a half-century of inadequate or failed efforts to improve health outcomes or reduce costs, the HR industry is "now very confident" that its next version will satisfy corporate criticism and pressure to deliver on a 50-year promissory note to improve employee health and well-being.

The article highlights stories from rich companies who pay a premium for talent; they are spending more on fitness centers, meditation rooms, and services to help people better manage their finances and other key stress points of life. Except for adding the words "holistic," "individualizing," and "sustainable," the wellness industry is offering the same old programmatic approaches to addressing their employees' life challenges. But the source of most employee stress is the very structure and culture of the workplace. For example, sending Sylvia to a stress management class would not reduce her stress. Getting rid of two toxic employees would.[10]

Leaders, me included, mean well. When we see a problem, we reach for our bag of tricks or call in outside experts with their bags of tricks. But, when we do that, we operate with a diminished capacity to care. Part of the reason is that by the time we have climbed the ladder and reached positions as master problem solvers, our emotional intelligence has precipitously dropped.[11] We become numb to the ripple effect of our decisions on people. That mirror neuron installed at birth as a means of empathizing with others can (without continued cultivation) become tone deaf. (The TV show *Undercover Boss* is built on the premise of tone-deaf bosses discovering the impact of their decisions.) As a consequence, we seldom take the time to fully explore what a meaningful, practical, and caring response might look like. True care is personal, a gift to another. So, instead of actually caring, we busy leaders try to delegate care to an

Instead of actually caring, we busy leaders try to delegate care to an efficient delivery system that assembles the components of care. But that system does not, cannot, include the human touch.

efficient delivery system that assembles the components of care. But that system does not, cannot, include the human touch. Too often the solutions we parachute into various areas of need are imposed; done "to," not done "for" or "with."

Tom Emerick told me a story from Walmart of how the benefits world, his world, was so often a grand adventure in missing the point:

> *I met a bunch of cashiers in the store. They were all overweight. And I, the Very Helpful One from Corporate, said, "What if we gave you free gym memberships?"*
>
> *And one woman answered, "The only way I can come back here and do this all day long is I go home and soak my feet in Epsom salts every night. My feet hurt so bad at the end of my shift that I can barely walk. Don't ask me to get on a treadmill, or I won't be able to come back to work. If you want to do something to improve our lives, gives us shoes, or a mat that will keep our feet from aching an hour after we get here."*
>
> *Another lady said, "You know, I drive a 14-year-old car. I buy my furniture at garage sales. I've never had a vacation because I don't get paid enough money here. And a couple times a week I get a large pizza and a six-pack of beer and just go home. That's the only recreation I have all week long. Don't tell me I can't have that."*
>
> *And, you know what; she was right. I got to thinking, how arrogant am I to not have any idea what these people's lives are like?*

That is the threshold that only care can cross—knowing the sights, touches, textures, sounds, smells, and nuances of what people's lives are like. The mammoth delivery system that we often call "care" does not have (and will not allow) room for a human touch. The metrics measure participation and health cost, not care and connection. Organizations like the Mayo Clinic and Cleveland Clinic and companies like Barry-Wehmiller, Next Jump, W.L. Gore, Cummins, and GoDaddy have created different structures more aligned with grooming cultures than traditional pecking orders. They provide

And, you know what; she was right. I got to thinking, how arrogant am I to not have any idea what these people's lives are like?

leadership that cares, clear cultures and ecosystems of support, and environments that continually reinforce why and how employees are valued.

When Well-Being Becomes the New Norm

Perhaps the real problem is stress seems so normal. I do complain about stress with peers at the end of the day over a beer. We can all articulate the activities, demands, and curveballs that complicate our lives, but in fact we regard them as badges of honor. You and I know people who jokingly say, "There are two kinds of people, those who get stressed and those who give stress." But his knowing smile implies that the speaker is the latter. Stress is our modern-day Faustian bargain. We have willingly handed over our well-being in exchange for the promise of financial security, recognition, or feeling valued. It is another python.

As Bob Chapman told me, "Don't complain about the cost of healthcare. 84% of all illnesses are chronic. The largest cause of chronic illness is stress. The biggest cause of stress is work. Guys, you are the problem. Okay? You can beat up insurance companies. The dumb things we do to manipulate insurance companies and doctors and hospitals. Why don't we just reduce demand?"

Chronic disease is the steamroller that threatens corporate survival. When I share the statistics and stories with business leaders, I see true surprise, even alarm. I see a growing and universal acknowledgment that stress represents an existential crisis. But wellness efforts have had no effect against chronic disease, largely because organizations and companies have learned helplessness.

They also keep aiming at the wrong target. Stress is the target! It drives the steamroller that disables and kills so many.

They have acquired the reflex of throwing up their hands no matter how shocking or dramatic the numbers and details. They also keep aiming at the wrong target. Stress is the target! It drives the steamroller that disables and kills so many.

Increasingly, it seems that many leaders are starting to feel this. They are moving beyond cerebral acceptance to gripping it personally. It is no longer abstract, but painfully visceral. That is why I have hope. Many of the examples of cultures of care came through painful lessons, crossroads, and turnabouts. The road from reducing stress to achieving happiness is a road everyone wants to take and *can* take! The workplace can become a place of meaningful achievement, relationships, personal growth, and a sense of accomplishment.

Getting the Horse Back in Front of the Cart

According to Bob Chapman, "The person you report to at work is more important to your health than your doctor! *And* there is a 20% increase in heart attacks on Monday mornings. Furthermore, we know for a fact that the way we treat people at work affects the way they go home and treat their spouse and their children."

> *So, what does it mean that work is baking stress into the workforce and that work is the fifth leading cause of death in America?*

With 160 million workers in America, Bob Chapman's research shows they can and will have great influence on the health of the rest of America when they go home after work. So, what does it mean that work is baking stress into the workforce and that work is the fifth leading cause of death in America? That fact is a major contributing factor to everything else we will address. We must put the well-being horse back in front of the wellness cart. Our research found that well-being costs less in both the short and the long run—but it must come first.

Google is considered one of the best places to work. But they saw their culture was burning out too many people, and turnover was too high. So, they launched two efforts to understand performance and resiliency better. After studying 180 teams over two years, they

Figure 4.3   Well-being must come before wellness.

concluded that psychological safety was the number one factor in high performance. So, reducing the friction of work, as David Radcliffe says, or creating a safe place to work are not just nice soft skills for cushy workplaces. They are keys to survival for this new era of work.

The Leadership Nudge

Is your tendency to amplify or absorb stress in your organization? How do you know?

The Personal Nudge

Rate your average daily stress on a 10-point scale. Do you have healthy or unhealthy habits to deal with stress?

PART II

Is There Shelter from the Storm? A Search for Wellness

CHAPTER 5

In Search of Wholeness

The beginning is the most important part of the work.

—Plato

Bob, the CEO of a 2,000-employee global civil construction firm, brought me in to help his senior team navigate some thorny issues. But later, as Bob and I talked privately, I began to see the real reason for my visit. He was wrestling with hard realities built into the nature of his business. He just needed a friend, especially one who was an outsider, and a safe place to talk. I listened carefully. Because their projects cover the globe and last three or more years, Bob's firm often required employees to be away from their homes for months at a time. Bob slowly unpacked his thoughts through great emotion; I could see the concurrent pulls of his responsibility as CEO and his love and pain for the people who worked for him.

"We have a joke around the company," he said as he stirred his drink, "You can't make senior project manager until your second marriage."

Once again, I heard the same familiar hard business choice. It takes a strong leader to turn a project into a highly profitable success story. But that so often gets leveraged on the back of marriage and family. Conversely, a "good family man" has large and compelling reasons to avoid spending months away from home in remote sites.

"We have a joke around the company," he said as he stirred his drink, "You can't make senior project manager until your second marriage."

That is one of the classic dilemmas of capitalism. And the most common response to that problem has typically been some version of, "Look, it's not personal; it's business." Well, guess what? That position is no longer good enough in today's world. Real life has invaded our workspaces and places. Today, the truth is, "It's not business; it's personal." As Kate Lister and Tom Harnish wrote, "the whole person, not just the 'employee,' comes to work each day and goes home each night. And with them come and go all of their thoughts, worries, frustrations, aches, pains, ailments, and more."[1]

I can hear some of you protesting this as soft and cuddly thinking. I understand.

But consider this view (from an earlier MindShift project) of the new realities of the workplace in the twenty-first century:

Can you count on your personal assistant giving his best when he has to leave in an hour to drive his father to the kidney dialysis center? You can't avoid life outside the company walls. At the same time, you can have a significant positive impact that will influence and improve the life of the people that spend half of their waking day carrying out the mission of your organization.[2]

What Are Wellness and Well-Being?

After our January summit in Chicago, we looked for basic grounding in wellness and this new relationship between building science and medicine. We scheduled our next summit at the Mayo Clinic and specifically for the WELL Living Lab.

I drove in from the Rochester, Minnesota, airport to the Mayo Clinic in mid-March to prepare our first summit for this book. I passed several closed office buildings. Except for the Mayo Clinic, dominating downtown Rochester, the rest of the city looked like a lot of declining Midwestern towns. Rochester is, in fact, a "factory town": it produces health like few other places in the world. Their unique approach to team-based medicine attracts patients with complex medical needs. Speaking of his Walmart days, Tom Emerick said it was far better, and more cost-effective, to fly employees requiring expensive and complex treatment—and their families—to the Mayo or Cleveland Clinic than use local hospitals.

A decade ago, the mention of well-being in the boardroom would have been met with a round of blank stares, rolling eyes, or hushed giggles. While progress has been achingly slow, the concept is finally making its way into executive suites and workplaces around the world.[3]

—Kate Lister

The Mayo Clinic pays its doctors salaries instead of fees per procedure. That philosophy and practice stand opposite the traditional assembly line approach of seeing as many patients as possible and then quickly passing them on down the line. The Mayo doctors, instead, focus on whole care and outcomes. Of the 34,000 employees on its Rochester campus, about 4,000 are doctors. Rochester's next largest employer, the public school district, employs just under 3,000 people.

Mayo, ground zero for health in America, was the ideal place to begin our series of summits. And that is where we started with the ground zero of questions: What is wellness?

Webster's 1828 dictionary did not even include the word "wellness." Apparently, the earliest use of the word simply conveyed the opposite of being ill.[4] Webster now defines wellness as: "the quality or state of being in good health especially as an actively sought goal." And HealthCare.gov defines wellness through programs "intended to improve and promote health and fitness."[5]

The plot thickens when we turn to the Society for Human Resource Management (SHRM), the self-described "leading provider of resources to serve the needs of HR professionals and advance the professional practice of human resource management." It describes the means or tools a company may use for achieving wellness. Typical benefits in a wellness program include smoking cessation, weight loss, stress management, company gym/workout rooms, recreational programs such as company-sponsored sports teams, medical screenings, and immunizations/flu shots. Also included are educational safety and accident prevention programs that provide information and guidance on topics such as back care, cancer prevention, and AIDS awareness, as well as proper eating and exercise habits. All these benefits can be administered within an employer's employee assistance program or could be stand-alone programs.[6]

A lot of companies talk about wanting to improve work-life balance, but then only solve for "Work." It's time to make "Life" a factor in creating great workplace experiences with support that help individuals renew and stay energized throughout the day . . . "Work" will improve exponentially if we were to just focus on "Life."

Bryan Berthold, managing director, Workplace
Strategy & Workplace Experience, Cushman & Wakefield

But ask any person how they define wellness, and you will hear definitions as varied as the people responding. And that is where our problems begin. If we don't have a common understanding of what we hope to achieve, it's impossible to set a course.

Fuzzy Wellness

Because the definitions of wellness often have no context, they have no meaning. They are static, technical, and focused on means without anyone really asking, "To what end?" After the first few months of diving into the research, I felt a degree of vertigo about any attempt to understand or define wellness. Everyone uses the same or similar words, but each with different meanings, priorities, mixes, and intents.

I found that a few companies had an *origin story*, some form of epiphany or "aha" moment that set them on a search for wellness—not a wellness program. Those leaders talk about their journeys. They and their companies—GoDaddy, Barry-Wehmiller, Tuthill, Cummins, Next-Jump, Google, Idibri, MeTEOR, DPR, and others—knew their starting point, why they were on their unique journey, and they knew the distance to (and carried good pictures of) their destination.

I found that a few companies had an origin story, some form of epiphany or "aha" moment that set them on a search for wellness—not a wellness program.

Naturally, I also found some companies that had robust programs, but no story. They measured their success not by some image of a better future for their employees but in cold metrics like participation or health costs. It is hard to convey just how distinct those two camps were. With the first group, our conversations lasted several hours and included stories, authentic discoveries, failures, and lessons. Those leaders were open, comfortable, and not defensive.

My conversations with the second group seldom lasted an hour. Questions traveled well-paved roads. When I asked an off-road question, the conversation hit a wall of abrupt silence. Of course; my questions took them off script. So, they could only respond with, "How will you be using this information?" Or, "I have to check with our Communications department and get back to you." Before my conversation with one senior HR executive, I had to submit *all* my questions and allow five weeks for them to "research" the answers. I understand those responses, especially with an unknown outsider. I'm simply trying to describe the stark contrast between companies with healthy cultures and those trying to implement programs.

High Touch

We spent the first part of our Mayo Clinic time examining the terrain of health and wellness definitions, the differences between wellness and well-being, the meaning of "holistic," and other conceptual landscapes. Words fluttered about the room like butterflies. But then I watched them all settle around the need to *humanize* our approaches to humans.

That led to an observation that programs, in general, strip away the human experience and are too often delivered as a one-size-fits-all approach. What surprised us was that no one, even our wellness experts, considered corporate wellness programs and other efforts as helping or enhancing wellness or a sense of well-being (except some employee assistance programs).

> *What surprised us was that no one, even our wellness experts, considered corporate wellness programs and other efforts as helping or enhancing wellness or a sense of well-being.*

We discussed corporate cultures—known to us—that did express genuine employee care through a myriad of workplace initiatives, such as flexible work policies, paid time off, personal development opportunities, engaging workplaces, e-mail–free zones, and kid-friendly (and even pet-friendly) environments. We also learned that the efforts most valued by employees were inexpensive, creating connection, encouraging community, designing convenience, simplifying processes, providing coaches, and feeling valued in a time of need.

Thirty-five years ago, John Naisbitt captured the same tension between cold efficiency and the human touch: "Whenever a new technology is introduced into society, there must be a counterbalancing human response—that is, high touch—or the technology is rejected . . . We must learn to balance the material wonders of technology with the spiritual demands of our human nature."[7]

Our summary question became, "How do companies create that human touch?" You will read about the best of those in Chapter 14, Courageous Leaders and a Culture of Care, and Chapter 15, Emily's Story: Creating a Movement from the Second Chair.

What Does It Mean to Be Human at Work?

Corporate wellness was designed in the 1970s to detect and prevent the rise of chronic disease. As employee health-related costs began to double, wellness became a means for reducing cost and improving the return on investment. When that didn't happen, the rationale for wellness shifted to improving the attraction of talent. That didn't happen either. The most recent claim for wellness credibility is improving engagement, which it doesn't. Wellness is still in search of a clear identity and value proposition, with "well-being" as the latest addition to the conversation.

Steve Carter, a member of this MindShift project, raised the question, "What does it mean to be human at work?" Steve, who had recently completed his doctorate in virtues-based leadership, explained (over drinks and meals with the team) the relevance of ancient Greek thinking by describing human "well-being" as ευδαιμονία (eudaemonia). The modern English translation of the word comes down to *human flourishing*. If we peel this back one more layer, we arrive at the prefix eu-, "good" or "the good." The word "being" refers to soul or spirit. Thus, the roots of well-being literally mean: good + spirit.

The Greek concept of good is excellence, mastery, or virtue. Mastery is an intrinsic pursuit. Martin Seligman describes moral virtues as something we seek more of, not less. For example, we want more justice, honesty, wisdom, courage, and knowledge—not less. And these all have intrinsic worth and, therefore, do not require outside pressure, motivation, or manipulation.

Seligman's pioneering research examines the traits of those who flourish. One of his studies compared soldiers returning with PTSD. He found, however, a group with a different kind of PTSD, post-traumatic *strength* syndrome. These were soldiers whose traumatic exposures to death and violence proved to make them stronger and "more human." He found five attributes that they possessed. As summarized in his book, *Flourish: A Visionary New Understanding of Health and Well-Being*, the attributes create the acronym PERMA; positive emotion, engagement, relationships, meaning, and accomplishment.[8]

Aristotle defined happiness as human flourishing. If being human at work is the opportunity to grow and flourish through mastery, we must have completely different conversations about workplace wellness or well-being. We must realize that the workplace provides an opportunity for all the elements in flourishing: PERMA. This truth really does flip our assumptions about workplace health. It may also flip our strategies.

> *The workplace provides an opportunity for all the elements in flourishing: purpose, engagement, relationships, meaning, and accomplishment. This truth really does flip our assumptions about workplace health. It may also flip our strategies.*

Intrinsic desires more naturally succeed. Anything that relies on external levers will need to be continually propped, pumped, and hyped to stay alive. They may serve as a starting point but quickly fade. Employees instinctively feel the difference. One feels like it is provided *for* me, while the other feels like it is *done to* me.

So, What Is the Point?

As I told you in Chapter 3, a Japanese survey revealed that more than a million poll respondents named "spiritual aridity," or dryness, as the biggest threat to their country. You and I see some versions of that every day in America. Many in our workplaces seem to have lost a sense of why (purpose) and to what end. But that sense of futility starts well before work.

In catching up with an old friend over lunch recently, he surprised me by probing below the surface, "So Rex, how are *you* doing? What are your long-term plans?"

I paused, took a breath, and thought about his question. If a true friend digs that deep, I will try to answer from the same depth.

"Mark, right now I have a book deadline and three kids who are all freshmen in college. My mother-in-law just died, and my father-in-law moved in with us. We are temporarily taking care of a homeless person, and we have four dogs. I'm doing the best I can to keep up. I'm not sure I can see past these next several months let alone the next few years."

Mark understood, responded graciously, and shifted to a story of his cab driver, an immigrant from Congo who would love to have our problems. I nodded; sure, I got it. But his questions made me wonder if I'm among the multitude on a treadmill or on a journey heading toward PERMA.

Workplace wellness has too often become a means-driven conversation, focusing on the how, and not the why or the who. It has become a convoluted and complex hairball of competing constituencies, too many vendors, and big bandwagons. But, it seems that very few leaders or managers operate out of any vision of human flourishing.

But we must and can rise to that higher ground of leadership. We can discover, enhance, and increase the value of "being human at work."

Ed Strouth, who along with Laurie Ferrendelli runs Barry-Wehmiller's wellness and education programs, told me about getting "reschooled" by Bob Chapman when he was promoted to director of health and well-being. Bob's predecessor was a more traditional HR person, who focused on cost and risk. Ed naturally prepared for his first budget meeting with Bob as he would have prepared for Bob's predecessor; multiple spreadsheets, program justifications, comparisons to the previous year's spending, etc.

Then, Bob asked him one question: "Is this the right thing to do for our employees?"

"Yes."

"Then I don't want to see a spreadsheet brought to a future meeting."

> *Then, Bob asked him one question: "Is this the right thing to do for our employees?"*
>
> *"Yes."*
>
> *"Then I don't want to see a spreadsheet brought to a future meeting."*

Bob's message was clear. Barry-Wehmiller's justification, or WHY—"Is it the right thing to do?"—said that the numbers, while important, should not drive any wellness decisions. Josh Glynn from Google relies on extensive data but is equally clear on WHY. He said Google's mission is "We help Googlers lead full lives in order to sustain a culture that can change the world."

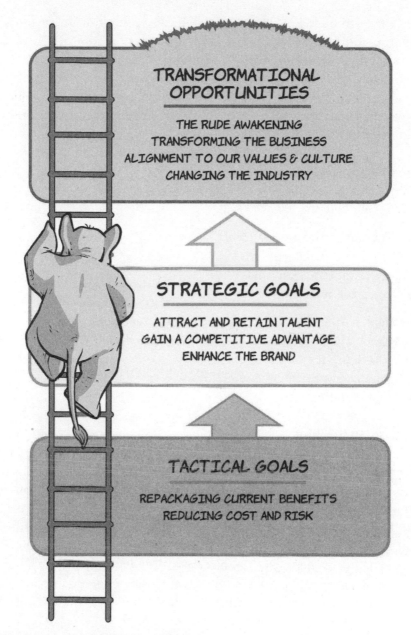

Figure 5.1 The ladder to wellness.

Our team built a "ladder" during our Mayo summit. It has proven useful to some leaders as an assessment of where a company is on its journey to wellness. The ladder begins with tactical challenges. The next rungs move into strategic goals. The higher rungs, transformational opportunities, require greater leadership participation, coalitions between departments, deeper stakeholder voices, and a reshaping of cultural norms.

The Bottom Rungs—Tactical Goals
- Repackaging current benefits
- Reducing cost and risk

The Next Rungs—Strategic Goals
- Attract and retain talent
- Gain a competitive advantage
- Enhance the brand

The Higher Rungs—Transformational Opportunities
- The rude awakening
- Transforming the business
- Alignment to our values and culture
- Changing the industry

Each rung requires higher and broader commitment and more resources. The calculus also shifts from budget line-item cost controls over to more complex relationships, influencing organizational performance. When you evaluate your company's current location on the ladder, you may find the program, messaging, resources and systems, leadership, and employee experience all on different rungs. That is more common than clean alignment, and it also offers an immediate opportunity for increased effectiveness.

The work of aligning these can be messy like cleaning out an attic. You may need an outsider to lift the process above the understandable emotions of the process.

Finding that common starting point with a "ladder" was, perhaps, the most valuable work we accomplished together at the Mayo Clinic summit. Our collection of leaders from different companies was probably like leaders inside any company. We came with different experiences, expectations, biases, and assumptions, and our first instincts were to bolt those onto existing frameworks and fuzzy notions of wellness. The ladder concept helped us to find the same sheet of music.

The ladder also helps companies ask, "Do we start with designing a better program?" Or "Can we use our program to build a better company?"

The Leader's Nudge

- How do your employees define personal wellness and well-being?
- What do I have conviction for, commitment to, and congruence regarding employee health and happiness?
- Can you explain the reason and the benefits of your company's offering to a 10-year-old? Would they think, "Cool"?
- Are your programs, messaging, resources and systems, leadership team, and employee experience on the same rung?

The Personal Nudge

- What do wellness and well-being mean to me?
- Do I feel like I'm flourishing at work using the PERMA model?[9]
- Where do I see my company on the ladder for flourishing?
- How can I start some conversations about grounding and aligning of our wellness efforts?

CHAPTER 6

Why Happiness
Before Health

We hold these truths to be self-evident, that all men are created equal, that
they are endowed by their Creator with certain unalienable Rights, that
among these are Life, Liberty and the pursuit of Happiness.
                                    —US Declaration of Independence

The journey that produced this book began at the Mayo Clinic. I chose
Mayo because of its unique approach to whole patient care, including
the patient's sense of happiness or well-being.

Dr. Amit Sood, professor of medicine at Mayo Clinic College of
Medicine, and chair of the Mayo Clinic Mind Body Initiative, opened our
session. Dr. Sood was born and raised in Bhopal, India, and began his
career witnessing the aftermath of the Bhopal chemical spill as a first-year
medical student. His view of suffering was shaped by his work with
patients maimed by the tragedy and living in conditions of extreme
poverty, malnutrition, and disease. That experience led to his belief that
external conditions were the key contributors to suffering.

His quest to help alleviate suffering opened the door to a two-year
residency in New York. His patients there were much different. Healthier
and stronger, they did not suffer acute and desperate conditions. Yet, they
struggled with the same level and duration of suffering and stress as did his
impoverished patients in Bhopal. He saw "a deep disconnect between our
material and emotional wealth." That surprising insight changed his career.

So, right at the beginning, Dr. Sood's message touched a deep chord and established a vital theme for our work. We learned the deceptively simple truth: Happiness comes before health.

We learned the deceptively simple truth: Happiness comes before health.

The Pursuit of Happiness

Incredibly, America is founded in an understanding that humans have the right to pursue happiness. Now, I admit that the word "happiness" has suffered erosion from the way the framers used it. Still, after 15 years of research and working with thousands of people, I haven't found a better word (because many readers will be more familiar with "well-being," we use it and "happiness" interchangeably throughout this book).

Let's drill down into the strata beneath happiness.

The 90-Minute Rule

In my work, I often overwork my brain. And I usually just try to push through it. That is a mistake. Dr. Sood says our brains fatigue after 90 minutes of focused work. We cannot feel brain pain because the brain has no nerve endings. But overworking our brain is like stressing a muscle.

Leo Widrich, cofounder and COO at Buffer, examined the origins of the eight-hour working day. Not surprisingly, he discovered it was created in, by, and for the Industrial Revolution. After exposing the total irrelevance of an industrial revolution idea for today's working world, he wrote, "One of the things most of us easily forget is that as humans, we are distinctly

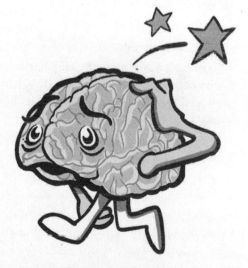

Figure 6.1   The brain can be overworked, just like a muscle.

different from machines. At the core, this means that *machines move linearly and humans move cyclically*" (italics mine).

> *For an efficient work day, that truly respects our human nature, the first thing to focus on are ultradian cycles.*
>
> *Our human minds can focus on any given task for 90–120 minutes. Afterwards, a 20–30 minute break is required for us to get the renewal to achieve high performance for our next task again. . . . So instead of thinking about "What can I get done in an 8-hour day," I've started to change my thinking to "What can I get done in a 90-min session."*[1]

I understand the origins of our working day patterns. But, why do we remain enslaved to an eighteenth-century model? Today is a time (in Tony Swartz's words) "to manage your energy, not your time." Yet the typical work patterns in the twenty-first century pull us right into brain-jarring work after a stressful commute. We start our day buried under an avalanche of company e-mails. And we often face a series of meetings, with little or no time to prepare. As a result, too many meetings wander and don't add value or make decisions. It seems that we walk in the door of our workplace, and then straight into a shredder. We have no time to focus.[2]

We walk in the door of our workplace, and then straight into a shredder. We have no time to focus.

So, is it possible to achieve happiness at work? Or is "the job" unavoidably and forever taxing, harsh, unhealthy, and dreaded? Shouldn't places of productivity consistently release those who work there to be the best version of themselves? Look at our cultural views of the workplace. The offices, factories, and other work environments presented in novels, movies, and TV shows always seem to revolve around negative views of managers, coworkers, and "company policy." Plots frequently include workplace hostility, injustice, sexual harassment, and psychological warfare. Do we simply not know how to create happy, engaging, collaborative, and productive societies around work? As New York Mets manager Casey Stengel once supposedly asked, "Can't anybody here play this game?"

An Engaged Mind Is a Happy Mind

In our work on this book, our team concluded that the workplace can and must become a happy place; a true haven. But that comes only by design. The money and time companies spend promoting wellness initiatives are wasted unless we first learn how to create a happy workplace.

For example, do you know it is not only possible but essential to remove friction from our workplaces? By friction, I mean the frustration and lost productivity that result from the failure of things to work. Things as simple as having enough outlets and easy plug-and-play electrical and digital connections are crucial to creating a frictionless work environment. Time spent crawling around under conference tables looking for electrical outlets, or waiting for someone from IT to fix the damned LED projector, is friction. To remove it, some companies have created living labs to test different work configurations, furniture solutions, and technology to resolve the friction points on the front end. That seems like a small price to pay to drive common friction from daily operations.

A frictionless atmosphere enhances focus and engagement. That's because the ability to focus and accomplish good work is key to experiencing happiness. I participated in a Harvard study a few years ago using an app called Track Your Happiness. The findings were the same. *A wandering mind is an unhappy mind.*[3] An engaged mind is happy. Think of the times and activities that took you beyond any awareness of time and space. That happened because you were so absorbed in creating, conversing, building, reading a book, walking alone through nature, spending a day in a museum, driving through the country, or completely lost in a work project. Those experiences and others like them release the happy hormones that restore health.

Leaders know engagement is the holy grail of business. If that is true, wouldn't it follow that companies would do anything possible to create an environment and a culture of happiness so that people could find the natural engagement that is so vital?

So, why does happiness in the workplace still trail the emphasis on physical health by a large margin? How did we get these backward? Why has it taken almost 50 years of failed *wellness* (health) efforts to begin to look at *well-being* (happiness)? Even companies most recognized for their wellness initiatives are just beginning to explore the well-being side of the equation in limited ways. Teaching meditation, mindfulness, and stress management just scratch the surface. We need a larger definition of wellness and a deeper exploration of how companies might do more to create it.

The new attention to well-being or happiness provides a new opportunity to rehumanize wellness efforts and reframe our thinking. But that has not, and will not, come by applying program thinking. The current system lets the tail wag the dog by focusing on programs, steps, and participation without asking, "What is the point of this?" Most businesses and leaders have a long way to go to decouple from the traditional wellness systems and mindset.

Most businesses and leaders have a long way to go to decouple from the traditional wellness systems and mindset.

What Makes Us Happy at Work?

I have worked with Dr. Mike O'Neill, a cognitive psychologist, for more than two years on this project. Dr. Mike, as he is called, has focused his career on the study of human performance and happiness in the workplace. His work combines cognitive psychology (how people think, learn, decide, and remember), positive psychology (human flourishing), organizational design, ergonomics, and workplace strategy.

After my 15 years as a performance coach, helping thousands of people to "find their sweet spot," he changed my practice by subordinating engagement to happiness.

Dr. Mike says, "The problem with engagement is that it has become primarily an instrument for achieving improved productivity. Employers are willing to spend money on engagement surveys to uncover where they can improve. These have proven strong predictors of retention rates, and it helps manage the risk of losing employees. All of this, however, accrues to the benefit of the employer. Our research indicates that focusing on the broader notion of happiness, a sense of well-being, *naturally* results in engagement.

"How do you operationalize the word happiness? We found four traits we could test and measure: (1) a sense of well-being, (2) happiness at work, (3) lower stress levels, and (4) feeling relaxed. Furthermore, in one of our tests, 4,000 office workers experienced real effects from two aspects of work across all four traits. First is the ability to focus. The second measurable aspect is the degree the workspace communicates that you are valued.

"Workspace that is easy to understand, navigate, and use sends a definite message, 'We value and want to support your role in our organization.' Giving people a choice of where to work, control over how they accomplish work, the right tools, and, surprisingly, the right storage and retrieval systems, all register as affecting workplace happiness. One critical but often overlooked happiness factor is job design. Poor job design is a major source of stress and disengagement. It all seems to come down to two factors; cognitive load and autonomy.

> *Workspace that is easy to understand, navigate, and use sends a definite message, "We value and want to support your role in our organization."*

"A job with high cognitive load with high autonomy produces positive stress. That's right, stress can be good, in fact, stress is necessary in order to filter out the world for focus. Senior architects fit this category. On the opposite end are jobs with high cognitive load but low autonomy. They produce the most stress. Think of a call center. You hear a beep, and you're on! You don't know if you're dealing with a happy or angry caller until you hear their voice."

PERMA—Five Keys to Human Flourishing

Dr. Martin Seligman is known as the father of positive psychology. The former president of the American Psychological Association, Dr. Seligman is director of the Positive Psychology Center at the University of Pennsylvania. He built on Dr. Donald Clifton's work beginning in the 1950s known as strengths-based psychology. In other words, building on what is strong instead of fixing what is wrong. In his search for what makes people happy, he coined the acronym PERMA: positive emotion, engagement, relationships, meaning, and accomplishment. Dr. Seligman identifies those dimensions as the keys to human flourishing.

One of Dr. Seligman's research projects examined 1.1 million soldiers to explore psychological fitness and resilience. Brig. Gen. Rhonda Cornum, PhD, MD, the director of the Comprehensive Soldier Fitness program, said of Seligman's project, "We don't assume people can shoot when they come into the Army, so we teach them how to load weapons and how to aim. . . . We need to attend to psychological fitness the same way we do physical performance."[4]

Part of the study examined soldiers who struggled with PTSD and those who eventually became stronger. Two factors separated the groups. Soldiers who became stronger worked at it. It was not by accident. Their lives also exhibited the five elements of PERMA: (1) a sense of living for something bigger than themselves, (2) work and activities they naturally enjoyed, (3) relational connection and interdependency, (4) their lives and work made a tangible difference to others, and (5) consistent achievement.

Shouldn't that also apply to the workplace? What if you turn PERMA into personal questions to be used as a framework for workplace strategy and design?

- How do the workflow, workspace, and leadership communicate a sense of purpose to me and others?
- Does the workspace offer me a choice to work in ways that leverage my strengths?
- How does the workspace facilitate a sense of psychological safety, connection, and access to vital workplace relationships?
- Does the workspace help me know how my work makes a difference, that I and my work have meaning?
- Does the workspace give me a sense of accomplishment?

Hope and Engagement

Sometimes hope is the first casualty in the push to achieve business goals. Leaders assume that everyone carries the compelling vision of the objective, that everyone is sufficiently healthy and zealous for the mission, and that everyone will rush the beach like soldiers in a war movie. But some people are damaged, broken, discouraged, and just barely hanging on. Those people are not engaged with anything or anyone. They cannot rise to the mission; they just want to get through the day and return home to bed, chemicals, or silence. They have no hope; it died long before they ever hit the beach.

Sometimes hope is the first casualty in the push to achieve business goals.

I am usually hired because of unhappiness. I've never been told, "Everybody's happy and productive; could you come in and make us a little happier?" I know the unhappy "Let me hide" employees and I know the "I'm unhappy and I'll make sure you are too" employees. I've coined an acronym for the second group, CAVE dwellers: consistently against virtually everything. According to Gallup 20% of your employees are CAVE dwellers, toxic. They cost companies 34% of their salaries.[5]

Early in my work on engagement, in fact, my very first workshop, I met Bob. To this day, he remains my largest image of a toxic employee. His body language told everyone that he'd rather be anywhere on earth than in that room. Bob didn't speak, look up, laugh, or go out for a cigarette. He just sat, with his head on his chest, and glared at the materials on the table. He didn't even look up when I stepped into his personal space.

When we broke for lunch a colleague from my firm and I invited Bob to lunch. We ordered, briefly covered the weather and sports, and then I had to ask. "Bob, what do you get to do in your job that taps into what you like to do?"

"Nothing."

I paused and dove in again, "So, what do you get to do outside of work that you enjoy and energizes you?"

"Nothing."

My stomach started churning. I could see Bob was hurting and I was not qualified to dig much deeper. But I did have a backup. My colleague was a top clinical psychologist and would rescue me if I fell too far into trouble.

I paused, not sure what to ask. But, I went back in, "How long has this been going on?"

"Twenty-five years." Then he helpfully added, "I hate my job and I hate the people I work with."

Ten minutes into a one-hour lunch, I was drained and nervous. So, I said, "Help me, Bob. Just play this out for me. What happens to your health, job, family over the next five years if nothing changes?"

He shook his head, looked at his plate, and whispered, "I don't know."

At that point, my colleague came to the rescue, changed the subject, and we returned to the workshop.

Bob didn't speak that afternoon, but he did seem to listen.

I returned 90 days later for a second session, a two-day session to prepare the managers to introduce the material to their employees.

When I arrived, I first ran into Bob.

"Rex, great to see you. I'm looking forward to the session."

I had no idea how to interpret that. Bob did participate and then on the morning of the second day Bob stopped the workshop and changed my career. He said he needed to say something. I gave him the floor, but thought, *oh no, what is this?* By the time he got to his feet, he was in tears.

"I've been an SOB to all of you and I just want to say I'm sorry. I love this job and I love all of you." Four or five people reached for Kleenex. I was in tears. After an awkward silence, I called a break. I immediately walked over to Dave, an executive officer, and asked, "What just happened?"

I've been an SOB to all of you and I just want to say I'm sorry. I love this job and I love all of you.

Dave gave me the short version of the story. As a result of the Gallup Strengthsfinder Assessment, Bob discovered that he was naturally wired to be creative, solve problems, and get things done—but was drained by people and politics. Yet, he was responsible for young, immature employees who, for the most part, did not have college degrees and were union members. That responsibility did not tap into any of his natural strengths. It forced him to work as if he were in a foreign country and didn't know the language.

In the final day of the first workshop, I explained that people experience a virtuous reinforcing loop when they are able to apply their natural strengths to their work. It comes easier, they begin to produce better results, and they get positive recognition. On the other side, when they must operate outside their strengths, the work gets harder and more draining. Drain turns to frustration, frustration to anxiety, anxiety to anger, and anger to rage. After 25 years Bob came in every day ready to go postal.

Bob gained some real insight from that. More than that, he found hope.

That lesson early in my consulting career completely reshaped my approach to CAVE dwellers. Someone said that hope is the oxygen of the soul. Hope is also a nudge. All by itself, it tilts people into the courage, confidence, and energy to do the right thing. So, managers should do all they can to find it, impart it, rebuild it, and restore it. Hope will go a very long way to turn people toward health. Like a building, hope is another potential nudge for a greater sense of well-being.

Out on the Frontlines

Josh Glynn told me, "We know your direct manager has more effect on your work life than anything."

That may be why Google invests so heavily in internal research on the factors that make a great manager. Josh said that he's observed that most companies have a serious disconnect in trying to create engagement or improve wellness. Success for both falls on the back of middle managers, which it should. But it also breaks down with middle managers, which is predictable. He explained that middle managers will get the blame, but it is really a leadership problem. In most cases when initiatives fail, managers are neither fully trained nor resourced to translate, model, train, and coach their employees into a new way of thinking and behaving. New initiatives are simply add-on responsibilities.

But, managers are stationed on the front lines. And for good reasons. They inspire, equip, direct, and oversee operations. They are the most immediate point of contact and traction with the workforce. Assuming a manager is trained and resourced, Gallup has identified 12 needs that employees require to find true engagement and perform at their best. The 12 requisites ascend Maslow's hierarchy from basic to aspirational needs. I've simplified them to the following:

> *Gallup has identified 12 needs that employees require to find true engagement and perform at their best.*

1. Focus me.
2. Equip me.
3. Help me find my fit.
4. Recognize a contribution, weekly.
5. Care about me.
6. Help me grow.
7. Hear me.
8. Help me see the impact of what WE do.
9. Help me feel everyone will be held to equally high standards.
10. Help me to find and form vital relationships at work.
11. Assess my progress and areas for growth.
12. Challenge me.

Even a casual look over that list reveals the value and priority of happiness. That list communicates the heart's cry of people as they live out their roles and responsibilities. People have an integral need to be properly aligned with body, mind, soul, family, and other human relationships. They need personal integrity, a sense of productivity and meaning, sufficient degrees of safety, and adequate power to negotiate life. Of course, physical and mental health are important. But happiness is far more critical than physical and mental health. Furthermore, it often leads to greater health.

Social Emotional Literacy

Social emotional literacy is a language. It has become a growing field in childhood psychology, especially working with at-risk kids. It goes further than emotional intelligence. It forms the practices and habits for mental health and happiness.

We opened our Dallas summit on social emotional literacy with a presentation from Michelle Kinder, executive director of the Momentous Institute. The century-old institution started as a therapeutic outreach to at-risk communities in Dallas. Today the institute includes training and a lab school. They work directly with about 6,000 kids and family members every year. According to Michelle, many of their kids live with the toxic stresses associated with poverty and adverse childhood experiences (ACE). ACE are divided into three categories: (1) abuse, (2) neglect, and (3) household struggles such as violence, addiction, divorce, or incarceration. Without intervention, a child coming out of these conditions will likely experience a disruption in neurodevelopment. That leads to social, emotional, and cognitive impairment, and eventually to unhealthy and destructive behavior. Without intervention by those who care, these journeys do not end well. Interventions must start early, engage the family, and be led by teachers well trained in social and emotional literacy.

I carefully selected the Momentous Institute because of earlier research into education. The institute is a positive outlier. They achieve incredible outcomes with kids who come in abused, neglected, and psychologically scarred. They are an educational MASH unit. Their philosophy, methods, and tools have been designed not only through their therapeutic lens but in the day-to-day encounters with kids, families, and the communities they come from.

After more research, I discovered and alarming statistic: 50% of the kids in our nation are being left behind. Most of those will not graduate and those who do will not have the academic or life skills necessary to survive, contribute, grow, and build hope for a better tomorrow. Half of these kids will fall through the crack because of socioeconomic reasons and the other half will face a lifetime of struggle with their learning differences. These kids do grow up. But, without vital skills and social emotional maturity, that often means a fast lane to prison.

Michelle explained the vital connection between chronic and acute stress on the brain. Stress is cognitive load. When it is constant it shuts down the learning and decision-making side of the brain. In other words, many of the kids who arrive at school are in no condition to jump into learning. When the additional load of learning is added, they either withdraw or act out. She calls that, and has helped her students recognize it as, an "amygdala hijack."

Think for your moment when you were at your wits' end. When I've encountered deadlines or other pressures, my survival gene came alive! I felt like a scuba diver sucking on a suddenly empty tank. If the garbage disposal gets clogged and my innocent wife pleads for help before dinner, my amygdala is likely to pop. If I were constantly on the razor's edge, I'd have a very difficult time trying to create a safe place or help an employee needing emotional support.

The Momentous School provides a safe, positive, and connected environment for their three-year-old to fifth-grade kids. But they also know they must work with parents and others who shape the home lives of the kids. When Michelle took me to the parent resource room, she explained, "Parents are welcome to come here anytime. In addition, the parents of our three-year-olds participate in

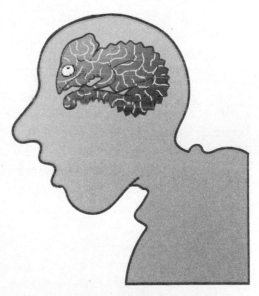

Figure 6.2 Too much stress leads to an amygdala hijack.

a home visit that includes leaving behind a box of books and educational toys. The box also has a journal, so they can describe how they used the material and read what other families wrote."

Parents also receive coaching and training so they can be equipped to improve the family and home environment. Michelle took me to the vision wall, where parents write their visions for their children's future. Some were simple, several were hopeful, and many were very specific and quite moving. Some stories just took my breath away. Throughout the tour, I found numerous subtle details, nudges, that reveal the "momentous" attention to each child and the environment. The hallway walls were painted in textures that invite kids to sweep their hands along the wall as they walked, stimulating their senses. Photographs of the brain, highlighting different areas and brain functions, are posted throughout the school. A three-year-old told me that she had a brain and it was in her head and it was very, very important. Five-year-olds knew where frustration, anger, and sorrow come from in the brain. They also knew the coping skills that calm it down.[6]

I was struck by the seamless integration of teaching and environment that extended to the home and family. The Momentous Institute recognized what too many companies miss—it takes an ecosystem to reprogram and create sustainable change. The institute has built what Jeffrey Pfeffer begs leaders to create: supportive systems, environment, and culture.

> The Momentous Institute recognized what too many companies miss—it takes an ecosystem to reprogram and create sustainable change.

I've met with a few companies and institutions that build such thinking into their culture. Cummins is famous for their policy on "invisible diversity." Google hires many with Asperger's and others along the autism spectrum. They train managers to create a psychologically safe environment. Parkland Hospital and Kaiser Permanente provide opportunities for those on the lower economic rungs to be trained and mentored in life skills.

Dr. Ron Anderson, former CEO of Dallas's Parkland Hospital, told me about a woman who ran the laundry service, a difficult job. Many times she was offered a promotion. And she turned each one down because she saw the laundry room as her calling, a place where she could do the most good. Because it was one of the lowest entry positions in the hospital, she found it to be an ideal place for recruiting people who needed a chance in life. She worked with and developed them until they could get a promotion and foothold on the upward ladder—an incredible and improbable dream for most of them. It was a moving story, but more so because I heard it from the man who planted and cultivated that garden of care for Parkland Hospital. It is one thing to recognize talent or give a person a break in life; that what good leaders do. Extraordinary leaders, however, have learned to place others at the center, see a person's greater calling, and give that calling a garden in which to grow.

I was honestly not sure how a group of business leaders would react to our summit on social and emotional literacy. I knew it would take us outside our comfort zones. Most, however, were deeply moved. We responded to the innocence of kids, their inherent worth, and the skills to nurture the wounded and hurting. But that built a bridge to recognize, as Bob Chapman reminds us, that "Each of us is someone's precious child." That lens is an incredible reframe, a powerful nudge when you can look beyond the value that someone brings to the table and see their intrinsic worth. Michelle and her kids reminded all of us that happiness is the bedrock below the human capacity for working productively and living as healthy and contributing members of society.

The Leadership Nudge

Do you have time to care? How well do you know the lives, interests, and challenges with your direct reports? What provisions do you have to give opportunities providing both job and life skills? Do you have someone to reach out to, a safe and trusted listening ear? Or, do you feel isolated by your role and demands?

The Personal Nudge

Do you have times when you feel you're about to have an amygdala hijack? Do you have a habit that helps you to restore calm? How do you cope with daily work and life stress? Do you have a friend at work who provides a safe place to talk, process, and support?

CHAPTER 7

Where's the Data?

Inconvenient Truths

For fifteen thousand years, fraud and short-sighted thinking have never, ever worked. Not once. Eventually you get caught, things go south. When the hell did we forget all that?

—Mark Baum, *The Big Short*[1]

The wellness industry is built on the quite reasonable premise that prevention is better and less expensive than a cure. But, from that premise, the industry ventures deep into embellishment. It promises that early detection through screenings and assessments will prevent debilitating and costly diseases. It swears it can deliver behavior change. Finally, insisting that education and incentives can change bad habits, it claims programs for personal improvement, such as weight loss and smoking cessation, will provide 300% to 600% returns on investment.

None of that is true.

Traditional wellness programs have not improved health outcomes, lowered costs, reduced chronic disease, changed behavior, improved engagement, or helped to attract and retain talent.

Wellness has become a culture or a system of belief that defies the data and common sense. For example, if wellness (or any other) programs give 300% or greater ROI, every company would be increasing—desperately increasing—their investments in those programs. And they're not.

Programs, departments, bureaus, and other power centers very naturally build support for their own existence. As part of a pure survival instinct, they tell good stories that everyone hopes are true. They also weave equally compelling stories of what would happen if they went

Traditional wellness programs have not improved health outcomes, lowered costs, decreased chronic disease, changed behavior, improved engagement, or helped to attract and retain talent.

away. Finally, they build or borrow the strongest planks of credibility they can locate.

That's why, if you dare peek behind the packaging, the narrative, and the logic of wellness, as I did, you may come face to face with a fierce reaction. I learned that the hard way when I stumbled across a book, *Why Nobody Believes the Numbers: Distinguishing Fact from Fiction in Population Health Management.*[2] That blockbuster caused me to reach out to its author, Al Lewis. Al, as I mentioned in Chapter 2, is a certified heavyweight in the industry, the founder of the Disease Management Association of America, and is also one of the fathers of the preventative health movement.

However, Al experienced the personal crisis of coming face-to-face with the evidence that his work had not measured up to its claims; it had produced no improvement in health or drop in health costs. Because of that, he disavowed most of that work. Today Al walks in a wonderfully earth-bound view that math is real, not a matter of opinion. In fact, he dedicated *Nobody Believes the Numbers* "To my fifth grade math teacher for apparently

Figure 7.1   Al Lewis.

doing a better job than the other kids' fifth grade math teachers."

His basic point is that health costs calculations are not representative of the true population health costs or risks. Al's conversations, blogs, and e-mails can be incendiary. But he makes total sense. His many critics never attack his data, only his "style." In fact, his sheer grasp of numbers

The wellness industry is (like any industry) a self-serving, self-preserving, narrative-clinging, somewhat dark and deceptive smoke-filled room of fast and loose dealing from consultants and vendors.

and his sense of reality is why he fits so well on the island of wellness castaways. And that's why all of them have become a collective wrecking ball to the wellness industry.

Strangely, most of experts and advocates I have interviewed essentially agree with Al. The only difference seems to be that they have not concluded that the foundations were fundamentally flawed, but rather in need of reform. That is the core of what I learned from my ringside seat at the food fight. In trying to navigate the realms of workplace wellness, businesses need to know that the wellness industry is (like any industry) a self-serving, self-preserving, narrative-clinging, somewhat dark and deceptive smoke-filled room of fast and loose dealing from consultants and vendors.

Part of our purpose in this book is to help you find better ways to invest in the health and well-being of your employees than traditional vendor supplied wellness programs.

As I told the story in Chapter 2, when I was disinvited to a wellness conference simply because I talked to Al Lewis, I knew I had to become a film noir private detective and untangle the mystery behind my rejection. Along the way, I found a cadre of wise and credentialed leaders, who had decades of direct experience and deep research. Like Michael Burry and Mark Baum in the movie, *The Big Short,* this small and eccentric group focused on the numbers, not the narrative; they cared about math, not myth. Their quirks fit their purpose—they didn't care about being published in the leading journals, invited to the right parties, or booked to speak at the most elite wellness conferences. They all seemed intellectually honest in their mission: "Stop wasting money on wellness programs."

In addition to Al, that group of alternative voices included Tom Emerick, an author (and coauthor with Al) and the former head of benefits for Walmart, BP, and Burger King. Tom introduced me to Soeren Mattke, an internationally recognized scholar and managing director of the RAND Health Advisory. It also included Salveo Partners, a wellness and culture consulting firm focusing on culture change. Josh Glynn, director of health and performance at Google is another member of the group.

The Wellness Industrial Complex

Tell me the difference between stupid and illegal and I'll have my wife's brother arrested.

—Jarred Vennett, *The Big Short*[3]

First, to gather some perspective about the wellness industry, please consider this snapshot. The Global Wellness Institute divides the entire industry into the following segments:

- Beauty & Anti-Aging ($999 billion)
- Healthy Eating, Nutrition & Weight Loss ($648 billion)
- Wellness Tourism ($563 billion)
- Fitness & Mind-Body ($542 billion)
- Preventative & Personalized Medicine and Public Health ($534 billion)
- Complementary & Alternative Medicine ($199 billion)
- Wellness Lifestyle Real Estate ($119 billion)
- Spa Industry ($99 billion)
- Thermal/Mineral Springs ($51 billion)
- Workplace Wellness ($43 billion)[4]

As you can see, the workplace wellness realm is the smallest slice of the $3.7 trillion industry. But, because it enjoys daily access to the nation's workforce, it is the one part of the industry holding the largest platform for change.

Because wellness programs have daily access to the nation's workforce, it holds the largest platform for change.

The US part of the global $43 billion workplace wellness world is a $14 billion industry. Of companies with over 200 employees, 92% have some form of wellness program.[5] And those companies spend an average of $693 per employee per year.[6] In recent years, the cost per employee has grown about 15% annually (not including the larger hidden costs).[7]

Most programs are divided into two elements: (1) disease management, and (2) lifestyle management. Disease management focuses on the 5% of the work population who rack up 80% of health-care costs, including those who are in the early (and therefore undetected) stages of chronic disease.

The alarming rise of chronic disease, a catalyst for the growth of preventative health programs and interventions, is the most threatening part of the entire landscape of health and wellness issues. It was a central part of the Affordable Care Act. President Obama was right when he said, "the health care system was not working. And the rising costs of health care burdened businesses and became the biggest driver of our long-term deficits."[8]

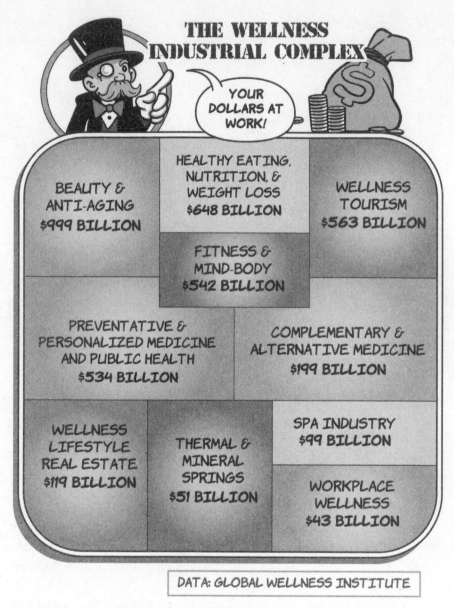

Figure 7.2   The wellness industrial complex.

The Great Train Wreck

Told with enough persistence and conviction, what was once untrue can become true, in a self-fulfilling prophecy sort of way.

—Jeffrey Pfeffer

Those realities about chronic disease marked the boundary lines of the new battlefield for health. And wellness programs became the central strategy in the battle. And then the whole train flew off the track. First, some of the arguments presented before Congress included experts, studies, and projections that fell somewhere between embellishments and BS.

For example, the "Safeway Study" was heavily promoted by the Obama administration and congressional leaders as a worthy private sector initiative. Some saw it as part of the great bundle of better ideas that would soon tumble across the land. But then the study hit the wall. Washington wonks woke up January 17, 2010, to this headline in the *Washington Post*: "Misleading Claims about Safeway Wellness Incentives Shape Health-Care Bill." After recounting Safeway's claims and Washington's hopes, the story told us:

> . . . *a review of Safeway documents and interviews with company officials show that the company did not keep health-care costs flat for four years. Those costs did drop in 2006—by 12.5 percent. That was when the company overhauled its benefits, according to Safeway Senior Vice President Ken Shachmut.*
>
> *The decline did not have anything to do with tying employees' premiums to test results. That element of Safeway's benefits plan was not implemented until 2009, Shachmut said.*
>
> *After the 2006 drop, costs resumed their climb, he said.*[9]

Some of the arguments presented before Congress included experts, studies, and projections that fell somewhere between embellishments and BS.

In another study, a Harvard economist claimed that, for each dollar spent, wellness programs returned three dollars in health cost savings and another three dollars in reduced absenteeism. But a 2014 RAND Corporation brief disproved the report.[10] The Harvard author later retracted her report's claims.

Then it all broke wide open. Conversations and e-mail threads among policymakers, insurance professionals, health-care leaders, and other stakeholders exposed deep anger and accusations over what some felt was a fabrication of data to promote self-interests over truth. Although I don't know the intent of those using false data, I understand the emotions. I spent eight months convinced of the accuracy of the dollars and data the industry provided. I'm sure many of the human resource and wellness professionals did too. And here's the problem: A few case studies have become major pillars of information or misinformation, and they have been repeated over and over for more than a decade.

Figure 7.3   Soeren Mattke.

It's actually not clear at all when people say "Our program works," what they really mean by "works."

During my interview with Soeren Mattke, lead author of the congressionally mandated RAND analysis of wellness programs,[11] he said, "It's actually not clear at all when people say 'our program works,' what they really mean by 'works.' How did they measure that? Most importantly, who measured it? Most of the time your vendor measured and declared victory.

"When wellness became such a hype, the claim was, okay, you spend a dollar on wellness and you get six, eight, 10 dollars back in savings. Of course, that was total bull. After a while, they said, 'Okay, it might not save you net health care costs, but you will break even on health care cost. Then anything else like productivity gains, morale or retention, whatever; that's kind of a bonus.' So, it was presented as a deliberate value proposition.

"Then people kept asking, 'Where are the numbers?' Nobody actually has ever quantified this. Instead, they said, "Well, it's still good. You shouldn't really look at it from an ROI perspective. You should look at it from a value on investment (VOI) perspective,' whatever that is."

Rachel Druckenmiller, director of well-being for SIG, jumps into the conversation, "We've started with something like ROI, right? We said, first it's the ROI, that's really the thing that we've got to focus on, and then it's about health care costs. But, when that gets too difficult, we move on to talking about employee engagement. But then we back away from that because that's a loaded topic. So, let's move on to culture. And that's the biggest challenge of all. So, what do we actually do, what do we actually measure?"

Figure 7.4 Rachel Druckenmiller.

Two Nagging Questions

In my search to understand the wellness case, I struggled with two nagging questions:

1. If wellness is working, why are chronic disease and health costs rising at the same alarming rates?
2. If $1 produces a $3 return, why are companies trying to reduce their cost in wellness programs?

I knew the wellness industry promises improved health outcomes, reduced risk, lower health costs, improved engagement, and a competitive advantage in recruiting. But I needed to know *how*. My ignorance was my saving grace and the turning point in our research.

I could not find how the positive returns were calculated or verified. What were they measuring? I tried following the story upstream, but they always stopped at the rosy outcome. I got tired of being caught in a cycle of circular reasoning. When I mapped the footnotes and sources, they all pointed back to one another. I never found an explanation of how the analyses were conducted or what was actually measured. The story was always told as "$1 of investment = $3 in return."

I discovered what happens when a claim or strand of logic resonates intuitively, in theory, and as a darn good story. It attracts early adopters and opportunists. When I reached the global director for health and performance for the most cited case study, he admitted that he did not know where the numbers came from or even who had actually created the report. So, that study seemed to be nothing more than a very high profile and very respected urban legend.

Meanwhile, back in the company of my new castaway friends, the misfit provocateurs, I kept hearing simple declarative sentences and specific and sourced data. Moral, logical, and grammatical clarity are as refreshing as clear mountain stream. I felt like Anne Lamott, who said, "When people tell the truth, it's like finding an English language station in Morocco."[12]

The RAND 10-year study tracked the cost savings comparison for an employee who participated in a wellness program versus one who did not. After five years, a company would net $157 over the employee who opted out. The report qualified that as "statistically insignificant."

The study also found that less than 15% of eligible employees participate in wellness programs. Josh Glynn told me that he came to despise the word "engagement." It had become synonymous with just signing up for a health risk assessment or participating in a wellness event. I believe that. One human resource team for a global manufacturer showed me their "engagement" graphs. For most of the year, participation remained flat at about 10%. Then it slowly rose in September and continued until just before to the November enrollment deadline. At that point, it hit 40%. That meant the employees received the typical incentive, signed up, and then went back to doing what they were doing before. Everyone knows that programs measure success by the number of people who sign up, take an assessment, or attend an event. Dr. Roizen says that those don't mean a thing; that's why the Cleveland Clinic only measures outcomes on five numbers: (1) blood pressure, (2) triglycerides, (3) cotinine (found in tobacco), (4) body mass index, and (5) LDL cholesterol.

Tausha Robertson, cofounder of Alterity,[13] said, "When you put numbers in front of the financial folks that I work with, they're like, 'Yeah, that's cost mitigation. That's not savings. I want savings. But the wellness industry presents cost mitigation as savings.'"

The industry also shows cost shifting as savings. When I poked into the details, I often heard comments like, "Yeah, when our plan changes its deductible, I just cost-share more of it to the employees." I also found that most did not have reliable data on true health cost reductions. Not only is there a lot of noise in the system, but the data and analytics go far beyond the skills or background of most benefits managers or wellness account managers.

> *. . . employees received the typical incentive, signed up, and then went back to doing what they were doing before.*

Wellness Claims Ignore Biology

Leaders must consider the four primary reasons that traditional wellness programs won't stop the influx of chronic disease:

1. People with chronic disease are less likely to participate.
2. Education and incentives don't change unhealthy behavior. If you think they do, show me the data.
3. Because wellness programs often reshuffle every November, they lack the continuity to address long-term health.
4. Chronic disease takes years to develop and years to manage or reverse.

Soeren Mattke explained how we get it wrong at the outset:

> *We conclude chronic disease results from smoking, bad diet, and lack of exercise. Hence, if we provide a program that tinkers with those conditions, it will reduce the cost of care. But that ignores the pure biology of chronic disease. The symptoms we see today are the consequence of poor health behavior decades ago.*
>
> *If I start eating like a pig today and only get off the sofa to fetch another six-pack, it'll take me maybe five years to get obese, and ten years to become diabetic. At that point, I'm not really expensive because early-stage diabetes can be handled with a few pills, a few tests, a few doctor visits. That's really not anything that shows up in any statistics. Then it'll take another five to 10 years for me to develop vascular complications like heart disease, blindness, renal failure. At that point, I'm getting expensive.*

Figure 7.5   The state of American fitness.

Dr. Roizen identified more warps in the wellness programs. "Most employers have a period in November called Open Enrollment. And most insurance companies don't look past the next year of owning that person. They have to sell a good story because they can't deliver health."

Tom Emerick told me:

A lot of people report losing weight within 12 months. But, when I went back and checked on it three years later, they had all put the weight right back on. Every pound that came off and stayed off for three years cost about $50,000. Too many wellness vendors do a survey and report that employees are losing weight. But they don't go back and check three years later. They deliberately don't check because they know it doesn't stay off.

Figure 7.6   Tom Emerick.

The RAND study looked at the average obesity program in America. The average person lost one pound per year for three years then stopped. So, in other words, they dropped from 300 to 297 in three years. That's just irrelevant.

Change or Die

Sometimes life seems uncomfortable and that's actually when life starts.

—M.H. Rakib

Do you think that people who smoke do so because they missed all the health warnings? Smokers know smoking kills. Doctors and nurses smoke, probably because they work in stressful jobs. People who are overweight aren't confused about the problems of obesity; they live with the effects every day. Telling people to eat more vegetables and exercise does not shift behavior. Only a very small part of the population who hear or read warnings about smoking or eating will actually make a life change.

Alan Deutschman, the author of *Change or Die*, wrote about IBM's rude awakening at their 2004 Global Innovation Summit. Health care looked like a good field for IBM. A market that represented 15% of the country's GDP and rising health-care costs appeared to present a promising opportunity for a company that tackles large complex problems through data analytics. However, a report from a panel of experts took all the wind out of their sails. They told the summit that 80% of health costs related to the five lifestyles, the same ones we've covered. And they admitted that medical science had been dealing with the same problem since 1955.

Deutschman described what happened next:

> *The knockout blow was delivered by Dr. Edward Miller, the dean of the medical school and CEO of the hospital at Johns Hopkins University. He turned the discussion to patients whose heart disease is so severe that they undergo bypass surgery, a traumatic and expensive procedure that can cost more than $100,000 if complications arise. About 600,000 people have bypasses every year in the United States, and 1.3 million heart patients have angioplasties—all at a total cost of around $30 billion. The procedures temporarily relieve chest pains but rarely prevent heart attacks or prolong lives . . . many patients could avoid the return of pain and the need to repeat the surgery—not to mention arrest the course of their disease before it kills them—*by switching to healthier lifestyles. *Yet very few do. "If you look at people after coronary-artery bypass grafting two years later, 90% of them have not changed their lifestyle,"* Miller said. *"And that's been studied over and over and over again. And* so we're missing some link in there *[italics mine].*
>
> *Even though they know they have a very bad disease and they know they should change their lifestyle, for whatever reason, they can't."*[14]

> If you look at people after coronary-artery bypass grafting two years later, 90% of them have not changed their lifestyle.

The Hidden Cost of Wellness Programs

As he gazed out the window, Tom Emerick turned me and almost groaned, "So I asked these groups, 'When you're talking about getting ROIs, how do you measure it?' They go, 'We look at the cost of the program compared to the savings.' I said, 'But that's the smallest part of the cost. Do you look at what it costs for the HR team to be set up to run it internally? If employees are spending an hour a week in a wellness program, do you add up the lost productivity? You're sending people down for a lot of tests. Are you looking at the cost of the false positives?' And they said, 'No, we don't look at that.' So, they are not looking at the whole cost of the program."

He continued, "When I ran a 3,000-person executive exam program, I saw that people were always going down for a standard exam and getting a false positive. For example, they have a squiggle on their EKG and get a thallium stress test baseline and then a second thallium stress test. They are told nothing is wrong, but the company spent $25,000 to get there.

"I spoke to one of the industry's top advocates, who said he had never looked to see if people were having false positives on all these tests.

"I said, 'If you haven't looked at that, you haven't looked at one of the biggest costs of the programs. If everybody in the company spends four hours a month in wellness meetings, did you add up all the lost?'

"'No, we don't look at that.'

"'But that's the second biggest cost, lost productivity. And the higher the profit per employee, the worse those lost wages are.'

"At Microsoft, their annual profit per employee is about $350,000. Do you really want somebody that's making that kind of a contribution sitting in wellness meetings and activities 60 hours a year?"

Ron Goetzel, senior scientist at Johns Hopkins Bloomberg School of Public Health, founder of HERO, and the leading wellness evangelist, explains one of the largest problems in collecting accurate information:

> When we think about wellness programs, we're talking about vendor programs. *Vendors sell to their customers, human resource and benefits personnel. They say, "We're going to save you money. We're going to produce an ROI. We're going to lower absenteeism and disability, workers comp." But they never really think about the end user, the real customer, the employee.*

It is very, very, very, very hard to change human behavior.

One company brought in meditation yoga people for their employees, and nobody showed up. That's because the employees were young and wanted to do aerobics, they wanted to climb walls, to do stuff on bicycles. Nobody bothered to ask them, "What would you like?" It sounds pretty extreme but that actually happened.

I asked Ron about the promises and effort in changing behavior.

It is very, very, very, very hard to change human behavior. The way to get there is a combination of different activities. They may include culture; they may include physical design. They may include incentive programs, communication, dissemination, strategic thinking about how to do that and expertise in the science of behavior change.

All of those things are interwoven with one another, and most companies in America don't know how to do that. They don't have the expertise; they don't have the background, and they don't have the knowledge.

Dr. Goetzel describes the unachievable challenge. Think of a company that has neither the expertise or resources to administer the level of complexity he describes. On the other hand, the companies we found with effective programs shed complexity for a very human approach. We found a handful of focal areas, not 25, 50, or 100 things to juggle.

So Why Is Everybody Doing Wellness?

It is a fact that 90% of companies over 200 employees—we're talking a total of 56 million employees—have wellness programs. And the average annual expense per employee, for these programs, is about $700.

I asked Tom Emerick why would companies even invest in wellness if it doesn't do anything? He said:

It's just a giant fallacy. Why were people putting money in these mortgages during the run-up of the real estate crash? Everybody was doing it. It's momentum. Everybody's doing it, so it's got to be good. These companies would be far better off dumping their wellness programs. There's some evidence that it's actually doing some harm to people.

Al Lewis told me in an e-mail, "If I were a company with a lot of employees, I would be spending my money on environment long before I would be spending my money on wellness programs."

Nail in the Coffin

In January of 2018, the NIH Health in Buildings Roundtable issued, "What Do Workplace Wellness Programs Do? Evidence from the Illinois Workplace Wellness Study."

Their conclusions confirmed our work:

- High incentives get people started but don't last
- Healthier people self-select into wellness programs
- Unhealthy people are likely not to participate
- 4.5 percent of additional participation for unhealthy employees pays for the cost of the program but that cost does not include soft costs, productivity loss or false positives for HRA's.

According to their report, "At large incentive levels, further increases have little effect on participation and thus primarily represent compensation targeted to inframarginal participants." In other words, marginal participants are those who would not normally participate at all. But, *inframarginal* people are those who would likely join the program, even without an incentive.

The study concludes, "Finally, we find no significant effects of wellness programs on the outcomes we examine . . ."

For the NIH to announce that they "find no significant effects of wellness programs" is like General Motors announcing they find no reason to continue producing internal combustion engines. At this point, it is not possible to know the effect of this report on the wellness industry. But, it surely seems that it is at least *a* nail in the coffin.[15]

How Do We Ever Get to Reality?

Even the most skeptical critics of the wellness industry admit that some companies, like Johnson & Johnson and Cummins, *are* operating good and effective wellness programs. Cleveland Clinic is another exception: they have achieved high and active participation rates among employees with chronic disease, and they have bent the rising cost curve downward. Google, GoDaddy, Next Jump, and some other companies go far beyond programs and premium amenities to create cultures and a closed universe that promotes and provides wellness *and* well-being.

> *One starts by asking are employees* **human** *resources or* human *resources.*

So, how can you help your company find traction in achieving a truly healthy culture? There are several roads and all lead to different destinations. Each road reflects your current assumptions about those you employ. Steve Carter described those assumptions as a starting crossroad. One starts by asking if employees are human *resources* or *human* resources. One is relational and human centered. The other utilitarian and focuses on output.

Which road is your company taking?

Most companies want to take the higher road but are completely unware they are traveling rapidly toward a dead end. Companies like Barry-Wehmiller, MeTEOR, Next Jump, and GoDaddy told us they were once on dead-end paths and didn't know it. Then each experienced an awakening and arrived at Steve Carter's crossroad of assumptions. That process revealed the heart of their business. Each leadership team had to choose which path to take. Once they chose to put the welfare of their employees at the center, all the other choices came into sharp focus. Every decision had a grounding reference point and was not subjected to the churning confusion of complex vendor offerings and sleight of hand tricks to make the numbers look better.

Chances are your company is on one of those dead-end roads that never gets to wellness. If you are not sure, refer again to the RAND report, our interview with Ron Goetzel, my band of castaways, and Dr. Roizen, who all confirm typical wellness programs are tactical, ineffective, and anything but people centered. As a starting point, your team should discuss the ladder. Determining the rung where your company stands will take you into a crossroad conversation. You will soon discover if this is a deeply personal issue to your company or just a program. The higher road begins when it becomes a deeply personal corporate conversation. I admit I was on the "Let's do wellness better" road until it became very personal.

When I had to convince more than a hundred leaders and experts—most of them my personal friends—to serve our MindShift Wellness project, I discovered just how personal it was to many of them. They weren't interested in simply making wellness better.

And it became more personal eight months later when I concluded that wellness programs don't reduce cost or improve health outcomes as claimed. Because I had some 'splainin' to do, I proposed a new mission that seemed too high.

Then, on the heels of that, it became personal again when I met leaders like Calvin Crowder and Wade Lewis with GoDaddy, who were making wellness and well-being a reality. And they signed up to help us in our new mission.

I saw the personal intensity again when Tom Carmazzi, CEO of Tuthill, went out of his way to answer my questions. After he kept saying, "I don't know," he brought in an outside accounting firm and invested three months looking behind the numbers to help me see exactly what kind of visibility CEOs must live with every day. But what is scary is to realize that most don't or can't achieve Carmazzi's focused persistence; they are driving blind.

If you make it personal, you will pull it from the clutches of the bureaucratic control, the inevitable embellishments, the spins, the outright deceptions, and all the other compromises that defy data and math. Peek, as I did, behind the packaging of all the presentations, stories, and numbers. Insist on what is true, not what you hope is true.

The Leadership Nudge

How engaged are you? How well do you know your trends and demographic numbers? Which rung of the ladder best represents your current location? What road are you driving? Dig deeper.

Personal Nudge

How well do you understand your benefits? Do you have (and are you using) an employee assistance program? How can you nudge your company down the higher road? Can you share this chapter with your leadership?

CHAPTER 8

The Mystery of Hospitality

Experiencing the Human Touch

When the idea of this book first appeared in 2015, I assumed I was sufficiently knowledgeable about the concept of wellness. After all, I've worked across a wide landscape of American business and culture for several decades. I don't miss much that bursts forth from that soil. And my work on two earlier books had touched on the topic in some depth.

So, I felt equipped and ready. Surely, researching and writing a book on workplace wellness would be a simple extension of the work we did in *Change Your Space, Change Your Culture*. We had addressed stress, health risks, and even mentioned the emergence of well buildings. Our mission appeared straightforward: how do we adapt and bring the best of workplace strategy and design into support of workplace wellness?

I knew what to do: assemble the best and brightest from the wellness, architecture, construction, workplace, real estate, health-care, and academic worlds; convene in quarterly summits across the country; research, synthesize, and write. I knew we could move this conversation forward in significant ways. Yes, I got this.

And then it became personal.

Death of a Project; Birth of a Story

In a profound irony, reality struck as I clawed my way to a deadline for a book about health and well-being; three members of my family—my brother, my mother, and my mother-in-law—died. And my 25-year-old daughter was diagnosed with multiple sclerosis (MS).

I had already written the chapter of despair zones when my brother stepped out of that zone and fell into a hospital bed, kept alive by artificial means. I had heard of families agonizing over the decision to end life support. But then my sisters and I had to do it.

And my mother's life was compromised by iatrogenic issues (caused by or related to medical treatment). Wow; I wrote about that in my first book. But, that's when I was an expert, a writer on a book project. The next time I encountered the word, I did so as a son. Iatrogenic medical treatment is now an integral part of my personal story.

MS was just another disease. Until it came home. That's the first time it ever brought tears. More recently a charming and wise, and very Southern, lady died several hundred miles away from our home. But she gave birth to Lisa, my wife. She was the grandmother of our children. Her singing filled our house, and her life, values, and insights are woven throughout the tapestry of our lives.

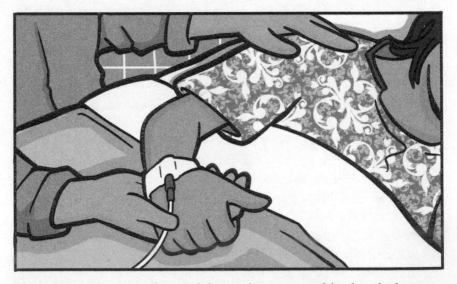

Figure 8.1 It doesn't take much loss to become sensitized to the losses borne by others.

It does not take much loss to sensitize people to the losses borne by others. So, what happened while writing this book that made me stop when I heard others speak certain words or phrases? Those human sounds rose far above "research." I had to stop and listen to colleagues, friends, and

> *Truth that has not been lived is stolen.*

family as they described their struggles with losing family members, children battling drugs or depression, and their constant skirmishes with a dehumanizing health-care system.

My friend Charles Simpson once said, "Truth that has not been lived is stolen." Only after I lived it, could I really see the truth of chronic disease, painful and exhausting struggles, and the human reach to be well. I never realized how hard some wrestle every day to get their bodies to cooperate so they can just get through another day. And now I understand their unrelenting need for predictable routine. And I also know the domino crash if one thing fails to follow the requisite pattern for living.

I recently attended Hope for Hemophilia, a charity event that provides support for families fighting for life against a rare disease. I had known the founder, Jonathan James, since he was in diapers. I attended the event because he is a friend and I was completely ignorant about his life or this enemy he battles daily. I was humbled and overwhelmed; I felt inadequate at every level of comprehension. My empathy could not lift me high enough to understand what it's like to live dependent on drugs that cost over $100,000 per month just to stay alive. That war, that struggle, and that weariness took on names and faces as well as revealed graces, grit, and hope.

My ability to compartmentalize turns out to be a very thin veil. I now know how easily and quickly a seam can open through that veil to a parallel universe in the lives of friends and families. I'd like to say I always had awareness of them and their situations, but I now see that wasn't true. It is now, and I am discovering how to be a more supportive friend, an encouraging colleague—someone who pauses to ask those standing near, "How are you doing?" I'm embarrassed to know the times I asked that in a perfunctory manner.

I just didn't know. I didn't know that on any given day, just staying alive can be a severe struggle.

> *. . . a seam can quickly open through that veil to a parallel universe in the lives of friends and families.*

When health and well-being, or their absence, become personal, lives change. A friend, Rich Blakeman, vice president of alliances and partnerships at *Four Winds Interactive*, recently explained how the personal showed up in how he viewed the terrain of health: "When I looked at the scales, my food and drink, and my exercise, I realized that I wanted to be as healthy at 60 and 70 as I was at 50. That changed my life."

What This Means for Leaders

Leaders want happy and healthy employees. We all know that. But why do they want them? Yes, of course: ROI. Companies invest a great deal of money on wellness and engagement for that purpose. Nothing wrong with that realistic view. But does it go any deeper than that? It can and does when leaders go beyond the mechanics of their decisions, policies, and programs to see how these ripple through the lives of individuals. Without that counterbalance of personal consideration, any program, well intentioned or routine, turns into a blunt instrument that delivers components of care without ever reaching its intended goal.

How do leaders pierce the veil to prevent good intentions from having unintended negative effects? Vanderbilt's Dr. Shari Barkin sees this trap in medical academics and concludes: "We end up delivering a lot of health care without ever reaching health." Dr. Roizen describes his "aha" with a patient who was not heeding his life-saving advice. He realized he had to move from professional prescription to human description of what he called an "empathetic positive future." As a watchful CEO, Bob Chapman knows he must stand guard against cold rationality's continuous assaults on common sense.

Since passing through my own crucible, I go back to these pivotal statements that have become grounding. I think of them almost daily:

It is easier to spread influence with people you know.
—Dr. Nickolas Christakis

Leaders have to care, and they can't care for people they don't know.
—Bob Chapman

People feel like wellness programs are done to them, not for them.
—Al Lewis

If I could cure loneliness and depression, 70% of my worries would go away.
—Tom Emerick

We end up delivering a lot of health care without ever reaching health.
—Dr. Shari Barkin

Leaders have to care, and they can't care for people they don't know.

If every leader—if *you*—read these statements every day, it would radically change our approach to those people who show up in our shops, factories, office buildings, courthouses, schools, and other institutions every day.

When a Workplace Cares

Our daughter Michelle recently worked for a telemarketer for school fundraising campaigns. She immediately liked the culture and the support. But in time, the pressure of making 60 calls an hour created a sensory overload for Michelle, as she struggled with her Asperger's. We watched her come home day after day, emotionally and physically exhausted. But because they provided insurance that covered her medication, Lisa and I did the best we could to coach and encourage her.

But, after a while, as she learned more about of her MS, Michelle decided to quit and find something else. But the vice president of HR knew Michelle's challenges, perhaps better than most. Because her mother has MS, she fully understood how stress triggers flare-ups. So, the VP found a solution for an employee she cared about: she opened a new position for Michelle that was not offered to anyone else. Michelle got to work from home, part-time with benefits. They praised her work and she continued to learn and receive coaching. Michelle is now excited to return to college, largely because of the added confidence from her supportive work environment. Small acts of hospitality like those shown to Michelle don't show up on spreadsheets, but have real life-changing effects.

I think I get it now. I see why our project was —and this book is— about far more than reducing health-care costs or finding a way to engage another 10% of employees in a weight loss program. Michelle's HR director treated Michelle like she would like to see her mom cared for. It was personal!

That is the kind of bridge we should all try to build in our careers and in life. But, we can't care for, or show hospitality to, people we don't know. When we offer kindness to people, we also influence their network (out to

three levels). Bob Chapman, CEO of Barry-Wehmiller, certainly understands this principle. He reminds his managers that a good day at work also
produces a life-giving evening at home

When we offer kindness to people, for the family.
we also influence their network.   Bob captures this vision well: He
"imagines a world where every per-
son matters. He imagines a world full of caring work environments in
which people can realize their gifts, apply and develop their talents, and
feel a genuine sense of fulfillment for their contributions. Chapman
imagines a world in which people leave work each day fulfilled and are
better spouses, fathers, mothers, sons, daughters, neighbors, citizens of the
world. Because everyone—including you—matters."[1]

Does Anyone Here Care?

Many of my clients happen to be companies concerned about safety; in
fact, it is a top concern. The construction industry, for example, has the
"highest mean annual crude mortality rate . . . of all industries."[2] I've sat
in on several high-level conversations tackling this problem. I know the
difference between sitting in a room of leaders, shuffling through stats and
numbers, recommending different policies and interventions, and listening to leaders discuss people they know.

I sat in on a senior executive meeting for a global construction firm
when the discussion turned to safety. The company's chief safety officer
reported an increase of accidents over the past two months. The leaders,
obviously concerned, drilled into the report with numerous questions:

- Do we need better training?
- Do we need an app to help remind people?
- Do we need better oversight?
- Are we conducting thorough project audits?

I agreed that those were valid questions, but then asked if they were
sending a clear message that safety is really a foundational value. What I
really said is, "I don't think safety is a priority for this team." Two leaders
reacted and recited the company's value statement on safety.

When the voices of disagreement finally settled, I observed the entire
meeting focused on how each division president was progressing against

their revenue target. But the topic of safety only raised lots of questions; it didn't produce one personal example of having a conversation with someone in the field, visiting a site, or coaching anyone on his or her safety process. Outside of the report, no one really knew how those in the field were addressing safety.

My questions tried to humanize what sounded like a scorekeeping conversation. Because the score was bad, it drew senior leadership scrutiny. I think I was able to effectively break the scorekeeping trance by reintroducing common sense. A week after the meeting the COO called and asked if I would interview an internal candidate they wanted to lead the company's safety efforts. I was skeptical because it felt like he was offloading leadership's burden of safety and checking a box by assigning it to someone down in the organization. But I learned that was not the case as soon as I talked to the candidate. My first question: "So Steve, why do you care about this position?"

Steve didn't give me reasons. He told me a story.

"On one of my first jobs as a construction manager I lost a guy. He was a good person, great team member. It should never have happened. I still think about it. I promised I would never allow that to happen on a future project of mine."

I never got to my second question. The moment was emotional for Steve; it was emotional for me. I knew Steve. He's crusty, doesn't give a damn about spreadsheets, and would rather work in his woodshop than attend a company event. However, there is no one I'd rather have ensuring safety than Steve. He would make safety a personal and top of mind priority inside the leadership team. I told the COO he chose the right person.

It's About Being Human

At its best, leadership is social and engaging. Everyone has a stake in happiness and health. Leaders can start improving the health, happiness, and vitality of their organizations by reducing friction. "Tone at the top" refers to leaders creating an environment of honesty and integrity for improving accountability. Although it began as an accounting term, I think it is time to expand it to humanizing the workplace in general. What is the tone for a healthy culture? It starts by being human, real, approachable, interested, and grateful.

But too often we see the workplace as a zone where people must leave the best parts of themselves outside the front door. Everyone must wear the employee mask and pretend to agree, understand, be on top of it, and having a good day—for eight hours. No wonder workplaces are so stressful.

Rachel Druckenmiller, director of wellbeing for SIG, recently wrote:

> *Most of us have a deep fear that who we are and what we have to offer is not enough, that we won't measure up. That fear can drive and propel us to work hard and to strive. But the pressure to be "on" and productive can be relentless and exhausting. Proving ourselves at work often means sacrificing some other area of our lives, especially our relationships and our health and well-being.*[3]

> *. . . the pressure to be "on" and productive can be relentless and exhausting.*

A couple of years ago, I met with several Millennials at Cummins in Columbus, Indiana. I wanted to hear what they thought of working for a blue-collar manufacturer in a small middle-America town. In one meeting, I met with five people who loved the company because they felt safe, valued, and challenged. In trying to express what she liked about working for Cummins, one of them, Kimberly, said, "The leaders here are real people, and they treat me like a real person. I can talk to them like anyone else." She went on to describe a causal after-hours mixer at CEO Tom Linebarger's home. She was invited along with several other new employees. Most of the senior leadership team attended! If an old-line, 100-year-old manufacturing company with 55,000 employees spread across the globe can create and maintain a human touch, then anyone can. That is also how you attract and retain millennials.

Can the Workplace Be Restorative?

When Bob Fox, one of our MindShift members, visited the CBRE headquarters, he asked the CFO how he measured the ROI for their new office.

And he, a "bean counter," replied, "Smiles."

Patrick Donnelly, principal at BHDP Architecture, told me about an encounter between one of his designers and a client's employee in the lobby of their new office building:

> *A woman started calling out, "Hey! Hey"; then she caught the designer, grabbed both his hands and bubbled, "I recognize you. You designed our offices. Thank you so much for what you did. I've been working here for the last few months, and it has changed my life, saved my marriage. I left my last job because I couldn't take it anymore. The space was depressing, and no one was happy. I didn't realize how much of that I was taking home with me. I love my new home, and you were part of it."*

Incredibly, a workplace proved to be restorative, even far beyond the office where that woman worked.

> *We have an opportunity to restore human dignity through good work.*

Bob Chapman, CEO of Barry-Wehmiller, told me that he believes there is an intimate connection between workplace happiness and health: "We know for a fact that the way you treat people affects the way they go home and treat their spouse and their children. We know we're kind of self-destructing as a society because we're not teaching people to be stewards of others. We're teaching people to use people for economic gain. We have an opportunity to restore human dignity through good work."

Have you noticed in recent years that the lobbies of offices and even hospitals have started looking and feeling like upscale hotel atriums? Some companies are turning receptionists into concierges: a push to bring human warmth to a cold and sterile environment. CBRE sends receptionists to the Four Seasons for concierge training. I see potential magic hidden inside this trend. It's called "hospitality," and it's an ancient virtue that is being restored to those places where people spend so much of their time.

I felt that magic when I met Carli at GoDaddy. I arrived early to set up our summit (for this book). As our team pulled the details together, I left our workshop room and walked out into the hall. I used my Boy Scout skills to determine the direction to the supply room. That is when Carli walked up. With her face about chest high to my 5'10" frame, she took a firm posture.

"What are you doing out of your area?"

I was caught. "I was looking for the supply room," I stammered.

"My job is to make sure you focus on your job. Give me a list of everything you need, and I'll make sure we take care of it."

"Really?"

That was not a one-time conversation. Carli became a mother hen to our team; she anticipated what we needed. As we were tearing down after the event, Carli walked in and asked, "What can I ship home for you?"

The Power of Hospitality

Hospes is the Latin root for guest, host, or stranger. Showing kindness, especially to strangers, is deeply rooted in ancient Greek, Eastern, and Middle Eastern Cultures. Traveling strangers had the right to expect to be taken in and treated well.

Dr. Ron Anderson, the former longtime and widely respected CEO for Parkland Hospital in Dallas, told me about Parkland's unique mission.[4] As a county hospital, it serves those with no insurance. So, it is where society's most vulnerable go for medical treatment; it's the hospital for strangers. Dr. Anderson, knowing that "hospital" and "hospitality" share the same origin, told me the ancient text that guided his role as CEO: "Do not forget to show hospitality to strangers, they may be an angel in disguise."[5]

Do not forget to show hospitality to strangers.

Bob Chapman takes this same attitude to the workplace: "Everybody is somebody's mother or father, brother or sister, son or daughter; they have the same hopes and dreams as we do for our own families."

Hotels and restaurants are the natural stewards of those traditions. That's why they're part of what we call "the hospitality industry." If I asked you to describe a memorable time with a close friend or family member, you're likely to tell me about a restaurant. When I ask people for restaurant recommendations, they usually tell me about a small, hidden, and intimate restaurant where the owner greets you like family and the menu is only a suggestion. The décor fit the restaurant's personality, but is seldom lavish. In fact, many describe their favorite place as a "hole in the wall."

I once met Jeffery Pfeffer at Ecco Restaurant in Burlingame, California. Although I arrived early, the owner knew who I was. He smiled, "Let me take you to Jeffrey's table." When Jeffrey arrived, the owner greeted him like a brother. While seating him, the owner told me why Jeffrey was such a splendid human. When it was time to order, I didn't see exactly what I wanted on the menu. Seeing my brief hesitation, the owner said, "We can make anything you like. Just tell me what you want." That is hospitality.

Starlette Johnson, former president of Dave & Busters, told me, "Hospitality is the last industry in which you can ascend through the ranks without an advanced degree because it requires high emotional intelligence." She said that the best servers must pick up on a person's mood and desires in order to provide a personalized and memorable experience. It's all about reading people and situations, focused listening, and being present. What comes naturally to many in the hospitality industry are rare and treasured skills. Today, they are strenuously taught in workshops, conferences, and corporations.

My niece, Janelle Weber, is the general manager for Publican Quality Meats (PQM), part of the One-Off Hospitality brand in Chicago. They

> *Hospitality is the last industry in which you can ascend through the ranks without an advance degree because it requires high emotional intelligence.*

are considered one of the premier restauranteurs. When visiting PQM, Janelle makes each visit memorable. For a gifted server, the menu is a living and interactive dynamic; it goes well beyond just the written document (or chalkboard, or iPad). Janelle tells a riveting story about "today's selections." She is fully absorbed in the chef's planned adventures for that day. Her interest aroused our curiosity. After our selections, Janelle breathes a hint of some possible surprise. "Let me see what the chef is up to today."

And, yes, surprises: a complimentary charcuterie plate, a new spread for fresh bread. "And the chef would like your opinion on this." Well, of course!

When the food was served, Janelle made sure we had extra plates to share. The entire presentation was choreographed. We could see that Janelle took great satisfaction in watching our very animated joy. After we were full, really full, came complimentary dessert. On the way out, I got a big hug and a small bag with two fresh oatmeal cookies for her grandpa, my dad.

Perhaps the reason this has so much fascination for me is that I did not grow up in a food and family culture, where meals were integrally related to family and fellowship. Some of my Irish, Polish, and Italian friends describe *every* Sunday growing up as adventures in such a culture. I grew up as the oldest child in a family of two parents, two boys, and two girls. We lived in a split-level tract home in a middle-class suburb of Chicago. Because Dad traveled during the week, dinners would usually find only one or two of us at the table at the same time; we were all involved in after-school activities. Meals consisted of Ragu spaghetti, fried pork chops from an electric skillet served with applesauce, pot roast, and canned peas, corn, or string beans. We ate Wonder Bread with Oscar Meyer bologna and Kraft yellow mustard for lunch. You get the rest. Our grandparents lived in Florida and New York. We had no big family meals. Life was very good; I have no complaints at all. I'm just saying that we lived outside the old-world charm of family and food.

Many workplaces very naturally included a version of that kind of food and companionship. When I worked for Southwestern Bell in Dallas many years ago, I ate in the union lunch room, sitting next to "some of the guys." I could see a distinct culture as they played dominos and talked hunting, fishing, and the Dallas sports teams.

That lunch room was more than a company cafeteria; it was a gathering place, an expression of classic hospitality. Over the past decades, a lot of companies lost the culture of those lunchrooms and cafeterias. Google and GoDaddy are among many who are bringing them back. In addition to well-stocked and inviting microkitchens, the chefs in the cafeterias love to create off-menu adventures for their patrons.

The Big Takeaway: It's About Leadership

Rachel Druckenmiller asked a splendid and very probing question: "Would the community around you notice if your company disappeared tomorrow?"[6]

Think about that. Here's another view of the same question: Why do neighborhoods grieve the closing of an old and favorite restaurant? Because it contributed more to the culture, health, warmth, and conviviality of a community than it ever took in payment for those grand liturgies of life at the table. The leadership—chef, restaurant owner, maître d', and sommelier—saw and pursued the magnificent vision for the restaurant as a vital and active partner in the community.

Yes, they had to make a profit in order to remain alive. But the balance sheet was simply a way of measuring the quality of their participation in the swirling communal celebrations of graduation and wedding parties, quiet anniversary dinners, family gatherings, company award presentations, power lunches, and other table-based events.

Shouldn't a place of work represent an even larger gift to the community?

To create those great workplaces that are good for people—inside and outside the company—ultimately requires active and engaged leaders. Leaders who have a personal stake in a better future together and can impart a compelling picture of what it can look like. That is the challenge. Programs, regardless of how well they are designed or written, carry no magic.

Joseph Campbell told Bill Moyers, "The influence of a vital person vitalizes."[7] We need vital leaders and their vitalizing influence within our times and spaces. But most are pressed, stressed, distracted, and drained by accelerating demands and disruptive forces. We live in a time that is driven by ever-increasing means but without the anchor of life-affirming ends.

The influence of a vital person vitalizes.

Finding personal health and happiness is a continual journey of discovery and struggle. It takes on greater meaning and has more power to help or harm when wrapped inside a family, a community, or a company. The best examples we experienced saw personal challenges as a "we" journey. Too often, however, it feels like me against the machine. Health and well-being are never static; yet programmatic solutions deal with those hurdles as if they were linear, rational, binary, and unalterable.

President Eisenhower famously said, "Plans are worthless, but planning is everything."[8] In the same sense, it is not the programs that deliver health or well-being. It is the collective road of discovery, planning, testing, learning, and growing—together. The WELL building that CBRE built simply embodied what that office had collectively discovered, tested, and implemented together. They are still learning and changing. It is still evolving, as it should. There is no cycle of starting over when November's open enrollment comes around. Health and well-being have become the culture.

Replace the word "wellness" with "health," and you will see how wellness can quickly take on a programmatic or bureaucratic connotation. Health, on the other hand, is personal and intimate. It seems that more leaders today are seeing their job as a calling to create a better community around their workplaces and better culture for those they lead. Those leaders and their companies form a growing list adopting the practices of firms of endearment (part of the conscious business movement),[9] social entrepreneurs, benefit corporations,[10] servant leader[11] organizations, or deliberately developmental organizations.[12] Their goals revolve around releasing people to discover and pursue what they do best and enjoy most. And the financial performance of most exceeds their peers.

If leadership builds a bridge to new worlds, then leaders must:

- Appreciate—give a damn about—their employees.
- Walk the talk and deliver a compelling vision.
- Take the long view.
- Build and maintain a healthy culture.
- Weed out resistance to change.
- Stand strong during good times and down cycles.
- Build an ecosystem with such excellence and strength that the culture will endure in all seasons and under new leadership.

The following sections will show you how to create a workplace that is good for people, a place that releases them to flourish. Naturally, that produces great and profitable work (ROI is a valid measurement). But it also makes them better citizens, neighbors, volunteers, parents, and cheerleaders for a thriving community.

Leadership is a high calling and in rare supply. Potential leaders, however, are too often left sitting in the wings untapped because they are not your usual suspects. The technical caretaker era of business is gone. Leadership today must also be personal.

Everyone wants to contribute. Trust them. Leaders are everywhere. Find them. Some people are on a mission. Celebrate them. Others wish things were different. Listen to them. Everybody matters. Show them. We don't just need a new guide to leading in times of change or adversity. We need a complete rethink, a revolution.[13]

When health and well-being become personal, you will find fewer answers but so much better questions. The great leaders are more interested in a thoughtful exchange and hard questions than defending decisions or practices. The companies and leaders we profile in the upcoming chapters provide a fresh tone at the top that resonates far better with their employees. Let's get set for a wellness adventure together. Through it I think you'll find answers to your questions, a framework to guide you, and examples to follow.

The Leadership Nudge

Reflect on some of the health and happiness peaks and valleys in your own family? What are some stories from employees on your front lines?

Personal Nudge

What kind of personal margin do you have in your life? If you were to rate on a five-point scale your satisfaction with work, time with friends or family, fulfillment, health, and finances, which category would you like to improve? Can work play a part in that improvement? If so, how would you start? If not, what could you change?

PART III

Magical Nudges: The Road to Health and Well-Being

Any sufficiently advanced technology is indistinguishable from magic.
—Arthur C. Clarke

CHAPTER 9

Nudge Thinking

How Small Things Lead to Big Results

I'm all for empowerment and education, but the empirical evidence is that it doesn't work. That's why I say make it easy.

—Richard Thaler

Before he won the 2017 Nobel Prize in economics, Richard Thaler was most known for changing our nation's approach to 401(k)s. In 2006, his research persuaded Congress to change 401(k) enrollment from an opt-in structure to an opt-out. That difference, that little nudge, increased 401(k) participation from 30% to 90%.

A nudge makes the right thing easy. It tips the better choice into the "automatic" realm. A fuel efficiency gauge near the speedometer is a nudge toward slower and gentler driving. Displaying bottled water and healthy juices at convenient reach (and hiding soft drinks) nudges people toward healthier consumption. Those kinds of cultural nudges flow out of behavioral economics. The positive reinforcement or the gentle suggestion shifts people toward greater

> *The positive reinforcement or the gentle suggestion shifts people toward greater safety, better health, economic improvement, and other individual and group benefits.*

safety, better health, economic improvement, and other individual and group benefits.

Think about the application of nudges. The old way—informing, training, begging, encouraging, inspiring, pushing, tempting, threatening, poking, or punishing people into compliance with policies or actions—is expensive, frustrating, and ultimately ineffective. That's because people are not rational beings. We thought they were; they're not. Move on.

Society could try to coerce people to become organ donors. That should be easy, right? After all, people already know that donating healthy organs when they no longer need them (like, after a deadly car wreck) is a selfless and generous act toward others in society. But, here's the problem: that beautiful reason just doesn't work. That's because people don't want to think about the circumstances or the process of slicing their vital organs out of their body and sewing them into other bodies. And they surely don't want to go through the hassle of finding and hiring a lawyer to execute the requisite paperwork to make it all happen.

But, a simple statement on the back of your driver license is easy. Just sign it and go. Done. No need to think about it any further. You don't even realize that you were gently nudged to bestow your heart, lungs, kidneys, eyes, and other vital organs to people you don't know and may not even like. No one had to attend a meeting, go to court, or pay anything. A nudge made it free and easy.

Nudge and Wellness

We've all heard the expression "An apple a day keeps the doctor away." Well, I've got a question for you: What if it's true? Wouldn't that be easy to do—to eat an apple a day? Here's the problem: It's also easy not to do.

—Jim Rohn[1]

Traditional corporate wellness programs have assumed that if employees only had information about healthy choices and received a $300 discount on their health insurance premium for achieving their modest goals, that would be enough to persuade them to change.

That hasn't worked and won't. That's because humans are not rational decision makers.

And that is why behavioral economics has become such an emergent force; it certainly formed a major part of our research for this book. Behavioral economics is built along the difference between our autopilot, intuitive side, and our more deliberate and reflective side. A nudge is often all it takes to make a good choice easier and a bad choice harder. Designed nudges can influence policy, programs, work design, workplace strategy, purchasing decisions, physical environments, social network effects, and other features of contemporary life. Nudges are much less intrusive (and expensive) than efforts aimed at changing people.

> *A nudge is often all it takes to make a good choice easier and a bad choice harder.*

Daniel Kahneman, the cocreator of behavioral economics, spoke about this during a recent podcast: "Instead of asking, 'How can I get him or her to do it?' start with a question of, 'Why isn't she doing it already?' Very different question, 'Why not?' Then you go one by one systematically, and you ask, 'What can I do to make it easier for that person to move?'"[2]

The Homer Simpson Effect

My associate Michael Lagocki and I drove out of Dallas very early one morning, headed for a 9 a.m. meeting at Texas A&M's School of Public Health. The first 90 minutes of our road trip down I-35 flew by so very quickly. But, when we took the exit to College Station at Waco, we ended up on a mostly two-lane highway. That's when we began to get stuck behind farm tractors, pickups, and big tractor-trailer rigs. Our conversation suddenly tapered off as I began to concentrate more on the road and my driving duties.

That is the first principle of behavioral economics. Our brains work in two modes. Autopilot, our default mode, is designed to conserve energy. It works about 80% of the time. That's why we can usually safely drive (a modern automatic function) and talk at the same time. But, our intentional, focused, reflective mode is necessary for high-demand times, like driving through downtown Chicago during rush hour.

> *Our brains work in two modes. Autopilot, our default mode, is designed to conserve energy. It works about 80% of the time.*

For another trip, I flew to Holland, Michigan, to make a presentation at an event. Since I had to arrive the afternoon before the event and spend the night in downtown Holland, I walked through the beautiful April evening down to Butch's Dry Dock for dinner. As I walked, I firmly decided to order their healthier salmon Caesar salad. But I ran into some colleagues at Butch's; they asked me to join them for dinner. Now, I was absolutely committed to salmon Caesar, until I wasn't. Two of my colleagues said, "You've got to try the smoked pork!" And they didn't stop there: they described it in sensual detail. So I ordered the smoked pork, fully aware that I just abandoned the healthy choice I had been so determined to consume. The moment got worse: a round of appetizers; a nice local stout beer, possibly two; and a flaming, cascading, volcanic desert.

I got "Homered." You must remember the forbidden donut—season 5, episode 5 of *The Simpsons*, "Treehouse of Horror IV." Homer became so enamored with the donut that he sold his soul to the devil.[3] The Homer Simpson Effect is what happens when your autopilot chooses the tangible and delicious now rather than the healthier, but too abstract you, way off in the fuzzy and distant future.

Our autopilot looks for shortcuts when we confront complicated, hard, ambiguous, or risky situations. Most of us don't read our insurance policies. That's because we're not rational beings. We've learned it's far better to look deeply into the insurance agent's eye and discern whether to trust her. Of course, we are smart enough to read and comprehend the policy, but we conduct a quick, instinctive, gut calculation comparing the pages of small font content against a set of cognitive biases and rules of thumb. In my case:

• Jerry recommended her—third-person credibility
• The company is a brand name—availability bias
• Pricing is comparable to competitors—confirmation bias

Our autopilot looks for shortcuts when we confront complicated, ambiguous, or risky situations.

Insurance companies, banks, mortgage lenders, and software companies can certainly provide easy-to-read, plain English contracts that highlight the areas of most interest or concern. But they count on people like me, who will quickly scan a document and think, *Do I really need to read all this legalese?* I mean, nothing bad has happened so far (subjective validation bias), so I will take that as a sign for the future. But, the devil is in the details, and it is after my roof needs to be replaced that I learn we have rain and hail coverage, but that doesn't cover wind damage. What?

Predictably Irrational

We already know that we are irrational beings. But, we are *predictably* irrational.[4] That is why supersizing works. And that's why checkout lines are filled with impulse items. Now, you know how Netflix has elegantly nudged us into binge watching. And, face it; you are simply not built to resist Aunt Martha's extra helping of apple pie. Our predictable irrationality is also why people smoke, even doctors who have the knowledge that cigarettes are killing them. They even smoke when they have financial incentives to quit.

Our predictable irrationality undermines efforts to introduce new programs, new technology, new compensation plans, and relocations—even when the new is much better than the old. But, because it is predictable, we can use it to help counteract irrational fears, shift from harmful to healthy behaviors, and embrace change.

Traditional economists start with the premise that humans are rational decision makers who optimize their gains and minimize losses. Behavioral economists start at a different point. As psychologist Dan Ariely explains, they begin by watching how people actually make decisions, and then reverse-engineer these observations, looking for common patterns. That difference in approach explains why traditional wellness programs have never been successful at changing human behavior.

Incentives, information, and willpower are no match for environmental triggers that only have to catch people off guard, as they did for me at the dinner in Holland.

Sirens in the Workplace

The classic story of the Sirens in Homer's *Odyssey* provides a splendid example of how to overcome irresistible temptation. As you probably remember from high school, the Sirens sang such beautiful and seductive songs that they lured ships to destruction and death on the rocky coast of their island. So, Ulysses ordered his crew to push wax into their ears to avoid yielding to the Sirens' songs. But he wanted to hear their songs, yet live to tell the story. So, he ordered the crew to lash him to the mast to prevent his steering the ship into the rocks.

Being tied to the mast is a commitment device, a tool to overcome the temptation that compromises long-term goals. Through behavioral economics, we can employ nudges and commitment devices to assist us in the higher, nobler, healthier, and more profitable patterns of life.

Bob had a 7:30 a.m. meeting at the office. So, after a late night, he chose to stay in bed until the last minute, skipping his wife's healthy breakfast. He knew coffee and some food would be waiting at the office. Sure enough, when he arrived, coffee, orange juice, and great and seductive pastries, pancakes, and biscuits and gravy were beautifully spread over a table. Most workplaces are littered with tempting Siren songs: they fill our bodies with sugar and empty calories. We don't seem to know or care that we're headed for the rocks.

The Power of Framing

Choices can be worded in a way that highlights the positive or negative aspects of the same decision, leading to changes in their relative attractiveness.[5]

Dr. Roizen discovered 20 years ago that his main job was motivating patients to live healthier. The traditional model armed him with compelling information about his patient's health risks. He could and did use scare tactics if necessary, but found they seldom worked. He learned that a person's habits and unhealthy social networks were more powerful than information, warnings, and pressure.

A person's habits and unhealthy social networks were more powerful than information, warnings, and pressure.

But, when his research uncovered six areas that could dramatically reduce risk and improve mortality, he reframed the conversation: *How would you like to live 10 years younger?* He calls this the empathetic future. It was a future that was imaginable because it brought new life to the realm of the possible.

Dr. Roizen's Real Age assessment is a great reframing device. It calculates chronological age against biological age. It is sobering and hopeful. When patients score poorly, he explains, "You are 55 but have the body of a 65-year-old." Once that sinks in, he asks, "How would you like to feel like 45 again?" That is a powerful and effective conversation, especially when the patient holds the Real Age score and assessment in her hands. Dr. Roizen confirms the patient's current state, clarifies the stakes, and makes the better future tangible. He reframes the issue, and reframing engages the focused side of the brain. Removing the clutter allows the brain to stay engaged.

Why do people not do what serves their long-term best interest? If we can step into their shoes and observe their surroundings and the social habits, can we begin to reframe and redesign their environment to remove those constraints?

Reframing is a critical, but often overlooked, device for managing. When CBRE proposed to move all paper files to the cloud, that news brought anxiety, especially among the many "digital immigrant" brokers. Anticipating that anxiety early (a key to good nudge thinking), they hired digital coaches to help employees scan, tag, and learn how to retrieve their files. Because they did, the narrative quickly shifted from, "I'm losing years of files that are crucial to my work," to "I'm a better broker today and can work from anyplace."

Calvin Crowder, vice president of global real estate for GoDaddy, describes their challenge, in a previous building, to encourage employees to use the recreation area to take breaks and have fun with colleagues. Because of its back-of-the-building location, people felt like they were sneaking off to have fun. In their new Global Technology Center in Tempe, Arizona, Calvin placed the recreation area in a central and highly visible place. When our group convened there, we watched people playing table tennis, ascending a climbing wall, riding pedal go-carts, and simply hanging out. Placing a recreational break room in a central space took away the old stigma.

Freedom of Choice and the Battle for M&M's

During our Google summit, someone raised the question, "Are nudges inherently evil?" In other words, are they manipulative? Do they represent Big Brother? Can our companies and our local, state, and federal levels of government be trusted to nudge us in appropriate ways?

The short answer, at least for Google and their director of health and performance, Josh Glynn, was that, for example, the dining areas do not remove unhealthy food and drinks. They are simply less visible to the autopilot brain but in plain sight to the focused brain. In the microkitchen refrigerators, the top half of the glass refrigerator doors reveal healthy waters, coconut water, kombucha, etc. But, if you look at the bottom frosted-glass displays, you can see some blurred red, burgundy, and green cans that contain favorite sodas. The glass is just sufficiently opaque to slightly blur the branding cue of major soft drink labels.

Google's first employee, Craig Silverstein, reportedly created their early M&M's culture. I love peanut M&M's. If there is a bowl on the table, I will start with the very subtle thumb-and-two-finger grab, just a few; easing into a second and third swipe using all five fingers. One peanut M&M contains 10.3 calories. So, my 20 M&M's added 200 useless calories; 100 of those calories are fat. And, for me, 20 is just getting started.

In 2006, Google used regular (nonpeanut) M&M's, 3.4 calories each, for a seven-week experiment in their Midtown New York office. They placed the M&M's in an opaque jar among several clear jars of healthy nuts and dried fruit. That office of 2000 people consumed 911,765 fewer M&M's, 3.1 million fewer calories, and 885 fewer pounds.[6]

But, then, Google took note of the recurrent weight gain (averaging 15 pounds) of "Nooglers" (new Googlers). That became known as the *Google 15*. So, Google implemented several nudges on a path to improve choices, reduce food portions, and encourage physical activity. They seem to be working. I don't know if M&M's are really the Google snack of choice, but I like the project because it captures all the elements of an intervention aligned with Google's values: their willingness to experiment, learn, rigorously measure, remain transparent, and use feedback as reinforcement.

The Seven Pillars of Wisdom

Okay, here's the real essence, the secret sauce, the elixir, the Seven Pillars of Wisdom behind nudge thinking:

1. **Default:** Make the healthy choice the default option. Haworth's headquarters placed the elevators at both (and very distant) ends of a

very long building core. But the centrally placed stairs provide a beautiful and panoramic view of the interior of the office and its exterior landscape. Taking the stairs is automatic, even desirable. I have been going to that headquarters since it was built in 2008 and didn't even know the elevators existed until recently.

2. **Appealing:** Give the nudge a solid appeal. The Haworth stairs *invite* you to climb. Four Winds Interactive wants everyone to pause for a few minutes each hour. So, at five minutes to the hour, all vertical display monitors rotate images of employees with their dogs. That brief happiness break has had the serendipitous effect of connecting employees to each other through their pets.

3. **Intuitive:** The City of Fort Worth painted a simple sign above the stairwell door in their elevator lobbies: *StairWELL.* That clear, intuitive prompt nudges everyone into thinking "Sure, why not?" As you leave the Four Winds Interactive office for lunch, the interactive monitor provides a map of the surrounding areas and highlights healthy restaurants and a round trip step count.

4. **Simple:** Less is more. Barry Schwartz's research found that two or three really good healthy choices are far better than a dozen options. When I'm at GoDaddy, I can go directly to the healthy food island, located very prominently in front of the area that serves pizza, burgers, and barbeque. Ergonomic chairs that provide a few easy adjustments work far better than those with highly complex chair adjustments. One ergonomic chair company that sold expensive chairs with multiple adjustments received many complaints about discomfort. They quickly discovered that very few users knew how to adjust the chairs.

5. **Feedback:** Giving people immediate positive feedback reinforces behavior. Receiving recognition on the cafeteria receipt for a healthy choice or getting a small discount on the next purchase signals "Good job!" The new Delos space in New York installed an interactive digital display in the stairwell. It responds to the number of times employees go up or down the stairs, but does so in a fun and artistic way. That interaction adds a gamification element.

6. **Forgiving:** Okay, I mess up; something will break, or I just didn't read the instructions. Does the system have airbags for these "oops" moments, or do I get penalized? My sister's Fitbit band broke. For the three days it took to replace it, she was unable to track her steps that

counted toward their insurance discount. Because she could not make up the difference for the month, her company reduced their discount by 8%. The system provided no forgiveness despite calling to ask for help. Barry-Wehmiller's health concierge provides airbags for employees who run into problems with their medical providers, including billing issues.

7. **Norms:** Leaders produce the positive behaviors they desire by modeling, recognizing, measuring, and rewarding. The Cleveland Clinic measures five outcomes: (1) blood pressure, (2) BMI, (3) triglycerides, (4) LDL cholesterol, and (5) cotinine (an alkaloid found in tobacco). A family who meets all five metrics receives a $2,400 discount on their insurance. They give doctors who smoke six months of support to quit, or they are gone. Their program is the extreme. But, if measured in participation and cost savings, it is one of the most successful. Sixty-eight percent of their employees with chronic disease participate compared to less than 12% for most companies.

The Domino Effect

If you watch a very simple but brilliant YouTube video called "Domino Chain Reaction," by professor Stephen Morris,[7] you'll understand why it has over 2.5 million views. You will see 13 dominoes, ranging progressively larger from just 5 millimeters high up to the largest, at 1 meter high and about 100 pounds in weight. The first very small domino falls into the second one, releasing one small unit of energy. But when the largest one falls, it releases 2 billion units of energy.

And that is the secret of the domino strategy of progressively bigger nudges. It's the old cliché: "The larger they are, the harder they fall." Each domino nudges the gravitational pull of the next larger domino.

When some people hear about nudge thinking, they ask, Why we don't just start at the top with leadership and culture? We don't because they are the biggest dominos. They are the hardest to budge; they need some well-designed momentum to shift their mindset and behavior.

Most wellness approaches try to get individuals to change instead of shifting the dynamics of the system. But think about the public health "dominoes": public service announcements, news media warnings,

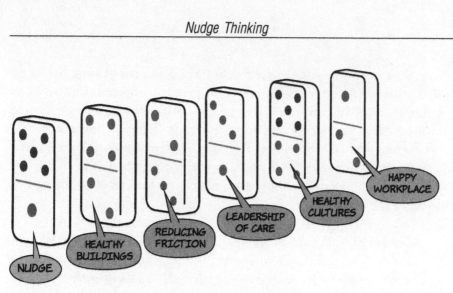

Figure 9.1 Small nudges lead to big change.

Centers for Disease Control and Prevention reports, surgeon general's warnings, and other information strategies use the domino chain reaction strategies. They first alter the environment; that shifts choices, which leads to influencing behavior until it becomes habit, and that builds a societal norm. Habits eventually change our thinking. For some reason, the wellness world ignores effective chain reaction strategies and continues targeting individuals.

The Nudge of Norms

Norms create powerful social nudges. They encompass leadership, environment, and the shadow culture. Norms—the pattern or model of what is normal—impose the constraints that prevent the adoption of new policies, behaviors, programs, or new ideas.

Boomers and Gen Xers remember when casual Fridays were first introduced. Of course, that shocked some. We joined a great debate: "What if someone showed up in *shorts*?" But, once in place and with the rise of the dotcom industry during the 1990s, business casual became the norm. And then it was full casual (skating to the very edge of what was socially acceptable, or even legal) on Friday.

Norms create powerful social nudges.

New norms provide powerful opportunities for shifting behavior. The most effective ones capitalize on inherent interests and work to strengthen and legitimize emerging ideas or trends. Google knows that people who feel connected to others are happier and tend to stay with the company. So, instead of starting a program called We Are Connected, they look for natural, organic groups and offer to provide structure and even training to help the tacit leaders strengthen the group.

> *Engagement with social norms, and an appreciation of their powerful influence on the well-being of populations, can be an important part of the work of public health [and the workplace—my addition], consistent with our emphasis on prevention, and our aspirations for healthier populations.*
> —Sandro Galea, MD, DrPH at Boston University

Betsy Price, the mayor of Fort Worth, Texas, told me about the new norms she has begun to introduce. Like the Walking School Bus, kids walking to school with an adult. It was developed to address growing child obesity. Because of that initiative, kids who normally get less than 30 minutes of exercise a week now walk 30 minutes a day and up to five miles a week.

Mayor Price also talked about her other initiatives. "We started our 'Rolling Town Halls,' on bicycles so that we could see different parts of the city and talk to people while we were cycling. We also have 'Walking Town Halls' on Saturday morning. We walk in different neighborhoods and different parks. We all soon realized that could be a big draw for businesses. If you've got a community that's beginning to take responsibility for their own health, that'll be a big draw and put us on the map and set us apart from other communities."

She also explained the very important issue of pacing: "You need to pace your employees and communities, so it doesn't feel like it's a push. "'Take an extra 15 minutes and walk on your break.'" Or, "'We will put healthier choices in our cafeteria.'" Blue Zones, a holistic wellness program, tells people to eat a "'plant centered diet,'" mostly plants. But, this is Texas. This is beef country. So, we just try to make healthy choices a little easier. We just said to people, "'If you're used to having beef six days a week, think about having it three days or four. Think about adding in more fruits and vegetables. Think about taking your

family to the park.'" That's why we're increasing our trail connections, increasing our parks so that they're available. They're close to everybody's home or everybody's business, and the closer you are to parks and to outdoor spaces, the more likely people are to use them."

Fort Worth has adopted nudge thinking to remove barriers, improve choices, and invest in the environment that affects everyone. Mayor Price added, "Our goal of the city is to work on the built environment. We're working on making it easier for our employees to find a place to walk. And we've set up a lap counter in City Hall and encouraged the department heads to get up from their desks and do some standing meetings, and to get their staff out walking. We're in the process of changing some of our vending machines so that when you walk up to the vending machine, the first thing you see is the water. People will still have that choice of sodas, but they'll be higher or lower. Same thing with the healthy choices in the snack machines. Just very simple things. Our 'Blue Zone parking' spaces are a little further away from the building."

So many of these ideas represent low-hanging fruit, not radical change. For example, did you know average dinner plates were 9 inches in diameter in 1900? And the average grew to 10 inches by 1950, and to 12 inches by 2010.[8] Today, for obvious reasons, the 9-inch plates are coming back. They reduce portions by 30% but still look full. That, and other beautiful nudges like hiding M&M's or sodas behind frosted glass, are helping many to live healthier, safer, and more prosperous lives.

And that doesn't require spending great sums of money or devising severe or coercive measures to force change. Nudge thinking begins by asking "What's keeping someone from already doing the good thing?" The work begins by uncovering the various constraints and experimenting with one nudge after another to discover the tipping points of acceptance and adoption.

Leadership Nudge

Take a walk through your offices and note of the number of temptations or constraints to healthy choices. Also, notice the bright spots th[a]t encourage positive choices.

Personal Nudge

What triggers in your environment cause you to give in to temptation? How can you swap those triggers for healthier ones? Start a
conversation at your next team meeting about adding healthy nudges
in the environment and routine. What or who might become helpful
commitment devices for you?

CHAPTER 10

The Healthy Building Nudge

The Invisible Power of the Workplace

The messages encoded in architecture and systems can foster a sense of mastery or helplessness.

—Charles Montgomery[1]

Ron Goetzel is the senior scientist and director of the Institute for Health and Productivity Studies at the Johns Hopkins Bloomberg School of Public Health. When I interviewed him, he explained why most companies just cannot pull off the creation of a healthy culture:

It is very, very, very, very hard to change human behavior. The way to get there requires a combination of different activities . . . culture, physical design, incentive programs, communication dissemination, strategic thinking about how to do that and expertise in the science of behavior change.

All of those things are woven together, and most companies in America don't know how to do that. They don't have the expertise, they don't have the background, they don't have the knowledge. Many don't have the money.

So, how do you create a culture of happiness and health?

Let's get started on the answer by stepping into another interview. I have learned that when Al Lewis speaks, you really don't want to miss anything. So, when he recently summarized the best corporate approach to wellness, I leaned in and listened very intently: "If I led a company with a lot of employees, I would spend money on environment rather than spend money telling them to change their bad behaviors. It's not even a question. If someone's environment is going to dramatically impact their health, productivity, and retention—that is where I would focus."[2]

If someone's environment is going to dramatically impact their health, productivity, and retention—that is where I would focus.

So, why, despite the invaluable perspectives of Lewis, Goetzel, and so many others, are most companies and organizations still trying to "do wellness" by requiring change at the individual employee level? That is not only futile, it is also very expensive. Because of our 18 months of research, I can tell you that improving the physical environment will prove to be a more effective and economical path to improving health than trying to force people to adopt behaviors which are in the best interests of their own physical being.

Figure 10.1   Money is wasted on ineffective wellness programs.

We found the best companies had two things in common; (1) committed and engaged leadership and (2) they invested the time and hard work to build healthy cultures. We know that leadership is the key. But without the hard work of building a robust ecosystem to support the leader's conviction, commitment, and congruence, those efforts become beautiful sandcastles that wash away under the next regime, budget squeeze, or market drop.

Just 5% of companies have the committed leadership *and* the necessary support structures and culture to nurture and protect employee health and well-being. So we think it's important to find a strategy that works for the 95%. When we concluded that most wellness programs are ineffective and a waste of money, we faced the question: What's the alternative? We believe it starts in designing healthy buildings.

Begin with a Healthy Building—A Slam Dunk!

Every time I meet with Paul Scialla, I learn new wisdom about our lives in a walled world. In each conversation, I hear three consistent themes.

1. Our species is still trying to adapt to living—90% of our time!—indoors.
2. The immediate space that surrounds us carries positive and negative health implications.
3. We have the ability, at a relatively low cost, to eliminate the harmful effects of buildings and transform them into delivery systems of health.

When I first met with Paul, he shot straight to his first point.

An individual, just by being in the space, whether at home, office, or school . . . just being in that space could have positive exposure to cardiovascular health, respiratory health, immune health, sleep health, cognitive health. This is a slam dunk!

Look at your built environment, where you spend 90 percent of your time. Take your age, multiply it by 0.9. That's how much of your life you have lived inside of four walls and a roof. What if we could activate that space to provide a passive and constant delivery of preventative medical benefits that wouldn't require the occupant to do a thing? An individual, just by being in the space, whether at home, office, or school . . . just being in that space could have positive exposure to cardiovascular health, respiratory health, immune health, sleep health, cognitive health. This is a slam dunk!

Figure 10.2   90% of our lives is spent indoors.

In the past few years, the International Well Building Institute,[3] FitWel,[4] the Living Building Challenge[5], Blue Zones[6] have distilled the best research into accessible information and guidelines. All corporate HR directors, wellness managers, heads of safety, corporate real estate executives and all those in the building service/supply chain should become familiar with the research. For the first time, we have a bridge of common language, which will help us move the discussion from building sustainability to human sustainability.

How Can a Building Make a Difference?

Paul Scialla imagines a day, in the not too distant future, "When our phones or wrist devices will warn us about toxic VOC's or unhealthy CO2 levels. Your phone could tell you that the EPA reports exposure inside a building is up to five times more toxic than standing outside. It's all coming, but we can do something *now*. The cost of designing healthy buildings is marginal. A 1% add to construction, and even that will become zero in the next few years."

So, what was he talking about?

At its core, a healthy work environment can be considered a useful and competitive business strategy to retain employees for the long-term.
—Jessica Nicolosi, Master's thesis, "A Holistic Approach to Workplace Wellbeing"

The following summaries of our 11 body systems give a brief glimpse into how our places of work influence our health, well-being, and performance. For most of my career, I had evaluated buildings through an environmental and aesthetic lens. But that view misses the deeper relationships between body, mind, and place. After examining the research, I came to an "aha" moment: "Of, course our environments deeply impact us, how could it be any other way?" At the very least we should build spaces that "do no harm." At their best, buildings can become invigorating and inspiring—with little additional expense.

> At the very least we should build spaces that "do no harm." At their best, buildings can become invigorating and inspiring—with little additional expense.

You will see in these summaries that spending on your building is the place to begin if you want to achieve serious improvement in the health and well-being of your employees. As you read, remember that stress is a dominant factor in our ability to function. Buildings have enormous potential to improve lives through supporting greater health for these systems:

Cardiovascular: Sitting decreases the heart rate and blood flow, sending less oxygen through your body. Movement raises metabolism and flushes the stress hormone, cortisol, out of the body. Buildings can be designed to reduce environmental stressors (noise and distraction) and with nudges to increase movement.

Digestive: Eating properly helps your body recover. Relaxed eating, especially with friends, activates the parasympathetic nervous system, releasing dopamine (pleasure) and oxytocin (connection). Eating while working, alone, or in noisy or crowded conditions places our nervous system on guard; it stands vigilant against real or imagined threats. Building design can create the pleasant spaces and communal connections that lower stress.

Endocrine: The endocrine system regulates metabolism, immunity, mood, and digestion. Maintaining balance is key to reducing chronic disease. Daylight and circadian lighting curtail endocrine disruption and stress.

Immune: Our immune systems often overload from fatigue and stress. That results in poor sleep and susceptibility to viruses, disease, and metabolic syndrome. Proper building design and construction can reduce environmental stress and exposure to toxic materials and chemicals that overload our immune systems. Buildings can also provide recovery areas that nudge people to take short breaks, further decreasing stress.

Integumentary: This largest human body system provides our external protection and works with the immune system to ward off an attack. Building design can help by regulating body temperature, providing hydration, and reducing exposure to toxins.

Urinary: Building design plays an important role supporting our body's primary system for removing toxins. The reduction of stress, healthy food selections, and engaging hydration stations provide some of the nudges to keep the body cleansed.

Reproductive System: Stress, toxic materials, chemicals, and electromagnetic fields all affect our reproductive system, balance, and mood. Buildings that provide easy and abundant access to nutritious food and adequate hydration contribute to improving reproductive health.

Muscular: Building design plays a major role in allowing safe movement. Ergonomics for support and environmental nudges to move are key to maintaining muscular tone and flexibility, thereby removing the cause of neck, shoulder, and back pain.

Skeletal: In its role as "body armor," the skeletal system protects the organs and the nervous system, produces blood cells, and regulates hormones. Ergonomic design can help to lessen the muscle fatigue and stress that can lead to injury.

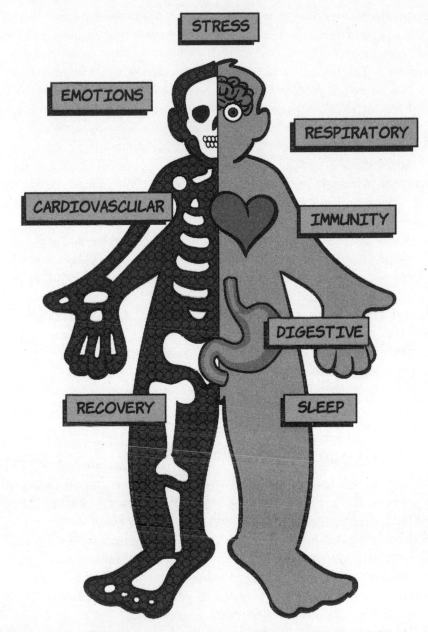

Figure 10.3 **The workplace environment affects most systems of the body.**

Respiratory: Building design can improve CO_2 levels; limit toxins, molds, and microbes; reduce particulate matter, and nudge people to more activity.

Nervous: The nervous system includes both cognitive and autonomic functions. The Academy for Neuroscience in Architecture at the Salk Institute helps companies to apply the latest research in neuroscience to "human responses in the built environment."

Shari Barkin, division chief of general pediatrics at Vanderbilt University Medical Center, told me how buildings influence our health and well-being from childhood:

> You're actually building your reactions to your environment during the critical windows of development in childhood. Buildings set your stress response and your reactions to certain things in your environment. That gets amplified over time. If you've created an environment that's more stressful, you're developing a physiology that's very reactive to stress. This pushes you in the direction of chronic illness.

"Let's Design a Better Planet!"

Whitney Gray, executive director of research and innovation at Delos, began her career in public health by focusing on domestic violence. After receiving her PhD from Johns Hopkins in health policy, she became a professor of nursing health studies. She was still searching for her purpose path when she saw the 2002 documentary *The Next Industrial Revolution*.[7] Susan Sarandon's voice opens the documentary: "Sustainable economy: an economic system that meets the needs of its current members without compromising the prospects of future generations."

Whitney saw a possibility beyond the film's message, a sustainable planet as the foundation for social justice and sustainable health. She kept looking for *her* place, the planetary spot that would release her to do *that*. When she met Paul Scialla, she knew she found a home. At the end of their first conversation, she said, "Let's design a better planet!"

When she presented to our group during our summit at Kaiser Permanente's Washington, DC, Center for Total Health, her natural intensity hit us hard. She rolled right into a forceful look at the ways humans have shifted natural rhythms, relationships, orientation to time, and definitions of home and play since buildings became a dominant influence in our lives. Her presentation certainly raised the question of why, if we spend 90% of our time in built environments, do we not also spend 90% of our focus and funds on *buildings*?

> *Why, if we spend 90% of our time in built environments, do we not also spend 90% of our focus and funds on buildings?*

When asked how much the new WELL standards would add to construction, Phil Williams, Delos president of business, told our team, "CBRE was our first commercial office project and so far, the most expensive. CBRE spent an additional 1.73% on the WELL upgrades. We're finding the cost premium can be $0. The average is about half of CBRE's cost."[8]

Lew Horne once told me, "Our WELL Building Certification is a tangible way for us to let our employees know we value them. As soon as they get off the elevator, they see the emblem. They know what we did. The certification is a simple reminder, but the space is the big reminder. Not a week goes by when I don't get a thank you."

How will we measure success in sustainability and wellness? Hopefully, the generation born today will wonder why we ever needed certification programs and ordinances to ensure energy efficient and healthy work environments.

—Dean Stanberry

Lew is emphatic when describing how their Los Angeles headquarters project transformed the behavior in the office, the lives of employees, and even their business. A change of space was a catalyst for a change in culture. He believes their process made the difference. They had no precedents and no best practices to serve as guides. It was a risky endeavor, but it created room to explore new ways of thinking and working. Lew recruited close to 25% of the office, working in small teams, to research technology, furniture, art, food, converting paper to the cloud, culture, move logistics, furniture, etc. Their Friday afternoon recaps were conducted in front of a full-height project learning wall. That provided a simple way to discuss what was, or was not, working. The weekly open meetings kept the teams aware of how the different aspects of the project were evolving and how to synchronize the work as the vision continued to take shape.

The process sometimes clashed with the linear prescriptive process from some of their consultants. We call that a design shift from PUSH to PULL. The old approach of PUSH is too cumbersome—have you ever pushed a chain? And it is too expensive to bring in experts in each category and expect them to play well together. The PULL process addresses integration challenges as well as creating a solution to uniquely fit an organization's needs.

In summary, PULL is like playing in a jazz band; PUSH is plodding through a checklist.

PUSH assumes:

- Leaders or experts have the answers ("Trust the expert").
- Leaders can accurately plan results.
- Achieving results is based on a "proven" and often proprietary path.[9]

PULL assumes:

- Leaders should challenge assumptions with fresh questions; they should trust the process.
- Leaders invite stakeholders into the process of discovery and testing.
- Achieving results is based on evidence gained from discovery and testing.

Your Workplace Is a Proxy for Your Health and Well-Being

Delivering a healthy building and one that transforms your culture and business may sound daunting, but is very achievable, increasingly necessary, and surprisingly economical. The largest catalyst to understanding and transforming our organizations is literally under our feet. When an organization thinks about changing their workspace, that very idea raises fundamental questions, excavates old assumptions, and causes everyone to roll up their sleeves to understand and rediscover "why we do what we do." Solutions that rise out of that process bring transformation.

Delivering a healthy building and one that transforms your culture and business may sound daunting, but is very achievable, increasingly necessary, and surprisingly economical.

Our workspaces send powerful messages about what our organizations value. Lew Horne explained that his employees walk in each day, see their WELL certification, and know that means something:

> *I think the WELL certification speaks to employees knowing we built this space with their health in mind. Our space is also having a positive effect on the home front. I hear employees talk about how they are eating differently at home, or becoming more active. We are in the building business. We believe buildings make a difference, but I have not seen anything quite like this before. It is also helping us with our clients. Because we've gone through our own journey, and it's made a huge difference for us, our clients seem to sense we can do the same for them.*

Let There Be Light!

The WELL Building Standard lists more than 100 health issues. Let's look at one, just one, feature to examine—light. This one area will give us a lens for viewing how buildings can contribute to greater employee happiness and health.

Maybe the reason I resonate to the subject of light is that my father graduated from Rochester Institute of Technology, specializing in reprographics. So, I grew up hearing and knowing about light frequencies, UV waves, additive and subtractive lighting. Light is a magical essence that invades our bodies with electromagnetic radiation, influencing both happiness and health. Light plays a profound role in physical and mental health.

The sun, in its daily or circadian cycle, regulates our biological clocks. Body temperature and cortisol elevate during the morning hours, responding to the rising blue light spectrum. But body temperature decreases and melatonin elevates to prepare us for sleep. That's why light is such a significant health issue. As the WELL Building Standard reminds us, "Given that people spend much of their waking day indoors, insufficient illumination can lead to a drift of the circadian phase."[10]

During an interview with Paul Scialla, I noticed a light fixture I had not seen before. I asked him about it. Now, understand, asking Paul a simple question ignites his authentic curiosity. He confidently gazes at objects, people, and ideas as a genuine seeker of knowledge. As he seeks, he talks.

"Forget the fixture. You see that lighting? It's a very high-lux temperature light. It's supposed to match the sky. It's doing that for a reason. We are conditioned to be outside, active, energized, and mentally acute during the day, and asleep at night. That's stems from tens of thousands of years of biological history. That was until we created these little boxes around ourselves; now we spend 90 percent of our day *inside*.

> *100 years ago we invented artificial light, and for the first time, the human body was exposed to artificial light in the evening. That completely disrupted our natural circadian rhythm.*

Even more disruptive, 100 years ago we invented artificial light, and for the first time, the human body was exposed to artificial light in the evening. That completely disrupted our natural circadian rhythm.

"The more we can match lighting to what we're supposed to get outside during daytime and adjust to a softer yellow and lower lux light in the evening, the more we're going to have the right hormones created in the evening for sleep and in the daytime for activity.

"Do you know there is a nerve in our eye that was only discovered nine years ago? It's called the circadian optic nerve. It is the first time medical science has realized there's a mechanism in your eye that has nothing to do with vision. It takes in peripheral light and darkness and controls your sleep–wake cycle. That's it.

Figure 10.4 The circadian optic nerve.

"We can extend the workday in a very healthy manner by applying higher lux, higher temperature, bluer, brighter, whitish light in an office setting to keep the body stimulated like it was still early afternoon, to keep mental acuity hormones and productivity hormones elevated, and stop the early secretion of melatonin. If you're already making a lighting decision, if your facility's manager is doing an LED swap, the health attributes of lighting can have a profound impact on the bottom line of the company. That could extend and enhance productivity for a couple hours a day for three months out of the year. That's your upside calculation. That additional performance factor comes at zero cost. The ROI for a simple swap is infinity.

"I installed circadian lighting in my bedroom. It's dynamic. It basically changes and creates the sunrise, midday, late-afternoon, early evening, and evening light inside."

Artificial light, and especially blue spectrum light, may be the single most harmful assault on our minds and bodies. Providing circadian lighting and harvesting natural light may also be the easiest, least expensive, and most immediate with the highest positive impact investment on 100% of your employees.

New York Times Building—The Magical Effect of Light

I met David Thurm in early 2008, about six months after the *New York Times* moved into their iconic headquarters. As the senior vice president of operations and in charge of the project, David had two design objectives for the building:

1. Lowering operational cost
2. Improving employee experience and health

He came away from two previous building projects with a guideline: "Push the limits on what you hope to deliver to employees: it's worth it." To push the limits on their project, the "gray lady" was forced to step outside its traditional role as a purchaser of goods and services to partner with key suppliers and push their limits.

That collaboration led to a most interesting feature in the building, a digital adjustable lighting interface (DALI). The building is designed to

The building is designed to harvest as much natural light as possible. Expanding windows to let the sunshine in was the easy part. Tuning the space to manage glare, changing light conditions and hot spots, required very precise science.

harvest as much natural light as possible. Expanding windows to let the sunshine in was the easy part. Tuning the space to manage glare, changing light conditions and hot spots, required very precise science. The building coordinates indoor and exterior conditions to optimize natural light and mimic the pattern of the sun. Three roof-mounted radiometers track the sun throughout the day. The signal is then processed through an algorithm to automatically adjust the exterior shades and internal lights. Mirroring the circadian rhythm may, perhaps, be the biggest health breakthrough in building technology.

In 2003, five years before the project, they hired Lawrence Berkeley National Laboratory (LBNL) to advise them on the project. In 2011, three years after project completion, they brought LBNL back to measure both building and human performance factors. That level of pre- and post-occupancy research reveals the level of intentionality that is essential for creating healthy buildings. Steven Selkowitz's "Daylighting The New York Times Headquarters Building" provides the full report.[11]

That report documents the significant energy and cost savings they had hoped to see. It also confirms that 78% of the occupants were highly satisfied with the lighting experience.[12] David reminded me of the business conditions in 2011:

We had just gone through another round of layoffs, people were understandably on edge and upset, but our satisfaction levels for the office simply confirm what we thought at the beginning of the project: our workplace could become something special and meaningful to our employees. I had the chance to visit the building earlier this year. The way natural light is captured in that space is still simply magical.

The Bridge to a Happy and Healthy Workplace

The first time I visited CBRE, I stepped off the elevator onto a cork underfloor (ah, the cushioned lumbar support). When I entered the open lobby, I was greeted by their concierge/receptionist. To her left, I saw a long, standing-height countertop. It displayed a healthy drink area and a several drawers filled with healthy snacks. Darcy, my tour guide, walked down the large central staircase; it was obviously designed to invite use. We entered a soft seating living room area called "The Hearth." Next, on the tour, we looked in on the nutrition and yoga classroom.

The CBRE office is divided into "neighborhoods." Employees can sit wherever they want, but tend to work in "their" neighborhood. Neighborhoods include a suite of glass-walled privacy offices, conference rooms, and low-height, open stations along the windows. Every station includes an adjustable sit-to-stand surface and two monitors with adjustable support arms. Darcy pointed out the circadian lighting and how the shades and light adjust over the workday. She explained that surface tops have antimicrobial laminates and each evening the office is cleaned using a UV wand with detailed cleaning protocols. Employees who chose to stand were given standing pads. The office is very open, but the distractions of noise are kept low, using sound-dampening materials and sound-masking equipment. Hydration stations serve purified water that meets WELL specifications. Their food areas displayed fresh fruit, nuts, and other healthy snacks. The last item I saw was the indoor biophilia landscaping.

Do you know what message speaks clearly to anyone walking through the office? That CBRE values health and their employees. Do employees feel that way about your company? Do they know the company cares? The CBRE project was a first of its kind, and the cost for its stunning upgrades was only about 1.73% more than normal construction. And that cost is coming down.

Paul Scialla is passionate about helping Delos customers "unlock human potential through your building." The best way to lift the health and well-being of your employees is to invest in the very place where they spend so much time. By doing that, instead of building complex and expensive behavior modification strategies that actually benefit very few, you can improve the lives of 100% of everyone who enters your built environments.

Leadership Nudge

Meet with your real estate and facilities group to identify the low-hanging fruit. Invite someone from Delos, FitWel, or one of the

MindShift members to meet with your senior leadership team to learn how you can turn your facility into a delivery system for health. Get the building to match the message—start with the vending and drink machines.

Personal Nudge

Standing is a proxy for movement. Your next position is your best position. Take micro-stretch breaks every 20 to 30 minutes. Take a walking break every 90 minutes.

CHAPTER 11

The Financial Nudge

The Return on Humans (ROH)

> *There's something that happens with the collection of a large amount of data when it's dumped into an Excel spreadsheet or put into a pie chart. You run the risk of completely missing what it's about.*
>
> —Aaron Koblin, digital media artist

Patrick Lencioni gets paid up to $70,000 and more to deliver the same, very simple, one-hour message that he's been delivering for more than 15 years: Healthy organizations outperform smart ones. Every time I watch him give it, I am reminded that organizational health is so elusive that companies will pay $70,000 for a one-hour reminder of what we already know.

Why is organizational health so elusive? Why is it so hard for leaders to stop, look, and listen to the messages all around, even in our own homes? Do leaders just not believe or understand the evidence? Are they too busy to pay attention? Do they simply not care?

These are serious questions. The evidence supporting well buildings, employee wellness and well-being, leadership engagement, and designed nudges is overwhelming and growing. We know a Grand Canyon full of data and details we did not have even a few years ago.

I sometimes imagine myself at a management meeting, armed with reams of that very compelling data. If I had my moment to take my best shot, would it make a difference? Would it suddenly change the minds around that boardroom table?

Probably not. In Lencioni's terms, it would likely be a smart presentation, but not one that penetrates the heart. I understand. I too have been making the Lencioni proposition for 15 years. I usually detect immediate interest. *Maybe this group will be the one.* But, no. I learn later that the flame died quickly. Part of the reason may be that I have no solid, urgent, and enduring relationship with the group. I only have intellectual capital, my expertise, references, and style. But it is also true that many would rather do the wrong thing they can measure on a spreadsheet than the right thing that, however obvious, is less tangible. That is what kills these efforts, or strips them of any potency. It's not ROI or data.

> *Many would rather do the wrong thing they can measure on a spreadsheet than the right thing that, however obvious, is less tangible.*

Is It Personal?

A group of Washington, DC, policymakers gathered in a sumptuous hotel meeting room to discuss the need for empathy in public policy. One of the presenters, a Hispanic community organizer, began to speak earnestly. In Spanish. The policy wonks looked at the event coordinator. *What was going on?* He spoke for four or five minutes. No interpreter. Then, he stopped, looked at the confused crowd and said softly, "Now, you know what first grade was like for me. I wet my pants the first day because I couldn't tell the teacher I had to go to the bathroom." He spoke another 20 minutes to a completely captivated audience.

Sometimes those sitting around the boardroom don't buy in because they sense the issue is not personal to the presenter. Until this project, I cared about health, joy, and engagement. But my care was too cerebral and detached. Then, I walked through an extended series of familial and friendship crises. I even had to face a serious disconnect between our oldest son and me. My type "A" approach to life clashed with his highly relational wiring. I never intended it, but my message was clear: "You're not meeting my expectations." It eventually blew up in my face, and it took that for me to reach out for help. I had to start with me; I slowly became the kind of dad who was, first, a safe place. My son had to know that I cared. No conditions, expectations, or performance clauses. It's been a long road. But, as we recently concluded a phone call, I said, as I often have, "I love you, son." And he said what he never says: "I love you too, Dad." What is the ROI on that?

If you get hired at Next Jump, you are hired for life. The company has walked an extraordinary journey to help people bring their whole selves to work. Simon Sinek has helped them on that journey. His oft-stated wisdom has helped Next Jump to build a culture of care and commitment: "A company is a modern-day tribe. Hiring someone for your company is akin to having a child. If you have hard times in your family, would you ever consider laying off one of your children?"

> *A company is a modern-day tribe. Hiring someone for your company is akin to having a child. If you have hard times in your family, would you ever consider laying off one of your children?*

Sinek carries a classic load of wisdom: *It's not business; it's personal.* How did we ever forget that life—all of it—is personal? Barry-Wehmiller's CEO Bob Chapman asks one question about employee policies: "Is it the right thing to do?" If it is, he expects leadership to find a way to make it work for the company.

Here is the crossroad we face. Can we stop taking the road of least resistance? Can we turn away from mere efficiency, short-term outlooks, and spreadsheet thinking? At one time, safety was a trade-off with cost. Then Alcoa made it a catalyst for transforming their business. Sustainability was always a trade-off with cost. But Interface Carpet made it a catalyst for transforming their business. Once upon a time, General Electric was famous for firing the bottom 10% of their employees. Next Jump has made lifetime employment a commitment device to force it to become a better company.

Are We Smart or Healthy?

Maybe we're too busy and myopic to see and feel the need. But it seems that our momentum drives us to become efficient (smart) instead of healthy. Spreadsheets have become the fast food for decision making (just as PowerPoint has become the fast food of presentations). They are convenient and inexpensive, but they strip out all the nutrients necessary to make healthy human decisions.

I once sat in on a national contractor's quarterly senior leadership meeting. Reports appeared around the table for each participant. Each report included brief summaries, dashboards of key performance indicators, and pages with spreadsheet back-ups. Most of the meeting considered revenue projections and project updates. When the meeting turned to the safety report, we all saw that incidences for the past two months had increased. That generated a lively debate of suggestions on how to fix the numbers. No one saw that the numbers were abstractions for the real people who suffered real harm, loss of income, potential loss of future employment, and a ripple effect through their families. No one in the meeting acted from bad intent. The meeting simply followed the matrix for how we arrive at smart but unhealthy decisions. And, true to that pattern, that company decided to resend its safety protocols, add another safety audit, and put more pressure on supervisors.

I later wondered how the meeting might have unfolded differently if a large picture of each injured employee and his or her family had been posted along the boardroom walls before the meeting. What if the numbers had been turned into stories? What if each executive had selected one of those injured employees for a personal and unhurried conversation? Could a culture grow up around learning, caring, and communicating why the company values safety?

At one point, I raised a question of safety's value to the company. And, to their credit, my question did generate a follow-up conversation. Together, with one executive, we worked to create a Team Health process and dashboard designed around crucial measurements.[1]

The Power of a Meme

Another reason that organizational health is so elusive may be that leaders simply don't believe the numbers. I understand—I don't believe them either. Let's face it: one reason we don't have sufficient buy-in is that the wellness industry, the whole narrative, suffers a lack of credibility.

One reason we don't have sufficient buy-in is that the wellness industry, the whole narrative, suffers a lack of credibility.

Most wellness experts are not numbers people. They throw out statistics with little context or documentation. And that is how memes are born.

For example, many people in the wellness world have heard and believed that each dollar invested in wellness programs will produce a three-dollar return. But that's not true. Doesn't matter—that calculation is entrenched. In fact, if you type "$1 of wellness equals $3 ROI" into Google's search engine, you will get about 276,000 results. Scroll down; you will see those numbers repeated by SHRM, the *Chicago Tribune*, the American Institute of Preventative Medicine, OSHA, and others. The references roll for many pages.

That is where the great ROI debate began for me. I tried, diligently and unsuccessfully, to track down the source of that "$1 = $3" fiction. What was measured? Retention, engagement, lower health costs? How was it evaluated? Was a baseline established, a defined period of comparison, a control group? Who did the measurement? Was it human resources, an outside firm, the health vendor?

That "$1 = $3" is the most resilient meme surrounding wellness.

The word *meme* has acquired great (and recent) cultural currency and is rooted in the Greek word meaning "imitated." As such, the word describes the great expansion of phrases, videos, quotes, and other units of information that explode through that uniquely suitable carrier that we know as the Internet. James Gleick explained that dynamic very well:

> *Memes emerge in brains and travel outward, establishing beachheads on paper and celluloid and silicon and anywhere else information can go. They are not to be thought of as elementary particles but as organisms. The number three is not a meme; nor is the color blue, nor any simple thought, any more than a single nucleotide can be a gene. Memes are complex units, distinct and memorable—units with staying power.*[2]

Scientist Richard Dawkins coined the word in his book *The Selfish Gene*.[3] His further explanation, now in the Merriam-Webster Dictionary, tells us: "Memes (discrete units of knowledge, gossip, jokes and so on) are to culture what genes are to life. Just as biological evolution is driven by the survival of the fittest genes in the gene pool, cultural evolution may be driven by the most successful memes."[4]

That's how "$1 = $3" has survived for decades. And a leader, or an audience, with no intellectual investment or emotional buy-in will simply confirm their biases. The meme becomes a Rorschach test, not a useful decision device.

So, What Are We Missing?

David Radcliffe, Google's vice president of real estate and workplace services, presented a question to one of our summits: "Are we squeezing pennies of support on the top and losing dollars of engagement on the bottom?" Great question.

Are we squeezing pennies of support on the top and losing dollars of engagement on the bottom?

We know that 82% of a company's costs is salaries and benefits (69% salary, 31% benefits)[5] and remains below the surface, out of sight. The tip of the iceberg is made up of design, construction, furniture, and equipment costs of 5%. You add operating costs of 3% and technology at 10% for a total of 18%. So, in summary, here is the iceberg of costs:

If I live on the tip of the iceberg, my responsibility follows a simple logic: Shrink my cost. I become a hero by shaving 25% off $20, thereby completing a task at $15. If instead I spend $25 and explain that I did it to improve productivity, I simply went over budget. There are no systems in place to ask, plan, or measure if squeezing pennies loses dollars of engagement or spending pennies adds dollars.

Kate Lister raises this question by looking at two snapshots of a $70,000-per-year financial sector employee. She first looks at the cost—about $6,000 for an office and $8,000 for technology, for a total of $14,000 per year—to support this employee. The second snapshot looks at his or her contribution to corporate financial health. Each employee averages generating revenue of $420,000 a year, or $210 per hour, *six times* his or her salary!

Lister writes:

Here is the reality that most fail to consider in their myopic pursuit of lowering costs: if an employee loses just six minutes of productivity a day because of their office environment, i.e., problems with technology, poor ergonomics, bad lighting, etc., it entirely negates the hoped savings from eliminating their office. Eliminating office space may be tangible, but if

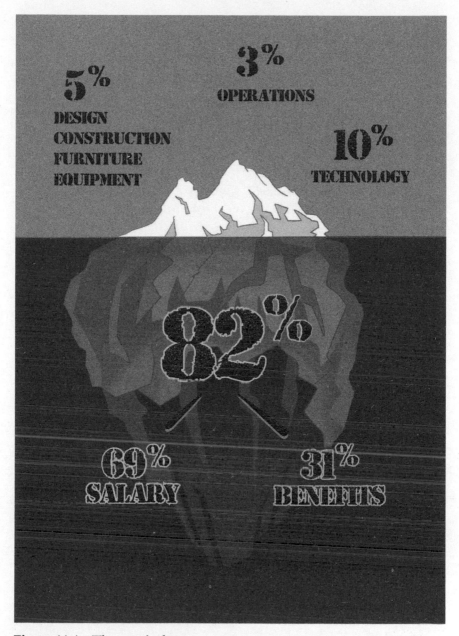

Figure 11.1 The cost iceberg.

unintended consequences make it harder for employees to do their work, the loss of productivity can completely negate the real estate savings.[6]

Companies like Apple, Facebook, and Google understand the true economy of talent. They fiercely compete in the talent wars. Their employees also generate an average of approximately $1.2 million of profit per year. *Each employee. $1,200,000 of profit.* Of course, those companies are disciplined and effective in their management. However, they use a different lens for viewing the value of human capital. They see it as an asset to leverage, not a cost to contain.

> *Companies like Apple, Facebook, and Google . . . use a different lens for viewing the value of human capital. They see it as an asset to leverage, not a cost to contain.*

In other words, could a 10% increase to enhance an office, just $700 per employee, result in just a 1% increase in productivity? If so, that would generate a 700% ROI.

Conversely, could a 10% "savings" result in a 1% loss of engagement and productivity? It only takes 20 hours lost (due to disruption, distraction, or disengagement) to drop 1% of productivity. That is one reason office moves or a new program implementation can become so costly. An hour of planning can prevent a loss of many hours in productivity due to poor coordination and resistance. Implementations that "go off the rails" can take weeks and months to work through. And they often leave a residual drain or stain on the organization.

Flipping the Argument

Are we playing defense when we could and should be playing offense? If so, that could be because people are often more comfortable defending something that doesn't work but that taps their personal sweet spot than to adopt something new that rode in from an unknown territory.

The first book we produced, *The Commercial Real Estate Revolution,*[7] tackled the dysfunctional process and culture for designing and constructing buildings. I was still learning to deal with gritty and skeptical subtrades and contractors who have survived by doing things a certain way. But one of our coauthors, Bill Black, grew up as a tradesman in Scotland, as well as a quantity surveyor. While I had research on my side, he also had years of hard-fought experience.

We addressed an event with general contractors, promoting integrated project delivery. That was part of our answer to flip the broken system. We argued that the stakeholders, brought in early and using a collaborative stakeholder framework, will perform much better than gathering everyone after all the major decisions have been made. The latter is a shotgun wedding. I told that meeting that such a marriage won't work. It is built on distrust. Owners won't support it. Others have tried and failed.

Even though no one took issue with our description of the then-current state of construction, it took a completely different mindset to consider a trust-based system.[8] But, when they asked for proof, I shared some anecdotes and found myself consistently playing defense. Bill, on the other hand, relished the brawl. He responded in a very cheeky tone, "So you're telling me that you'd prefer a late project, over budget, bogged down in claims with an unhappy client? Take a moment and defend that for me!"

The evidence for improving engagement and performance is deep and compelling, with one flaw. It does not fit the paradigm and falls outside the domains of real estate, operations, and procurement.

The tagline for an old Fram Oil Filters commercial gave a perfect summation of these processes: "Pay me now or pay me later." That is the problem that Dr. Roizen has with the RAND report. He says that Mattke is right: most wellness programs don't work. But that is because they are poorly designed and administered, they measure participation instead of outcomes, and they don't have meaningful incentives.

Kate Lister reports that only 17% of companies spend more than $150 per employee for wellness efforts.[9] The Cleveland Clinic provides incentives with a no deductible plan and caps out-of-pocket family costs to $3,000.[10] They have also reduced their average annual cost increase of 8% (the national average) to zero!

Maybe some leaders need to pay attention to the Cleveland Clinic.

The Strongest ROI: A Healthy Building

As you've probably gathered by now, investing in a healthy building is the most direct strategy for improving employee health and well-being. Because the immediate space that surround us affects every system in our bodies, Dr. Whitney Gray sees buildings as one of the most effective delivery devices for passive positive medical benefits. Those benefits are supported by exhaustive documentation of that impact on our systems.

In the fragmented system of budget buckets, the cost for upgrading a building comes out of either the capital or the maintenance budget. And that always evokes that standard objection: "This is going to be a tough sell." Assuming the organization is stuck in that logic, and either doesn't fully buy the business benefit of healthier employees or has no means of measuring it, I would (and do) compare a healthier building strategy to the cost and return of a wellness program strategy. Tom Emerick says the oft-stated annual cost of wellness programs at $700 per employee is just the vendor and rebate costs. He said, "That's not even half of the true costs." I asked why I've never heard that math at wellness conferences. He smiled.

Let's use Kate's example to build a scenario. And, despite Tom's adjustment, we'll use the average annual employee costs of $700. So, 100 employees will burn $70,000 in a year. Furthermore, only 15% of those employees will participate, most likely the healthy ones. If only 15 of 100 participate at a cost of $70,000, the cost of running that program is actually $4,700 for each! Obviously, the ROI for buildings just crashed.

> *If only 15 of 100 participate at a cost of $70,000, the cost of running that program is actually $4,700 for each! Obviously, the ROI for buildings just soared.*

We must have that essential conversation.

Let's use Tom Emerick's annual cost-per-employee of wellness programs, as shown in Table 11.1. A complete picture of wellness program costs must include the internal administration cost for running the program and the lost productivity of employee participation. You will need your company's actual monthly time investment per employee, on average. To get a true picture, use the lost revenue generation per employee, not salary and benefits.

Now, if the average employee turnover rate is 15%, whatever benefits an employee may have gained by his or her participation goes with that employee to the next company. But, improvements to the building and designed nudges remain and have a positive effect on whoever works in that space.

That should not be a "tough sell!" If it is, it is only because of budget and turf silos. We have seen that there is almost always enough money spread among different buckets to address employee health, well-being,

Table 11.1 Annual cost per employee of wellness programs.*

$700	Direct benefits
$300	Internal administrative costs
$2,520	Lost productivity participating in one workshop, online training, etc. per month
$1,125	False positives (15% participation x 30% false positives x $25,000 per incident)
$840	Events—health fairs—lost productivity for two hours per year per employee plus administration costs
$4,360	Total cost for wellness

*These are hypothetical estimates based on assumptions of soft costs. Tom Emerick tracked these costs while at Walmart. Few organizations, however, are aware of, or have the means to do similar tracking.

safety, service, etc. By coordinating resources, most companies would find that shifting dollars to a healthy environment creates an attractive and more effective strategy.

The estimated cost for upgrading a building to the WELL Building Standard, GSA's FitWel, or LEED v4 runs somewhere between $150 and $500 per employee. And that is a one-time cost. Paul Scialla elaborates, "That's the hard cost, the soft cost, the consultancy, the certification, all included, for what? For a constant and primarily passive delivery of prevention to enhance cardiovascular health, respiratory health, immune health, cognitive health, sleep health outcomes.

> *The foundation of enduring support for health and wellness investment is traditional due diligence analysis . . . Fortunately, such analysis is possible and often highly favorable. For example, returns of nearly 300% are possible, with limited risk, from healthy building investments and assume only a 0.5% increase in productivity.*[11]

—Scott Muldavin

That's the hard cost, the soft cost, the consultancy, the certification, all included, for what? For a constant and primarily passive delivery of prevention to enhance cardiovascular health, respiratory health, immune health, cognitive health, sleep health outcomes. Here's the best part: guaranteed 100% participation.

"Here's the best part: guaranteed 100% participation." And then Paul asked the key question:

What if there was a way to impact and introduce prevention into society in a manner that did not necessarily require behavioral change? What if there was a way to impact cardiovascular outcomes, asthma-related illnesses, respiratory outcomes, sleep outcomes, immune outcomes, in a manner that didn't require people to do something different, at least in the beginning? What's the best vehicle to deliver that prevention in a passive manner? Well, how about the real estate where we spend 90% of our time? Our homes, our offices, our schools, and other built environments can be used as a healthcare intervention tool, at $1 a square foot.

That is exciting.

Leadership Nudge

Pull together HR, corporate real estate, facilities, safety, training, and any other department that spends money to improve the employee experience. Where are the overlaps? How could dollars shift to more effective and proven outcomes?

Personal Nudge

Do you want to show your manager how much revenue they lose because of friction in their system?

Keep a journal for one week.

Log the hours of lost productivity because of interruptions or friction in the environment. Divide the revenue of the company by the number of employees to find the average revenue for your seat on the bus. Divide that number by 2,000 hours to arrive at your hourly contribution to the company. Take your weekly tally of hours lost, multiply it by your hourly contribution, and then multiply it by 50 weeks. You now have a starting point to look at how friction in the system costs the company.

What is the one thing you might recommend to reduce the weekly hours lost?

CHAPTER 12

Becoming Your Best Self

Rest, Engagement, Boundaries, and Deep Work

For thousands of years, humans kept their energy engines idling most of the day. They only accelerated to occasional bursts of exertion to hunt or escape danger. Pets give a good window into how the autonomic nervous system was designed to function. Our four dogs—Iris, Annie, Daisy, and Donnie—sleep most of the day and then spring to DEFCON 1 when the UPS delivery person comes within 100 feet of the house. When they finish defending the turf and letting the house and neighbors know it's all clear, they go right back to where they left off—full rest. Humans also go from rest to full alert in a split second. But it takes us a long time to return to full rest mode. Stress keeps our engines running high.

Dogs act in accordance with their fine-tuned senses for protection. But human responses include a very vivid imagination. Our imagination is powerful enough to activate fight-or-flight—with or without an outside trigger. That's why we live with the switch flipped "on" most of the time. We relive yesterday's regrets, coil like a panther against today's threats (real or imagined), and fret about tomorrow's unknowns.

Between those moments of stress, many distractions keep our brains in the shallows of life. That keeps us from finding recuperative rest or the vital restorative balance.

Part of the problem is the imbalance between our parasympathetic nervous system (PSNS) and our sympathetic nervous system (SNS). The PSNS restores our engine (the heart), sometimes called the rest-and-digest switch. The SNS's heart accelerator, sometimes called the fight-or-flight switch, turns on in the morning and revs up the engine to seize the day or when danger crouches near. Both work side-by-side and often in competition as the autopilot for survival called the autonomic nervous system (ANS).

The Corporate Athlete

Ever since I received my USPTA professional tennis certification shortly after college, I've carried a continuing interest in health and performance. Athletes train extensively, preparing for those short moments of competition. They must be at their best in those moments, and they also need to recover quickly from their spurts of exertion. That's why recovery is critically important for high-performing athletes.

The WHOOP athletic band is one of the first performance sensors in the new field of heart rate variability or HRV. Simply put, HRV measures a heart's ability to leap into action and, equally important, to slow down into a recovery or maintenance level. The WHOOP band, worn on the wrist or bicep, tracks the interplay between the sympathetic and parasympathetic nervous systems.

Heart rate is measured by the number of beats per minute. An average resting heart rate is 70 beats per minute (many top athletes have heart rates under 40 beats per minute). More important, however, is what happens between those beats. Your heart is constantly responding to its surroundings. When we breathe in, it accelerates slightly. When we breathe out, it slows down. For example, getting pulled over by a police officer races your heart. Even if the officer lets you go with a warning, your heart continues racing as you drive away, thinking what you should have done or said, anticipating the conversation with your spouse, and kicking yourself for not paying attention. In other words, your heart did not immediately shift to a rest level.

People who can shift on and off like a light switch preserve more energy and stay better focused. The others, who turn on and off slowly like a thermostat, are less prepared and focused during real-time action. That's why the escalating athletic competitive pressure is increasing the number of athletes whose bodies break down. Athletes are wired to push hard and through pain. Sports culture reinforces that drive. But over-training is a leading cause of injury, fatigue, and feeling off-balance on the day of competition. HRV measures that readiness.

I began wondering if there might be a similar problem with over-working. If so, how would one know? Is there a "peak state" for doing our best work? How does the WHOOP band compare the two?

WHOOP's vice president for performance optimization, Kristin Holmes-Winn, analyzed eight months of my activities and offered key insights and suggestions for improving recovery. I'll get to that later. I learned that stress can tax our system as much as an intense workout does. It burns up calories and shows similar levels of drain on our system. Stress, however, adds all the harmful effects that lead to metabolic syndrome. And it provides no benefit to your cardiovascular system. When I began focusing on recovery, using my WHOOP for feedback, I could slow or increase my pace of work based on my level of recovery and ability to handle cognitive or physical load. I also improved my sleep habits, which had the greatest positive effect on my health. That shift also made profound improvements in my energy and productivity.

I know many people who burn the candle at both ends; that applies to executives, truck drivers, nurses, construction workers, and people working double shifts. Their jobs are strenuous and stressful. Many go to bed late and get up early. Many of them get less than six hours of sleep, and much of that sleep is too light to give mental or physical restoration. And it's much worse when we travel. Studies show our sleep performance on the road drops as much as 40%. Too many road warriors do not wind down gently, clear the clutter out of their brain, or avoid screens before bed. Few get adequate sleep, take sufficient pauses throughout the day, or make meals social and restorative.

> *We don't understand the compromised condition we've created for ourselves. And to think I used to wear it is a badge of honor.*

We don't understand the compromised condition we've created for ourselves. And to think I used to wear it is a badge of honor. I didn't make

Figure 12.1 Employees have become corporate and business athletes.

the connection. Sleep deprivation had become normal until I collided with the data. That moment reminded me of the times as an athlete when I overtrained. We just did not call it that. After persisting in drills that exceeded the coach's instructions, I just called it being out of gas. It was the equivalent of being on the ropes in boxing. When you and I are overworked and not fully recovered, it doesn't matter if we wear sports gear or business wear: we are physically and mentally on the ropes.

Understanding the stress-work-life connection transformed me.

Walking the Talk

I wrote this chapter because I care about leaders and those they lead. Our bodies are the bridges that the heavy trucks of purpose, mission, vision, care, and career must travel. If they are not maintained, they will collapse under the weight of the cargo. We've all attended too many funerals for those who broke down under the load.

Pushing limits seems to be ingrained in the cultures of both athletics and work. But the cost of overtraining stays hidden until the breaking point. That is called "overtraining syndrome." Symptoms include insomnia, depression, fatigue, decreased physical performance, loss of concentration, and more.

How do you know if you've pushed it too far and *require* recovery? What does recovery look like? Dr. Amit Sood told us that because the brain does not have nerve endings, it does not register pain. That means we are all prone to overdo our exertion, ignore common sense, and fail to recognize signs of fatigue.

My Great Aha

When I started using my WHOOP band, my morning read-out would show low recovery. It simply did not compute. I exercised, ate well, and had a low resting heart rate. I'm very active, but this device on my arm was telling me that my heart was tired! I asked for a replacement band and tried moving up my arm for a potentially different reading. Looking back, I was in deep denial. The data and my version of reality did not align. So, guess which had to change?

The data and reality collided during a particularly stressful week in January 2017. My preparations for an upcoming summit hit several snags. Putting out fires kept me from fully preparing. One week before the summit, I had a very rough day. When I went to bed, my mind raced all night, solving problems and outlining the two-day summit. I woke up at 4 a.m. feeling wired. I captured some of my thoughts and got ready to work out. My recovery registered at 19, the lowest I had ever experienced. But I felt energized. I didn't realize that energy was simply the adrenaline of stress. I went to the recreation center for my morning workout, and 12 minutes into my elliptical routine I was depleted. Totally. I could not go any further. That is when "aha" walked into my head.

I was depleted. Totally. I could not go any further. That is when "aha" walked into my head.

My WHOOP told me I wasn't recovered enough to take on that level of exertion. Because my brain did not feel the pain, I had not paid attention. But WHOOP got my attention. I began taking note of other signs: a foggy mind, lethargy, a tendency toward negative thinking, being short-tempered, etc.

That was a crossroad experience. It created a mental diagram of a virtuous loop of rest, engagement, and satisfaction. I also saw a vicious loop of exhaustion and distraction. I needed that visceral connection, along with a feedback tool, to begin adjusting and adapting to new behaviors. I knew I had to build some new habits.

From that wake-up call, I started to notice when I was naturally my sharpest and best able to focus. My most productive hours for focused work were between 7 a.m. and 11 a.m. My biggest impediment was not just getting too little sleep, but poor-quality sleep. That feedback led to several changes in my evening routine. I gradually shifted to being in bed an hour earlier. I shut off screens earlier and bought a Kindle Paperwhite E-reader to cut exposure to blue light if I wanted to read before bed. Furthermore, I recapped the day in my journal to bring closure and to transfer ideas or tasks from my head onto paper. I also began listening to 10-minute guided sleep meditations.

The WHOOP app measures energy output and recovery throughout the day and keeps a running calculation of how much sleep I will need. It will let me know what time I need to be in bed if I want to wake up at 6 a.m. fully recovered. I use that app as a commitment device; it's so easy to announce, "My WHOOP is telling me I need to get ready for bed."

I learned and now practice ultradian rhythms from Tony Schwartz's book, *The Power of Engagement.*[1] These are periods of about 90 minutes of focused work, followed by a 20-minute break. A true break—stand, walk, listen to music, get away from your desk, go to the park across the street. This new work rhythm of intense focus followed by total breaks allows me to accomplish in a morning what used to take all day. It also conforms to Kristin Holmes-Winn's research on the need to decompress several times a day to reduce the effect of chronic stress on sleep.

Kristin Holmes-Winn

After finding my WHOOP to be such a valuable health management tool, I interviewed WHOOP's vice president for performance optimization, Kristin Holmes-Winn. Because of her long commitment to high performance and the essential cycles of restoration, I wanted to add her voice to this chapter.

"I've been in athletics my entire life; I even coached for 17 years. My whole life has been spent thinking about how to help people maximize or optimize their potential. How do they leverage their genetic gifts and their acquired skills and expertise? A lot has to do with how they live their life. What kind of performance lifestyle do they have? How do they eat, hydrate, and sleep? Those are huge factors on the physiological side. Are they building in purpose? Do they have a sense of competency? Do they feel in control?

"If you think about those factors in an intentional way, you will be able to design your day to optimize your energy production and your motivation. Through performance education, employers can help employees adopt a high–performance mindset.

"I think corporations should build a framework for educating their employees to understand the physiological and psychological factors. After all, they don't need to teach 1,000 things. It's just a few behaviors that in my view are most relevant to employee education:

Sleep Behavior: Those who care about their health must understand the physiological and psychological ramifications of sleep debt. From that, they must develop routines and strategies to optimize biological sleep.

Recovery Behavior: Today, we have excellent techniques and interventions that help to optimize rest cycles and limit the accumulation of stress.

Training Behavior: We can and must use technology to prevent overtraining. To do that requires us to create individual profiles that hold benchmark physiological information, periodization models, biofeedback, and recovery data.

"If people can get control of those few things, they can optimize their energy and motivation for the task. On top of that, a technology like WHOOP actually influences performance. Once people understand that, they start to act. When you use an HRV monitor, you really dig into your sleep and can see very vividly how behavioral changes improve physiology.

> *If people can get control of those few things, they can optimize their energy and motivation for the task.*

"To me, this is what corporations can do, because that is what we do with teams. Whether I'm working with the Clippers, the Texas Rangers, Jose Batista, or Florida State University Women's Soccer, it's all the same stuff. It's education on what's important to health and recovery. People can understand that, have a strategy and routine to build the right habits on a daily basis, and use technology to measure if they're living the healthy way."

Become a Champion Sleeper

Then Kristen told me: "I'm looking at your data right now; yeah, you were at a 35 HRV in January and you're now close to 80. That is unbelievable from a clinical standpoint. Whoa, your sleep performance is off the charts, that explains the improvement. You are a championship sleeper. Your average range is 92–100%, which is incredible. Whoever you're consulting or advising, they should listen to you because you're doing something right. Your Sundays are the best day, Saturday and Sunday are your highest sleep performance. Your least recovered day is Thursday, and your best months are May and July."

Kristen continued, "One thing we've seen in the data, as we work with high-level athletes who must perform, meditating or breathing deep three to five times a day improves sleep. What gets in the way and forces you to wake up in the middle of the night is chronic stress accumulation. Meditating three to five minutes right before bed is helpful to get you to go to sleep, but you're still going to be impacted throughout the night based on that accumulated stress.

"When it comes to daily productivity, task switching has one of the toughest impacts on mental well-being. When you're constantly being pulled out of concentration, it makes you feel less in control. It will sometimes take up to six minutes to get back to that flow state where you're completely engaged in what you're doing. I recommend you turn off the Internet and all your smartphone notifications while working on a project. Try scheduling your day so that you're giving yourself blocks of time when you really can dig in. Those blocks of time are probably best in the morning. Schedule meetings, interactive activities, or routine work for the afternoon.

When you're constantly being pulled out of concentration, it makes you feel less in control. It will sometimes take up to six minutes to get back to that flow state where you're completely engaged in what you're doing.

"I'm a huge fan of journaling. It is definitely one of the best things you can do to improve. We all have a strong internal clock, the circadian rhythm. Try to keep your sleep-wake cycles as consistent as possible. Two hours before bed, I dim the lights in the house. I minimize the blue light by 7:00 p.m., otherwise it will delay the melatonin onset (which enables us to feel sleepy)."

Mindset and Character

Happiness does not come from a job. It comes from knowing what you truly value, and behaving in a way that's consistent with those beliefs.
—Mike Rowe

Randy Thompson, construction specialist for Cushman Wakefield, reflected on some of the new trends in workplace design: "It's pointless to create a self-actualizing workplace without self-actualizing employees." Brilliant. We continue to focus on the hardware—the artifacts and tools for self-actualizing work—without developing the most rudimentary software—a healthy mindset.

Companies can no longer assume employees bring healthy attitudes and frameworks to work. Many employees lack basic life skills. Educators recognize the problem and have crafted a list of 13 twenty-first-century skills that look a lot like what used to be provided as life skills.[2] Collaboration, problem solving, communication, grit, and creative thinking are just some of the life skill gaps businesses are facing in today's job market. Their options are to accommodate and try to manage lower standards, or to take on the role of rebuilding character.

Cummins takes this challenge seriously. I asked Dexter Shurney, Cummins' chief medical director (recently retired), "What is Cummins doing to help manage stress beyond the normal breathing and meditation exercises that have become a baseline strategy?" He replied:

> *The most important quality is your mindset, your outlook on life. Part of what we try to teach is resiliency. One big component is forgiveness and thankfulness. People look at all the things that are wrong and seldom take the time to look at the things that are right. For example, do you have a job or a car? They may not be what you want, but you do have them. Be grateful.*
>
> *People are wallowing around with all these grudges they've been holding all their lives. We have to teach people that anger is messing up their lives. Look at what it's doing to your body, what it's doing to your T-cells, what it's doing to your immune system. This is the effect of stress. Stress causes premature aging. Holding on to anger and resentment and unforgiveness only hurts you. It's not affecting that other person.*
>
> *We provide different exercises. For example, we tell the Cummins people to write down all the things they are thankful for. What went well? What are you hoping for next week? As you accomplish those, be thankful. We do that every week. Try to go through a day only speaking positive things. Obviously, it's hard to change, but it starts to build a new mindset that says, "I need to think about things a little bit differently."*

I've talked with Dexter, Bob Chapman, Greg Kunkel, Josh Glynn, Calvin Crowder, Craig Janssen, and Mark Cunningham about their company's investments in leadership and employee training. Some of it is as basic as learning how to forgive, release negativism, balance a checkbook, go to bed at a decent hour, tell your kids you love them—basic but vital. These are the basic hygiene requirements in Herzberg's model of motivation. Employees need to master these basic life skills in order to do the required work from the higher levels of motivation in Maslow's model. The drive for accomplishment and deep work can only come if they have a reservoir of belonging, security, and safety. If an employee has trouble managing finances, talking to his kids, or is distracted by the pressures of life, how can he have the presence of mind to solve complex problems, navigate conflict, or come up with that next breakthrough product or idea?

> *If an employee has trouble managing finances, talking to his kids, or is distracted by the pressures of life, how can he have the presence of mind to solve complex problems, navigate conflict, or come up with that next breakthrough product or idea?*

The Puzzle of Engagement: Fit and Equipped

When you find a person who loves their work, you are likely to find someone happy, healthy, and inspirational. Employees who can work in a way they naturally do best and enjoy most are the most engaged workers. The key is finding how they naturally work best.

Back in the 1950s, Dr. Donald Clifton began conducting research with over two million people. He wanted to understand what the happiest and most successful people did differently than everyone else. He found one simple thing—playing to personal strengths. And, for each person, only a handful of strengths produced the stand out difference.

What are those strengths?

Clifton's research identified 34 measurable and predictive strengths. Consistently using the top five produces engagement. Engagement was also found to be the leading indicator of performance and satisfaction. His company, Selection Research, bought Gallup in 1988. In 2001, they created the Clifton Strengthsfinder Assessment, based on Clifton's research. To date, more than 17.5 million people have taken the assessment.

Now think of something you love to do. The energy of those thoughts and activities creates engagement. Think of the situations when you were so engrossed in an activity that you lost track of time. Operating in that range of natural talent accelerates learning, improves performance, and sustains it longer. Engaged work produces a feeling of satisfaction and recognition.

> *Think of something you love to do. The energy of those thoughts and activities creates engagement.*

Now flip your thinking to activities you abhor. Just thinking about them drains the blood from your face. I hate doing expense reports, taxes, or anything with tedious details. That all feels like a distraction; I procrastinate those things. I can turn a simple 20-minute task into a three-hour ritual that feels like penance. Why? It's anything but natural; it's hard work. I feel drained, my output is meager, and I am not likely to receive positive recognition. I still must get those tasks completed. That is where skills, tools, and partnering provide support for the areas that are not natural and easy.

I learned to use Strategic, my top Clifton strength, as my path to engagement and successful reading and research. You are far better using the top strengths to develop alternate strategies than trying to improve a strength low on the list. I could try to improve my Discipline talent, but it is number 28 out of 34. That's what my elementary school tried to do. The research is clear. I can improve Discipline from lousy to mediocre under a lot of strain and duress and lose it as soon as I release the pressure. Or, I can tap Strategic and others in my top five, and excel. The additional benefit is that over time my top strengths grow from natural strengths to mastery.

> *You are far better using the top strengths to develop alternate strategies than trying to improve a strength low on the list.*

Parallels Between Sleep and Work

Does anyone expect someone to sleep well if they are interrupted all night? I don't think anyone would say yes. Why do we expect people to work well if they are interrupted all day at the office?

—Jason Fried

After tracking and studying my sleep for a year, I clearly see the parallels between sleep and work patterns. I see four stages to both:

1. The first sleep stage is *awake*. The work equivalent is *distraction*.
2. The second level is light sleep. The corresponding work revolves around answering e-mails and routine work.
3. The third phase is deep sleep. The work parallel is engaged, present, or deep work.
4. The fourth sleep stage is REM, restore and repair. The work equivalent is rest and recovery.

Life, learning, energy, relationships, and mood all improve the more deep sleep/deep work and REM/recovery time we get. Easy to understand but hard to achieve.

When our dogs recently felt it necessary to warn the house of something around 3 a.m., I could not shut off my mind when the noise stopped. I laid awake until 6 a.m. My deep sleep and REM readings were half what they had been the night before. I felt weary when I had to get up.

If that night of sleep is translated into an eight-hour work day, it would be the equivalent of four hours answering e-mails, two hours of distraction, and only two hours of productive work. A very choppy day. That's why it's important to create hedges of protection around sleep and deep work. For example, Jason Fried's 37 Signals creates a sacred time for deep work, "No Talk Thursdays."

What if an office were designed around these four stages of work? Imagine a "distracted" zone designed for just that: positive distraction, conversation, or a moment for amusement. Next, a "light work" zone designed for answering e-mails and routine tasks. It is an open area and highly social. The sacred space for "deep work" provides a separation from any distraction and is available in 90-minute chunks. Last, "recovery" areas to give opportunity to take a five-minute walk along a nature path or a private space for a 10-minute guided meditation—even a mat to do a few push-ups or sit-ups to increase blood flow.

Activity workplace design uses a similar strategy to understand the distinct activities of work and define the space based on the ratio of this work. How might you rethink the workplace to encourage more deep work and recovery?

I know a company that has developed recovery areas, designed for 15- to 20-minute breaks. They are also tackling the challenge of employees arriving at the office after a stressful commute. They need space to transition between the road and the office. The idea of transition spaces is not new. Homes, for example, often have parlors to greet guests and mud rooms to shed remnants of the outdoors before entering the living space address similar needs. Maybe it's time to apply that thinking to the workplace. We also need transition time, and a space, for going from meeting to meeting. As professor and author Cal Newport says, "People who experience attention residue after switching tasks are likely to demonstrate poor performance on the next task."[3]

> *People who experience attention residue after switching tasks are likely to demonstrate poor performance on the next task.*

Deep-Present Work

We now know from decades of research in both psychology and neuroscience that the state of mental strain that accompanies deep work is also necessary to improve your abilities.

—Cal Newport[4]

Newport explains what happens to the brain when we give it a deep workout:

The new science of performance argues that you get better at a skill as you develop more myelin around the relevant neurons, allowing the corresponding circuit to fire more effortlessly and effectively. To be great at something is to be well myelinated . . . it's important to focus intensely on the task at hand while avoiding distraction . . . because this is the only way to isolate the relevant neural circuit enough to trigger useful myelination.[5]

The ability to consistently achieve deep and present work depends on recovery, mindset, engagement, and the vigilant elimination of distraction. Deep work is the place we create, solve complex challenges, gain mastery, deliver signature solutions, and achieve excellence. Deep work happens by design, with practice, aided by habits, and carried out in quiet and undisturbed places. Deep work demands fully engaged brains. And the only way to get them is from engaged humans.

That's why it is imperative for all those who work with you to find the way to become their best selves. But, first, you must find and travel that path. Blaze the trail for all who follow.

Leadership Nudge

Keep track of a few days and divide the time into segments of Deep Work, Light Work, Distraction, and Recovery. Did you have a 90-minute segment of undistracted thinking and work? If not, work with your assistant and peers to redesign your day.

Find a good sleep sensor and keep track of your sleep for a week. What does it tell you? What routines or habits can you adopt to improve your preparation for a good night's sleep?

Personal Nudge

Keep track of a few days and divide the time into segments of Deep Work, Light Work, Distraction, and Recovery. Did you have a 90-minute segment of undistracted thinking and work? If not, see how you might redesign your day.

PART IV

Haven in a Heartless World: The Need for Safe Places

CHAPTER 13

How They Did It

Creating Ecosystems of Care

If there is one "secret" of effectiveness, it is concentration. Effective
executives do first things first and they do one thing at a time . . . There
are always more important contributions to be made than there is time
available to make them . . . Therefore, there is always a time deficit.
                                                                 —Peter Drucker

Just as mountain peaks Rainier, Hood, and Shasta dominate the
Cascade Range, some companies always stand high above the rest.
The coming chapters will reveal the extraordinary success stories from a
few companies. More importantly, you will discover their secrets. The
most common trait separating them from the foothills is their focus on a
few essential principles and habits. You will see they maintain a strong
discipline rooted in a deep understanding of their own character, vast
ecosystems, and people. You will identify, perhaps for the first time, the
few fundamentals that can transform not just your wellness efforts but
your company.

Incredibly, while these companies kept a fanatical focus on a few
simple attitudes and practices, they each took very different roads to
getting there. Each company understood the unique elephant it rode and
how to nudge the beast to stay on the path.

The Cleveland Clinic: Clarity, Focus, and Simplicity

In 2004, soon after Toby Cosgrove became CEO of the Cleveland Clinic, he saw the writing on the wall. Despite being one of the premier medical institutions in the world, the health of its employee population mirrored the same chronic disease, stress, and bad habit patterns of their city and nation. If that continued to rise, they projected that, by 2016, the cost of health care for their 40,000 employees and 41,000 dependents would increase by $400 million.

> *Despite being one of the premier medical institutions in the world, the health of its employee population mirrored the same chronic disease, stress, and bad habit patterns of their city and nation.*

Cosgrove knew that if the Cleveland Clinic was also going to fulfill its mission, it would have to set an example. He hired Dr. Michael Roizen in 2007 as the *first* chief wellness officer—the first CWO for the Cleveland Clinic and first in the United States. The teamwork of Cosgrove and Roizen formed three key elements that have led to the Cleveland Clinic's success:

1. Clear, resolute, engaged leadership
2. A focus on five normal outcomes for employees
3. A comprehensive six-element push for culture change

Dr. Roizen explained the five normal: "If our employees hit five 'normals,' plus get their immunizations up to date, they get back to the 2009 insurance rates when we started the program. That is, essentially, a savings of 30% and for some, that means zero out of pocket cost." These five normals have recently been expanded to 6+2. Those normals are:

1. Blood pressure less than 130 over 85
2. LDL cholesterol levels under 100, 100 with no diabetes and no coronary artery disease, less than 70 with
3. A waist measurement of less than one-half the height or Body Mass Index less than 29.9
4. Blood sugar under 100
5. Zero nicotine as monitored by a cotinine level less than obtained by secondhand smoke

6. Stress management program completed
7. Fasting Blood Sugar or Hemoglobin A1C less than 107 or less than 6.3%
8. See a primary care provider yearly and immunizations up-to-date

In other words, they simplified and narrowed the focus: a dashboard of eight simple measurements. After all, if you're achieving the first five, you're most likely doing everything else right too.

Figure 13.1   Dr. Michael Roizen.

They also knew their campaign to bring radical change must be just as simple and clear. So they also narrowed and simplified that focus into six principles for change:

1. **Make culture a priority:** "Toby continually messaged how important being healthy is to the energy you bring to work, to your overall well-being, and to your ability to live well. You don't want to live with a disability. Every month, he rewarded someone who has reduced stress, lost weight, or quit tobacco."
2. **Make Room for "Aha" Moments:** "Aha moments are the sudden knowledge, like 'If that person can do it, I can do it too!'"
3. **Provide options:** "We found Weight Watchers worked for some people, a gym membership was preferred by others, e-coaching by our own program for many, and nutrition classes were key for other people. Providing options brings more people into the program. If you offer one program, maybe 20% will succeed; but if you offer 10 options, we've found over 70% can succeed, even to lose weight to get to a non-sickening BMI."
4. **Knock down barriers; reduce constraints:** "You have to knock down barriers and make it free. We used to reimburse the cost for smoking cessation treatments 83%–89% after the employee quit smoking. The day we made the first dollar free, we had four times as many people sign up that day as had signed up in four years."
5. **Nudge people to make the healthy choice:** "Make healthy choices the easiest. You can't buy a fried piece of anything on

the Cleveland Clinic campus because we took out all the fryers. You can't buy a sugared drink on the Cleveland Clinic campus. You can have a Coke, but you have to bring it in. If you're going to get sick, you have to make an effort to get sick. We want to help you stay healthy."

6. **Incentivize in a big way:** "We incented in a huge way, so more than half of Cleveland Clinic employees are still paying the insurance rates they paid in 2009. We also let people add a buddy, a social nudge, for all kind of things, for hypertension, etc., because being socially responsible and accountable to someone else (a coach, even an electronic e-coach, or telephonic or video coach) is a key component."

Whereas 6% of Cleveland Clinic employees had 5 normals in 2008, over 40% now do; whereas 12% with chronic disease participated in a chronic disease management program in 2008, now over 63% do (if you decrease the influx of chronic disease, medical care costs less and people bring more energy to everything they do). Unexpected absenteeism has decreased from 1.07% of days to 0.70 %. The clinics employees have also earned a boatload in incentive and costs saved. The Clinic saved over 254 million (all in medical costs including incentives and wellness program and administrative costs) according to its once very skeptical CFO in the last three years for its now 101,000 employees and dependents compared to where it would have had costs by 2017 if it had averaged the health costs of the rest of private hospital employers in the USA. And savings get bigger yearly. Cleveland Clinic estimates it will save over $150 million more this year—you see as employees and dependents get healthy, they progressively save more dollars.

In our study of companies and other organizations for this book, we saw that each approached employee health and well-being differently. But we also saw that the best all had two things in common: clarity and focus.

In our study of companies and other organizations for this book, we saw that each approached employee health and well-being differently. But we also saw that the best all had two things in common: clarity and focus. The Cleveland Clinic sets a high bar of expectations.

Barry-Wehmiller: "We Just Need to Care"

From its humble beginning in 1885, today Barry-Wehmiller is a St. Louis–based $3 billion global enterprise of more than 12,000 employees. Their primary business, supplying manufacturing technology and services, evolved from their roots as manufacturers of pasteurizing equipment. But the real business is acquiring and transforming struggling companies. B-W first caught my attention when I learned of their more than 100 acquisitions. When 70–90% of mergers or acquisitions fail, Barry-Wehmiller surely knows something most don't.[1]

Bob Chapman, the slender, energetic, constantly moving CEO for Barry-Wehmiller, carries a consistent message to every mile and every moment of his life: "Everybody matters" is not only the title of his best-selling book,[2] but it describes his life and passion. Solid life

Figure 13.2   Bob Chapman.

lessons, including some near-death business experiences, formed that message.

I reached out to Bob because I loved the book's story and philosophy. It confirmed the MindShift message. Upon my arrival at B-W, Rhonda Spencer, the chief people officer, built the onramp for my day with Ed Strouth, B-W's director of health and well-being, Laurie Ferrendelli, director of organizational development, and Bob Chapman.

The B-W story began, as it did with many companies, with a focus on health costs in the 1980s. From that, the company continued to push the boundaries until a culture of care began to emerge in 2003. Because the company grew so rapidly, so did the health and wellness needs of the employee population. B-W faced that growing need by making a new commitment to "everybody matters." To make sure leadership matched the commitment, they made Rhonda the chief people officer in 2014.

Barry-Wehmiller aligns with several of the principles described in the Cleveland Clinic Way: aligned culture, aha moments, options, knocking down barriers, and large incentives. They are also exploring and expanding healthy nudges. Four years into this wellness strategy, they are making progress like that of the Cleveland Clinic. That progress comes despite B-W's great differences from the clinic: they are spread across the globe, their US factories are often located in small industrial towns, and they have a much older population.

When Laurie Ferrendelli first took the director of organizational development position, she told Bob she understood B-W's focus on employee care, "If you take care of employees they take care of clients, and that results in taking care of business." But Bob said, "Perhaps—but that's not why we do it. We take care of people because that is the right thing to do. I expect our leaders to run the business to support that." He went on to say, "I do expect that we'll serve our clients better, but that is a by-product. It is not why we do it."

> We take care of people because that is the right thing to do. I expect our leaders to run the business to support that . . . I do expect that we'll serve our clients better, but that is a by-product. It is not why we do it.

When Laurie first entered the world of wellness, she quickly learned, "that a lot of vendors were selling this as another way to manipulate your employees for your gain. And if you start from that place, you're never going to really help people. We approach wellness from the standpoint of a fundamental value for people who are touched by our organization. We do it because we want people who have healthy lives. Companies that do it for any other reason have no chance."

After my time with Bob and his senior leadership, I asked him, "Bob, what happens when you're not here anymore? How do you scale this?"

He's a straight shooter: "We've been working on that question for 12 years. It started when someone asked, "'What's your greatest fear?'" My greatest fear was that we would build something great and find it to be too dependent on me. So, I kept thinking, *Okay, what are we going to do about it?* And I realized what great religions do over time. They articulate their beliefs. They tell stories that affirm their beliefs through disciples who pass it on. So I wondered, how are we going to create disciples?

And then he found the answer; he realized "We got to create a university. We got to teach people. We decided *that day* to start a university. We had to do it ourselves because our education system makes managers, not leaders. The beauty is we started with a clean sheet of paper. We said,

"'How do we teach people to care?'" It starts with listening skills, thinking like a leader, inspiring like a leader, acting like a leader.

"Now we offer this to senior executives from around the world. We didn't have any idea that we had been blessed with an idea that could change the world, but there's no question now, given where we are in the journey, that we have been given an idea that could begin to heal the brokenness that we're feeling in this world. We don't need taxes or politicians to fix our problems. We just need to care.

"As far as our mission for affecting others outside our company? We're giving people an appetite, we're not feeding them. Simon Sinek calls it the law of early adopters. We need to find people who believe what we believe. We're not trying to change what they believe."

Tom Emerick: The Human Touch

Tom Emerick ran the benefits program for Walmart's 1.3 million employees for more than 11 years. Before that he handled BP's 220 benefit plans. But, before all that, Tom started as an actuary. So he knows the numbers, what works and what doesn't. His years with Walmart and BP gave him a ringside seat for watching how the 10% of employees with complex chronic conditions often fall through the cracks of proper care. That results in tragic health outcomes and drives 80% of corporate health-care costs.

While wellness programs are focused and incentivized on the 90% of relatively healthy employees, providing quality care for the chronically ill brings a human touch to those who struggle daily.

Tom talks like a country doctor or pastor: "Folks in this outlier group have very serious conditions. Many of them are seeing multiple specialists, and they're being given multiple prescriptions, and there is gross variation in how patients like that are handled from tertiary center to tertiary center. There is also gross variation in quality, net cost, and even in the medical ethics for this population of patients. 20% receive bad diagnoses, 40% receive bad treatment plans. The cost impact can be more than 400% of what proper diagnosis and treatment would deliver."

20% receive bad diagnoses, 40% receive bad treatment plans. The cost impact can be more than 400% of what proper diagnosis and treatment would deliver.

Tom can burn hot when he talks about an American medical system happy to overdiagnose and overtreat patients. He held up a *Wall Street Journal* article that revealed coronary artery bypass grafts, given to patients with stable angina, offer no advantage regarding longevity or lifestyle for 97% of those patients. He pointed out:

In the US, we have 1% more heart attacks than in the UK. We do 350% more invasive procedures, and the British survive heart attacks longer. There's just simply no excuse for it. People say, "But we're less healthy." Come on; we have 10% more obese people than the UK, not 350%.

Tom recommends that we first educate ourselves on the vast range of quality and costs. Barry-Wehmiller was stunned at the differences when they began to use Compass as a health concierge. When an employee needed hip surgery, Compass learned that his doctor worked in three hospitals and the cost difference between the hospitals was as much as $12,000. Over the course of Tom's 28-year career, he helped hundreds of employees needing acute care. He found that sending them to the Mayo or Cleveland Clinic improved the accuracy of diagnosis but also provided long-term care and support.

He speaks persuasively from his depth of experience: "People are going to get sick, but the first thing we should ensure is that they receive the right diagnosis. If we're running benefit programs and we're letting 20% or 30% of the bucks get spent for people that have the wrong diagnosis, we can't say we have a wellness program.

"One specialist is looking at a blocked artery, another is looking at arthritis, another one is looking at a bad hip. Very few places look at the whole person. We can fix that. We need a new definition of medical ethics: Let's determine the desired patient outcome and use the safest, least invasive way to get there. That eliminates 60% of the heart surgeries in America.

"Only 5% of medical facilities practice this new form of ethical medicine. The Mayo Clinic, Cleveland Clinic, and Intermountain Medical Center in Utah are among the best. You know one thing they all have in common? Doctors are salaried. They don't get paid extra to cut. We talked a lot about wellness incentives. People behave the way they are incentivized to behave. If a doctor can make $3,000 or $4,000 for two hours' work in an operating room, why not? It's pretty easy to make that blocked artery look pretty severe.

"Lowe's set up a program to send their heart cases to the Cleveland Clinic, and they're having smashing success with it. The best care is the most cost-effective. How cost-effective can it be to do surgery on somebody that doesn't need it? What should HR people look for? The highest ethical standards, best outcomes, and lowest net cost. In other words, they want Centers of Excellence.

> *The cost of health care is doubling in 10 years. The folks running corporate benefit plans are the only ones in America that can stop this. You can absolutely call a complete halt to this for 80% of your claim dollars.*

"The cost of health care is doubling in 10 years. The folks running corporate benefit plans are the only ones in America that can stop this. You can absolutely call a complete halt to this for 80% of your claim dollars."

Ron Goetzel: 10 Principles

Ron Goetzel, the senior scientist at Johns Hopkins Bloomberg School of Public Health, vice president of IBM's Watson, and health and board chair for HERO, is a data guy at heart. He is probably more responsible than any other person for pushing the industry toward tighter standards of program effectiveness.

When I asked Ron what it takes to implement an effective wellness program, he outlined 10 criteria. He began by stating that there is no one-size-fits-all and that a variety of strategies and activities are needed. Here's his list of 10 criteria, including his comments about each:

1. **Culture of health:** "Wellness efforts have to go beyond a program. It's a way of being. Bob Chapman (Barry-Wehmiller CEO) has a good approach. The qualities of that culture include care for one another, and support; it's not a dog-eat-dog environment. Look at the positive culture of Chevron. The cultural imperative is supported by the environment, it's part of their strategic planning. The

plan is tied to performance metrics for managers, and even the line workers."

2. **Leadership commitment:** "None of these programs really work unless you have an engaged C-suite. They have to demonstrate that employee health and well-being is what they believe in. 'It is who we are as a company, what we do, what we practice.' They must lead by example so it permeates down to middle managers and supervisors. It cannot be a once-a-year message from the CEO. It's day-to-day operations of supervisors, and it manifests itself in all kinds of ways, including work/life balance, flexibility, stress, and decision latitude. All of these really do matter in terms of creating a healthy workplace. If the program is not properly resourced, it won't work. There has to be a budget commitment that includes a say from workers and union in the design of the programs."

3. **Specific goals and expectations:** "Like any other business idea, you can't just say, 'We're going to get people to lose weight and exercise and eat healthy.' What exactly do you mean? How much weight loss are we aiming for? How much exercise? How much and what kind of nutrition goals? How exactly are you going to figure this stuff out? What's the short-term goal? What's the long-term goal? Three, five, 10 years from now? Do you stick by those goals or let them fade when it becomes hard work? Are they measurable?"

4. **Strategic communication:** "It's like selling anything, any product. How many wellness champions do you have? The more you have the more likely you're going to get engagement. If I share an office with you, and you tell me, 'We're having a fun walk,' or, 'We're going to have a healthy lunch; come join us,' that's much more compelling than an e-mail from HR. The reason companies are successful is because they keep selling it, with variations on a theme, with humor, with a compelling narrative, you name it. It's marketing and communication. You've got to sell health just like you sell everything else. So, it's got to be consistent, constant, engaging, targeted, and often times direct person-to-person selling. That means you've got wellness champions scattered throughout the organization."

5. **Employee engagement by design and disciplined implementation:** "Here's the real story of most wellness programs: The vendors

are selling to the HR benefits people, and that is who they view as their customer. They say, 'We're going to save you money. We're going to produce some ROI. We're going to lower absenteeism and disability, workers comp.' But

they never really think carefully about the employee as the *real* customer. The vendors need to be asked, 'How are you selling it to the worker? Why should they be involved in any of these programs? What's *their* ROI for participating? How is your offering compelling to my employee base?'

"One vendor promoted meditation and yoga for employees, the company bought it, and nobody showed up. That's because everybody, young people, wanted to do aerobics, and they want to be climbing walls, and they wanted to do stuff on bicycles and all that. Nobody bothered to ask them, 'What would you like?' If the employees are not involved in designing the program; no focus groups, no surveys, and no ongoing feedback about what works and what doesn't, it ends up with good intentions that no one really cares about."

6. **Follow best practices:** "If I want you to quit smoking, giving you a brochure that tells you that you're going to die of cancer is actually not very convincing. However, something called motivational interviewing may be able to slowly, gradually get you to think about quitting smoking. There are different ways of doing that, those kinds of behavioral interventions, choice architecture."

7. **Effective screening and triage:** "You need to have ongoing annual assessments of people's behavior and risk factors. Now, does that mean biometric screening? No. The biometric screening part should follow the US Preventive Services Task Force [PSTF] guidelines. Some employers do too much screening, and they screen for stuff that shouldn't be screened. The PSTF people do systemic reviews of the evidence and say, 'Well, this is how often you need to have your blood pressure, cholesterol checked, glucose and weight checked.' They also provide guidelines for checking tobacco, alcohol abuse, and depression. An important part of the assessment is triaging people into high and low risk, with more attention being

paid to the high-risk people, and more of an outreach to that population."

8. **Incentives:** "Let's talk about smart incentives. They engage you, convince you to participate in programs. There are lots of ways to do it, anywhere from having lunch (or a walk) with the CEO, to a plaque you can put on the wall, articles in the company newspaper about you, and of course dollars. But I don't believe dollars is the best way to get people to change behavior. It's very effective to get people to show up for something, but I can't give you enough money to get you to quit smoking, eat healthy, exercise on a daily basis, and manage your stress. I really can't. Anybody who thinks otherwise is a fool."

9. **Effective implementation:** "You may have the most beautiful plan, wonderful brochures, lots of money and budget, and it is not working because people don't trust you or they are not integrated into the culture. It's being offered by a vendor. It's not flexible. It's not fun. It's not fresh. It's not interesting. This is a challenge, to get something that's a good idea and actually put it into place within your culture. This is the ecosystem."

This is a challenge, to get something that's a good idea and actually put it into place within your culture. This is the ecosystem.

10. **Measurement and evaluation:** "You can have fulfilled all the other nine things, but you have zero data to show that it's made a difference in anything. You need to set aside a budget for measurement and evaluation that looks at multiple dimensions of the program. For a small company, it can be as simple as an annual survey of your workers, asking them, 'What do you think?' Or, it could be a very extensive program evaluation done by people like myself and my team, using insurance claims and other data, financial analysis, to figure out whether the program is actually working or not."

J&J: Persistence, Data, and Continual Improvement

Johnson & Johnson is a 130-year-old company with about 130,000 employees. They are a lead supplier of medical equipment, pharmaceuticals, and everyone's favorite, Johnson & Johnson's baby shampoo. J&J is also held up as an exemplar for their corporate wellness program. Even the wellness skeptics like Soeren Mattke and Al Lewis admire J&J.

Dr. Mark Cunningham-Hill was their head of occupational medicine and global health services for 7 years. Although Mark recently left J&J to start his own consulting firm, he gave me an in-depth, behind-the-curtain look at J&J's wellness efforts.

As Mark told me: "My team designed the strategy around health, wellness, and mental well-being. A lot of our work considered the role flexible workplaces played in shifting culture and improving health by allowing employees to be more effective, focused, and energized.

"J&J has always been on the cutting edge of wellness efforts, building on traditional HRA (health reimbursement arrangement) wellness programs with fitness programs and fitness centers . . . very traditional stuff. Gradually, over the last five years, we've started to move into other areas. There's enough good data at J&J to know what the big issues are, and J&J focuses on them: movement, eating, mental health, and the quality of the workplace, both from an occupational safety point of view, but also from how the workplace drove and supported our focal behaviors.

"Alex Gorsky, CEO, is a great leader. He's the champion of these values. Every time he speaks, he promises more around health and wellness and the importance of it to the organization. He used to tell stories about his life, how he suddenly realized how important his family was to him and what he does, to focus on them. I think that kind of leadership, the storytelling can be really powerful.

"J&J's history of data has produced metrics that really work. Managers can track change over time and hold individual senior leaders accountable. The next five-year goals will be a big step forward. Data will continue to drive the future. Our ability to measure a change allows J&J to build and expand its support and culture of health. The ability to connect the dots through data gives J&J a unique advantage. Many companies express aspirations to provide a healthy workplace but can't connect performance to their values.

"J&J is known to provide a quality work environment on par with Google and Apple. But they deliver that quality to a much broader diversity of employees. That's why J&J's success in delivering a culture of health is sought out by companies around the world."

Are these efforts simply about return on value? If so, what is that value? Is it workplace experience, workplace culture, retention, attraction, or employee engagement?

Mark acknowledges that ROI is an important piece of the conversation, but emphasizes it is just that, a piece. For Mark, it gets back to a deeper question: "Are these efforts simply about return on value? If so, what is that value? Is it workplace experience, workplace culture, retention, attraction, or employee engagement? We know engagement leads to productivity. J&J is taking 100,000 employees through the corporate athlete program, designed for top executives by professional sports experts and Navy SEAL trainers. The program teaches employees how to live better, not just perform at a higher level.

"By the time I left in April 2017, we'd taken 54,000 through the program. We analyzed the people who had been through it and compared performance to those who hadn't been through the course. We looked at performance ratings, retention, and promotion. There were statistically significant correlations of superior performance from those who went through the program.

"The cost of the program for 100,000 employees globally is probably about $40 million. There is between a $200 million and $400 million return on that. But we didn't do this as an ROI. It was really about learning and seeing if the corporate athlete program has a real and measurable impact on the quality of lives and performance at work."

Mark told me that J&J stopped chasing after HRAs at the end of 2015, when they reached their goal of 80% global participation. That program never convinced J&J they got that much value. It just told them what they already knew, that high-risk employees were high risk. The people who were obese, smoked, or sedentary were unhealthy.

I asked Mark how J&J communicates a consistent and engaging message across the three families of companies and all of the sub-business units. He told me, "Perhaps that's where it gets back to the building; how to connect the dots for people, so they understand our program around employee flexibility, financial health, physical health, and understanding health-care benefits? Creating posters, sending out fliers or updates isn't enough. J&J has begun to look at the workplace as a way to tie together both the services and the messaging.

"We are using design nudges to encourage movement, especially in locations that are not typically thought to be places that embrace wellness. One of our facilities in Juarez has 3,000 employees in one manufacturing location. We provided walking paths and encouraged people to walk together more. We also developed an inviting staircase design to nudge people to use the staircases. We've used lots of little nudging tricks about how to get people moving that are successful."

I found that J&J's big lessons are consistent with other highly successful cultures; they begin with leadership conviction and commitment. In terms of making the strategy work, J&J's integration of HR, wellness, facilities, and IT, along with metrics tied to business outcomes, provide the ability to learn, adjust, and improve.

The Effective Leader

Each of the conversations in this chapter delivered solid, tested, and very real lessons in effective leadership to me. I heard the constant theme of picking the few priorities that will make the big differences, focus your time and attention to reinforce those priorities, resource the hell out of them, be that mission's first learning officer, and stay real.

No one ever said it better than Peter Drucker:

> *Management books usually deal with managing other people. The subject of this book is managing oneself for effectiveness. That one can truly manage other people is by no means adequately proven. But one can always manage oneself. Indeed, executives who do not manage themselves for effectiveness cannot possibly expect to manage their associates and subordinates. Management is largely by example. Executives who do not know how to make themselves effective in their own job and work set the wrong example.*[3]

Leadership Nudge

Are your wellness priorities simple and clear enough to put on a 3×5 index card? Could you explain them to a 12-year-old? Would he or she say, "Wow; cool"?

Personal Nudge

How well do you understand your company's wellness priorities, its offerings, and what your personal ROI is if you fully participate? Could you initiate a conversation within your department or team to discuss these questions?

CHAPTER 14

Courageous Leaders and a Culture of Care

Culture is what happens when you're not there.
—Rex Miller, Bill Latham, and Brian Cahill[1]

Most companies do not adapt to or even survive change. That is because most leaders assume they will know what to do when faced with a problem. Tom Peters captured the real issue more than 30 years ago when he wrote, "If you're not confused, you're not paying attention."[2] Adapting is learning while leading. We make it up as we go. But most leaders are not very good at that. They prefer to look magisterial and intimidating, like Jeremy Irons in *Margin Call* or Al Pacino in *The Godfather, Part II*. I do not enjoy looking like I don't know, so I don't play games like Pictionary or Trivial Pursuit at parties. Because I'm supposed to be pretty smart and creative, I had better perform well in those settings. Instead, I feel tight and anxious. *But fun is the point*. And I can't have fun because I feel pressure to perform. Pure and simple, that is why companies so often fail at change. Leaders try to maintain the image of supreme confidence and competence and always being in charge, when the whole point is to learn and have fun doing so.

The Trouble with Culture

Culture makes change difficult. So, how can we demystify that creature called culture? Yes, *creature*: it has personality, moods, a voice, and the power to act. It is a collective mind that prefers to remain silent and invisible. Until you cross it. Do you remember the moment during your child's adolescence when that wonderful, smiling, compliant child you nurtured, that perfect son or daughter, suddenly became a different creature when you had the audacity to cross his or her will? The familiar and beloved face contorted, the voice snapped or snarled, the eyes narrowed into an alien and bloodless gaze. In the blink of an eye, you wondered, "Who is this kid?"

Many corporate leaders have experienced the same disbelief, shock, and a twinge of fear when their brilliant and elegant plans turned on them. The leader simply caught a rare sighting of that shadowy creature. They don't even know that their leadership raised that snarling beast. But, in fact, it has grown into a little tyrant that easily asserts its will and runs the show.

Healthy cultures adapt, bounce back, learn, let go, cooperate across departments, serve one another, and add value to the whole. Conversely unhealthy cultures are sclerotic, prescriptive, political, and rigidly infallible.

Now you know why more than 70% of change initiatives fail. It is the reason the survival rate for the S&P 500 companies has dropped from 60 years in 1960 to under 15 years.[3]

Healthy cultures adapt, bounce back, learn, let go, cooperate across departments, serve one another, and add value to the whole. Conversely unhealthy cultures are sclerotic, prescriptive, political, and rigidly infallible. They impose pecking orders, resist cooperation, allow a sense of entitlement, fight through passive resistance, tolerate toxic actors, carry persistent low-grade anxiety and fear, react rather than flow, and view everything through tunnel vision.

The process by which culture becomes unhealthy is simple, far simpler than you've been led to believe. And getting back to a healthy culture is harder, much harder than you can imagine. There is no escaping the process or the work if your goal is a healthy and resilient culture that adapts with grace and bounces back when hit by adversity.

Hello, Shadow Culture

I once met with leaders struggling with their company's resistance to a large strategic initiative. They had done a good job assessing and communicating the business problem, articulating why the new constraints required change, presented a compelling vision for the future, and building a thorough execution plan. So, why so much resistance?

As soon as I suggested we need to work on the culture, the head of facilities pointed to a poster on the wall that featured five Corinthian columns with a triangular capital set on top. That gesture was meant to tell me, "Listen, stranger; here is our culture. So, that's not the problem. Let's move on." The group nodded agreement and then began throwing out ways to restore the magic:

- Improve communications.
- Achieve more employee engagement.
- Hold a town hall.
- Deal with resisters with more pressure.
- Find champions.
- Round up the ringleaders.

Like the new sheriff in town, I persuaded the posse to cool down and get off their horses. Then, I began to speak to the mob: "Culture is *not* that poster; it's simply what happens when you are not here. It is the attitudes, behaviors, and habits that preside when you are not here to direct, troubleshoot, and hold people accountable."

Culture is inevitable and invaluable. Healthy cultures are very intentional and carefully designed. This book contains many stories of how leaders did and are doing that. "Fuzzy culture" is something else. It is not designed; it seeps into a company through weakness and neglect. Unless leaders know how to eradicate the growth of negative or foreign workplace influences, they become a breeding ground for what we call "shadow culture." Shadow cultures spread like invasive species and hide in the dark shadows of any organization. Shadow (or fuzzy) culture causes employees to wait for someone to tell them what to do, how to do it, and then circle back to make sure it was done right.

> *"Fuzzy culture" is something else. It is not designed; it seeps into a company through weakness and neglect.*

Gallup reports 50% of the workplace is unengaged. That is largely because of fuzzy culture.

Fuzzy culture is also very expensive and time consuming. Of course, it is; it requires too many managers. That is also is why managers are overworked and often ineffective. If I could choose one magical power, it would be to enable leaders to see their shadow culture as clearly as young Cole Sear saw dead people in *The Sixth Sense*. It's hard, very hard, to find an outsider's view when you're on the inside. I am often blind to the shadow culture in my own family, even though I actually nurtured or modeled it at some time in the past.

Performance Cultures and the Art of Recovery

Edgar Schein, MIT professor and organizational scholar, wrote that culture is "a pattern of shared basic assumptions that the group learned as it solved its problems of external adaptation and internal integration, that has worked well enough to be considered valid and, therefore, to be taught to new members as the correct way you perceive, think, and feel in relation to those problems."[4]

That's true and it applies to designed culture and to the fuzzy or shadow culture that creeps in through neglect. Both forms exert astonishing influence over the health, direction, and endurance of a company. When Peter Drucker famously wrote "Culture eats strategy for breakfast," he described that influence, regardless of whether it is by design or by default.

Let's look at two companies that actually believe Drucker's maxim. GoDaddy and Next Jump have both endured successful overhauls that started with culture, not strategy. They are both high-performing athletes in the sense they understand their organizational bodies. No illusions. They are disciplined, ritualize their routines, practice and then practice some more, work with top coaches, fail often and with purpose, and (most importantly) excel at recovery. Leaders are player coaches, not executives who sit in the front offices.

New candidates literally try out, like athletes. If successful, they go through a second round similar to the NFL Combine. Instead of looking for "workout warriors," those companies look for people with an ethos of personal growth warrior. They must exhibit emotional intelligence and a habit of learning outside their comfort zone.

These two company stories, together, create a roadmap for other companies that understand that culture comes first and that creating a healthy culture is part of a future-proofing strategy.

Healthy culture is like the "Intel Inside" campaign. It is the invisible chip that powers strategy and execution. Part of that chip is the authentic commitment to care. GoDaddy and Next Jump both demonstrate a superior intuition about truly caring for one another. As we've said before, humans are not efficient creatures. They are not rational. They have hot streaks and slumps. They naturally clash with other humans for reasons that elude them. They come in with different hopes and baggage.

> *Healthy culture is like the "Intel Inside" campaign. It is the invisible chip that powers strategy and execution.*

If employees are going to perform at their peak, someone must care for and about them. In other words, people require time and attention. Jamie Casap, education evangelist for Google, says we understand the need to oil and maintain equipment, but we're not very good at maintaining our people. Culture is the human ecosystem. Companies must pay attention to it just as everyone must get serious about the natural ecosystem.

Creating a healthy culture is your company's only hope of survival, success, and sanity. GoDaddy and Next Jump have made culture a core competency. If culture is what happens when you're not there and is made up of invisible values, attitudes, habits, and behaviors, both companies turned that into a habit of creating habits, by design. Read on; you can do it, too.

Transformation in Tempe: The GoDaddy Story You Don't Know

If fewer than 30% of major strategic initiatives succeed, what are the odds of success for a company taking on four major shifts at one time? In 2012 GoDaddy, the largest web host and domain registrar in the world, took a high-stakes gamble. It was already a highly successful corporation. The chances of messing that up were far higher than reinventing the company and doubling in revenue over the next five years. That's why their transformation story will be studied for years.

Calvin Crowder, GoDaddy's vice president of global real estate, and Wade Lewis, vice president for local key accounts North America with ISS,[5] had just opened the new GoDaddy Global Technology Center in Tempe, Arizona, in the fall of 2014 when I met them. In giving me the tour of the new space, Calvin and Wade touched every theme our project was examining: leadership, culture, environment, and employee health and happiness. After my tour, I told them what we were doing. They joined the MindShift effort, made presentations in Denver, and hosted our final summit in Tempe.

The new Global Technology Center embodied the *new* GoDaddy. Until my tour, Bob Parsons (GoDaddy founder and former CEO) and

Danica Patrick still represented GoDaddy to me. They were, after all, both vivid and memorable characters. Every racing fan knows Danica. And Bob is forever stuck in my mind for saying "You put a tuxedo on me, it's like putting a saddle on a hog."

Calvin introduced me to Cameron Scott, chief brand officer. Cameron came with Blake Irving (recently retired CEO) from Yahoo and had been with him for more than 15 years.

Figure 14.1 Calvin Crowder.

Cameron told me the history: "Blake recruited me to Microsoft in the mid-2000s. I've also worked with him at Yahoo and now GoDaddy. When you find and work with great people, you tend to stick together. When I came to GoDaddy with Blake, there were several people already here that I had worked with previously. Tech isn't that big of a community, there's not that many of us, globally. During my first four-and-a-half years I led executive communications and corporate strategy. I'm involved with a lot of the current strategy work at GoDaddy but shifted over as our chief brand officer.

"GoDaddy was a subscription business, well before its time. With Netflix and Spotify we're all used to subscriptions. But a cloud subscription company was unheard-of back in 1997. Bob Parsons had grown it to almost a billion-dollar company and the financial fundamentals were very strong. Their ability to forecast and to be structured and mature as a business was just incredible.

"We expected everyone at GoDaddy would be like those really edgy, provocative commercials. It would be like a Wild West kind of thing. What we found was totally different. We experienced true core values of scrap-

We expected everyone at GoDaddy would be like those really edgy, provocative commercials. It would be like a Wild West kind of thing.

piness, grit, and determination with an incredible passion for the customer. This is what really jumped out, an incredibly strong business model and a strong customer-focused culture. And it only existed within the United States.

"And we had the opportunity to take that passion global, something we knew how to do. That seemed like a no-brainer. How could we take that internal passion and let it show up in the brand? Then position GoDaddy to go public. A lot of companies are challenged going public and have to adopt a whole different form of behavior. Not GoDaddy. The discipline and structure Bob built made it a company that was ready to go public.

Bob Parsons and the board were aware that the things that brought GoDaddy to its first billion would not get to the second billion. It is easy to say but very hard to acknowledge. Especially determining that first step. This is where Blake's leadership style built that perfect bridge. The company grew up lean and scrappy. That meant the facilities were very, very lean. The benefits at the time were meager, as you might expect in startup mode.

"Bob did not borrow, go into debt, or take extra capital to get GoDaddy up and running. That requires a special kind of scrappiness. Without it we wouldn't be here today. GoDaddy would have been like all the other rapid-growth tech companies that spent a lot of money, blew up, and disappeared.

"Blake stands out in the way he leads. He brings an incredible consistency to his job. In his process and style, you know exactly what you're going to get. Which makes him predictable, a really good thing for a leader. It's very challenging to work for a leader when you have no idea which side of something they're going to fall on in a key meeting or on key decisions.

"Blake was the chief product officer at Yahoo. He built Microsoft's first advertising platform. He is a product platform guy, and that was what GoDaddy needed to move beyond selling subscription domains and build a platform to support products. To do that we had to attract and retain the world's best talent. And so that's where Blake's idea of making offices a really compelling work space that attracted world-class talent came from.

"I remember the low ceilings in those first plans for the Global Tech Center. They were inexpensive and efficient. The original two-story design was a minimal-height, standard office building. When Blake first looked at the design, it made him claustrophobic.

"The design did not make an environment where our people would want to arrive early or stay late. It did not have a great cafe, workout area, or yoga center, and no showers to use after a workout. There was nothing in front of the building for recreation like volleyball or basketball. The structure of the office was just a boring-but-efficient grid. The message seemed to signal it was the best way to fit as many people into as little space as possible. Which can feel oppressive and regimented, right?

Blake asked Calvin to come up with a design to give the building air, space, light, and brightness.

"This is when Calvin was brought in. He was an IT manager, not really a construction or facilities person. Blake needed someone fresh and resourceful to step in. It was really late in the process, just weeks before construction. Blake asked Calvin to come up with a design to give the building air, space, light, and brightness. He wanted dynamic spaces where teams can huddle together, great conference rooms with really good tech. It was the beginning of reimagining our culture and environment not just for Arizona but all over the world. We would need to have progressive video-conferencing screens to have virtual team calls. Blake wanted to include amenities that make people want to be here.

"Calvin and the SmithGroupJJR worked almost around the clock and through weekends to completely overhaul and redesign the space through the lens of a new GoDaddy employee experience. GoDaddy received several industry awards for the facility, which features unique amenities like indoor peddle go-karts, a climbing wall, and central gaming and fitness areas to encourage movement.

More importantly, beyond the physical space, Calvin redesigned our relationship with ISS, our facility service provider. They began designing for a best-in class employee experience; what Calvin wanted was a cruise ship experience. Since ISS has a large global footprint, the Global Tech Center provided an opportunity to build that model.

"One of the great things about how we redefined the ISS relationship is it allowed them to go far beyond the traditional role of outsourced supplier, to really focus on creating an amazing employee experience, not what is most convenient for their team. Wade fully embraced that.

"With ISS, we took the traditional manager role and transformed it to be employee experience focused and outcome based.

"The traditional role of office manager is too prescriptive. With a thousand things to get done, they get spread very thin. That is the opposite of what we want. The first thing we want them to ask is, '"What are the outcomes that make the employee experience best?" How are we focusing on our people as individuals? How do we create physical spaces that promote our values and culture of community? The result was the birth of the experience manager (XM).

> *. . . a key part of work is to make sure you are fun to be around, be fun to spend time with, have a great attitude, keep a positive attitude, and radiate positivity.*

"Blake has helped a lot of people understand a key part of work is to make sure you are fun to be around, be fun to spend time with, have a great attitude, keep a positive attitude, and radiate positivity. You might be the best technical engineer or software developer or real estate guy, but if you're miserable to be around, people are going to push away. One of the biggest jobs executives at any C-level have is to recruit. To do that well you have to radiate positivity and be a magnet to attract talent.

"Before Blake went into tech, he was a jazz musician, a touring percussionist. He worked with several jazz legends. He keeps a full drum set in his office. I've worked with a lot of CEOs, and I've never seen anybody who brought their own passions into the office as much as Blake does. Sometimes, he'll show people how to do a little lick on the drums, before or at the end of the meeting. Sometimes he'll just think through a problem by sitting down and playing the drums. He comes in early and leaves late and it's not unheard of to hear him in the evening, just drumming away using it to churn ideas.

"Blake will retire after five years [he retired at the end of 2017]. His legacy will show how the leadership of care, a highly aligned and competent leadership team, and embracing the good that already exists

Blake's team built on what was already strong. He elevated the role of existing leadership. They also used one of the best tools to provide daily reinforcement and commitment of the new values——their new facility.

can overcome the traps that cause 70–90% of these efforts to fail. Even though it was clear the culture would need to dramatically shift to accomplish the aggressive growth goals of becoming a global $2 billion company, Blake's team built on what was already strong. He elevated the role of existing leadership. They also used one of the best tools to provide daily reinforcement and commitment of the new values——their new facility."

Next Jump: Happiness and Success for the Long Term

We are what we repeatedly do. Excellence, then, is not an act, but a habit.

— Will Durant

Every organization that achieves success lives through four phases: (1) birth and struggle, (2) formation and growth, (3) strength and maturity, and (4) peak and decline. A few fortunate ones get to experience a rebirth. Some have to tumble back down to death in order to find rebirth. Greg Kunkel, cofounder of Next Jump, knows that pattern. He shared some of those hard lessons that built Next Jump's uniquely vibrant culture, success, and continuous renewal.

The story of Next Jump's reinvention is described in Robert Kegan and Lisa Lahey's book, *An Everyone Culture.*[6] The phrase "deliberately developmental" is the golden nugget in their story. More than any company I've met or researched, Next Jump has found a way to embed the daily habits of personal and team growth. They have somehow learned to overcome the entropy of business cycles; they discovered a renewable resource——one another.

Figure 14.2   Greg Kunkel.

Next Jump lives out a question: "What if our business is simply the growth and development of one another?" That inquiry found expression in their core value of "Better Me + Better You = Better Us."

Greg met Charlie Kim, the original spark behind Next Jump, in boarding school. Greg described their complementary differences, "My grandfather was a small-town banker in Montana. Had one job for his whole career. My dad worked at Coopers & Lybrand as an accountant for 40 years. I did not grow up with the entrepreneurial gene. Whereas Charlie was starting businesses in high school. Charlie started the company to pay for his long-distance relationship with his college girlfriend by selling coupon books on campus.

"The company moved online and eventually transitioned into kind of an online B-to-B-to-C, like an e-commerce marketplace. But our mission is teaching our client culture. That is how we moved into what some call our "deliberately developmental culture." How can you build an environment where the collective responsibility for everyone grows? The notion of growing yourself plus helping others captures two basic human needs; we really design and adapt our programs, and we run our company along those two fronts.

Humility and Confidence

"That was always with us. But, around 2007, we started to focus on changing from being a marketing company to being an engineering company. We started recruiting against the top engineering companies like Microsoft and Google and Facebook, and we had this tipping point where we became successful at that. We had some amazing talent; the best and the brightest.

We looked around and realized we had hired what we called "brilliant jerks." That forced us to take a hard look at, "Okay, what is the culture we want to build? What is the type of individual that we want to bring on board?"

"But, a couple years later we looked around and realized we had hired what we called 'brilliant jerks.' We had really created an environment for all these jerks: they treated each other terribly and put themselves over the team. That forced us to take a hard look at, 'Okay, what is the culture we want to build? What is the type of individual that we want to bring on board?'

"That focused us on two elements. One is hiring. Who do you let into the organization and the family? Charlie Kim says there is far more value in marriage counseling before marriage than after. Two, what's the environment, the norm that you want? And that started us down this journey of reengineering and thinking about the programs. What's important to us?

"Next Jump has two stages to hiring. The first is our interview process, meeting 11 people. To get through that stage requires a unanimous decision. The two most important areas probed are questions reflecting humility and intentional failure. In other words, does this candidate embrace or react to feedback? When was the last time this candidate pushed outside their comfort zone, failed, but used failure to learn? If this isn't seen as a habit or mindset, the candidate is not selected."

Charlie recalls a pivotal moment: "After two years of tremendous investment in hiring, one day we literally fired half our engineering staff. And they were rock star engineers. That led to some deep reflection on the difference between those who did great work and seemed to really fit and the others. The brilliant jerks lacked humility. After turning the hiring process upside down and focusing on culture, the turnover dropped from 40% to 2%.

"The Personal Leadership Bootcamp makes everyone start in customer service. Bootcamp can be incredibly humbling. New hires work on customer service goals of quality and quantity. The real objective is to see what kind of person we're hiring, humble or arrogant, open to feedback, or a know-it-all. We expect everyone we send to Bootcamp to succeed. So, we create a custom graduation jacket at the beginning. When they succeed, we present the jacket in a ceremony and welcome them as a Next Jumper. It is a very moving experience. If they don't succeed or drop out, we pay them $5,000 and burn the jacket. When you become a Next Jumper, it is a lifetime commitment. If we see that the person needs help to continue, we provide training. And, some people have to go back to Bootcamp as long as it takes to bring that person along.

We create a custom graduation jacket at the beginning. When they succeed, we present the jacket in a ceremony and welcome them as a Next Jumper . . . If they don't succeed or drop out, we pay them $5,000 and burn the jacket.

"Next Jump has also worked with experts in several different fields to build a framework of fundamental practices aimed at building character. Jim Loehr of the Human Performance Institute gave us 50 key success traits. After a lot of experimentation, we saw that 50 was too many. Two continued to rise to the top: humility and confidence. So, that is now our lens for hiring, mentoring, promotion, and performance evaluation.

"Next Jump's health pyramid starts with physical training. Physical health permeates the atmosphere of the company. Their strategy for physical health is simple: Make it difficult to do bad things and easier to do good things.

"Next Jump then developed a buddy system called Talking Partners (TP) for emotional training. Next Jumpers are encouraged to pick a TP they feel comfortable with but to try to choose someone on the opposite side of the humility/confidence spectrum from themselves. They believe that each person tends to default to one side or the other. Humility can fall into insecurity, confidence into arrogance. The TP program is designed for daily mentorship. At the start of most days, each employee begins with his or her partner by venting, releasing the toxins or simply expressing what is on their mind. It can be anything. A tough previous day, bad commute, exciting news etc. Each then receives feedback from the TP and shifts focus to rehearse the day. That short session has been one of their most effective practices.

"Management meetings have shifted to Situational Workshops, a form of reflective coaching. Four employees meet and share very real challenging or failed situations. From that, the small group uses an inquiry-based approach to help each other unpack and process those experiences. They also convene a monthly session called 10x. Ten employees get up in front of a large group and provide a five-minute self-assessment of progress on business performance side and values. Four measurements frame each assessment: (1) Needs Improvement, (2) Meets Expectations, (3) Exceeds, and (4) Far Exceeds Expectations."

They have also created apps to provide feedback. The company registers each person's score, offers anonymous feedback, and then a panel of 10 evaluators offer their comments. It's like performing on *America's Got Talent*. The sessions are so intense that they often release deep emotions. Next Jump video records their response to the feedback. All of these values and dynamics have evolved for the purpose of building the skill and character of their workforce.

Charlie Kim does not believe culture is too hard to define or measure. I don't either. Culture is simply what happens when leaders are not there. Culture is always present. But Next Jump, like GoDaddy, has chosen to design the company culture. Because they did, they can also measure it.

Corporate cultures are either healthy or unhealthy, by design or by default. Next Jump arrived at their design by being clear on what they did not want: the entitled engineers, those "brilliant jerks," and the 40% turnover. Those negatives brought Next Jump to a crossroad. Many reach similar crossroads but do not pause to ask the reflective questions that Next Jump did. Most are also unwilling to weed out toxic behaviors and people. Next Jump hired for talent and drive. But, at the crossroad, they realized what actually worked was humility and confidence. When they changed their hiring practices, they redesigned the interview to look for signs of humility, comments about gratitude, and the ability to take and embrace feedback.

While their technology peers promoted culture as a cornucopia of external perks in an arms race for talent, Next Jump focused on individual character. Using Daniel Pink's three intrinsic motivators, they adapted one of the attributes, "mastery." Next Jump saw that those who experienced mastery also found purpose. Next Jump is now at $2.5 billion in revenue with 200 employees and growing revenue at 100% per year for the last five years. Workforce turnover has dropped from 40% to 2%. They have adopted a lifetime employee commitment if you pass the boot camp training. They allow employees 50% of their office time for service work.

Kim summarizes Next Jump's secret mindset: "Most of us try to solve things through shortcuts. But consistency is the basis of everything we do." To illustrate, he describes the process of losing weight by going on an intense short-term diet versus doing 30 minutes of exercise consistently twice a week. Next Jump provides daily coaching and mentorship, not just a perfunctory quarterly or annual review. Next Jump is designed for a journey, not just an event or a moment.

Dancing with Your Elephant

The shadow culture is the elephant all leaders have to ride. Because many have never learned to tame or teach their elephant, they are happiest when the elephant sleeps. When something new disturbs their habits or habitats, the shadow culture will ignore, wait you out, complain, resist, or sabotage the new initiative or change. This is very serious stuff. I once worked with a senior leader who was fired because the elephant he tried to beat into submission trumpeted so loudly that he woke the CEO. The new rider will have an even more challenging job ahead of her because the elephant is already disturbed.

GoDaddy and Next Jump learned what can grow inside the organization when culture is neglected. But part of their success is due to their skill at what we have earlier termed "elephant whispering": engaging, training, and transforming the relationship into one that carries the organization forward. When organizations push strategy and ignore the elephant, they often create collateral damage, harden divides, and/or settle into a low-grade stand-off.

The elephant can be a powerful partner, a sleeping dead weight, or a destructive force. As an old African proverb says, "When the bull elephants fight, the grass always loses." Guess what? You get to choose. GoDaddy and Next Jump effectively made the shadow culture a partner.

"The sustained success of companies has less to do with market forces than company values, less to do with competitive positioning than personal beliefs and less to do with resource advantages than vision."[7]

Leadership Nudge

What are some of the life skills that would benefit your employees and organization most? Who are good models for those skills in our organization? Could they teach these to others?

Personal Nudge

Do you lean towards confidence or towards humility? Is there someone who is a good complement to your style who could also become a Talking Partner with you?

CHAPTER 15

The MeTEOR Story

Extreme Ownership

Extreme Ownership by Jocko Willink and Leif Babin has become one of the biggest business books of the past decade.[1] And for good reason; it brought a kick-butt, scream-in-your-face, knife-between-the-teeth intensity to the issue of personal responsibility and owning every-thing—mistakes, successes, failures, improvement.

The authors, retired Navy SEAL officers, know that failure to own it is a failure to lead. Pure and simple. The only way to succeed is to accept responsibility for everything and blame no one and nothing, not even in your most private 3 a.m. thoughts. Own it, dammit, or sell the farm, move to town, and get a job bagging groceries.

When I read the book, I immediately saw MeTEOR Education, a consulting organization in Gainesville, Florida. But I knew MeTEOR when it was Contrax, a school furniture supplier. Even in those days, the owners—Bill Latham and John Crawford—had a much larger dream, an extreme dream: they wanted to transform education in America. Not Gainesville, not Florida, but the whole country. That's pretty extreme. After reading my book, *Change Your Space, Change Your Culture*,[2] they thought I was just the guy to help them do that. I listened to their proposition and, after a two-hour lunch, essentially told them I didn't know anything about education: "Look, I'm not your guy."

But Bill and John were like characters in a 1940s film comedy: when I would walk out my bedroom door in the morning, they would be standing there and immediately start talking at the point they were making last night when I shut the door in their face. They didn't know how to be discouraged.

In the end, they did such a good job at marshaling leaders and funding that I had to take the project. Bill and John made an incredible team: laser-focused, forceful, and unrelenting. I nicknamed them the Blues Brothers; they were on a mission from God.

Contrax's success was built on an intense sales culture and wrap-around customer service. Their compensation structure rewarded closing deals and moving quickly to the next. They reminded me of the old story of the extreme bear hunters.

The first guy leaves the cabin and disappears into the hills. Eventually, he sees a bear asleep in his cave. The guy goes in and kicks the bear till it wakes up, really angry. As the bear starts to give chase, the guy runs back towards the cabin.

Running down the hill, he screams, "Open the door! Open the door!"

His partner opens the door just in time for the guy to run into the cabin. The angry bear follows close behind and soon fills the cabin with his roaring presence.

The first guy jumps outside and slams the door. As he takes off for the hills, he shouts back, "You skin that one. I'll go get another."

John and Bill were those guys. They were unorthodox, but they built a highly successful, close-knit, work-hard, play-hard organization.

To Own Change

Halfway through that education project, John and Bill realized they had launched a journey of no return. To have the impact they wanted, Contrax would have to morph from a company that sold and serviced classroom furniture into an education and consulting organization. They had to show communities, school districts, principals, and teachers how to transform their schools. John and Bill began deliberately working to build the kind of culture they would need to support the company they were going to become.

John and Bill began deliberately working to build the kind of culture they would need to support the company they were going to become.

And they did it. Contrax did become MeTEOR Education. They created a new business mission and strategy, and rebranded and restructured from a centralized support hub to regional studios. But, then, when that rapid growth and increased complexity revealed cracks in the foundation, they invited me to help them.

I started by asking what kind of new work they would be doing? How would that work flow through the organization? What roles would they need to add? What kinds of skills? Would that require new people? Or could they teach old dogs new tricks? That conversation led to the more critical second conversation.

We shifted the focus to Contrax's current culture. I asked: "What is the current shadow culture? Help me understand the habits and behaviors that really run the place and have made Contrax a success."

Leaders and managers seldom see, let alone touch, the true shadow culture. Shadow cultures are like wolves in the wild. You rarely see one during daylight. I never fault leaders or managers for not having a grasp on shadow culture. However, without seeing and understanding that hidden side of the company, they'll never be able to shape, guide, and align it with the aspirational side of the company.

> *Shadow cultures are like wolves in the wild. You rarely see one during daylight.*

Then I took them through an exercise based on the television show *Hell's Kitchen*. We talked about the two sides of Chef Ramsay. The dining room Chef Ramsay is gracious and all smiles. But the kitchen Chef Ramsay throws sharp objects, curses, shows favoritism, and stand inches in front of faces and calls people "dirtbags." That is the differences between the publicized culture of an organization and its shadow side.

When I left, I gave them an assignment, an exercise at looking for the gaps. I asked them to keep a journal for the next month. "Observe and capture two kinds of behaviors. First, those spontaneous behaviors that impress and make you feel proud. Second, those that make you shake your head and wonder, 'What were they thinking?'"[3]

At the end of that month, the team gathered in a conference room and shared stories. Many stories evoked that knowing familiarity with what everyone knew. Naturally, some stories were extremely funny; some were sobering and emotional. But the act of sharing stories gave everyone a textured portrait of the company. The process revealed very constructive patterns and insights.

Next, each participant selected the top five positive and negative examples, and wrote brief descriptions on sticky notes. We put all the sticky notes on the conference room wall. The notes were then sorted into five positive and negative categories. That pulled everyone out of their chairs and into engaged conversation around moving the notes back and forth until categories took final shape. Once the categories were created, each column became a theme.

When we stepped back and looked at the wall, the collage became a portrait. Everyone saw five explicit themes, values, traits, and stories. The group also saw how the attributes added or drained value. Then the team reflected on where those behaviors came from and how the current culture reinforced them. Everyone stepped back and looked in the mirror.

"We Are a Numbers Culture"

The exercise included the critical questions about shadow culture.

- What messages do we, as leaders, send?
- What behaviors do we formally and informally reward or punish?
- Who feels entitled? Why?
- Who feels like they are second-class citizens around here? Why?
- What behaviors do we tolerate, and why?
- How does our environment reinforce the attitudes and behaviors we want to change?

As we gazed at the questions, I asked the team, "What do you value? And Bill spoke first, "I guess we value numbers. You get rewarded for numbers, and you get spanked for numbers."

That was a moving moment. I said, "No judgment here, Bill. Numbers are very significant. But, the real

> *I guess we value numbers. You get rewarded for numbers, and you get spanked for numbers.*

question is, do you want this to be a value or a by-product? If you want it to be a value, then you can begin to align your organization around the behaviors you want and the collateral costs you will incur."

Figure 15.1   Bill Latham.

Bill looked around the table, "That is not who we want to be."

That moment impacted everyone in the room, including me. I've facilitated many of those meetings; I typically hear a positive spin or a rally speech. That, however, was a rare moment of acknowledging a hard truth, but it also brought clarity and freedom. Everyone in the room needed to hear Bill take ownership and resolve to change.

That moment revealed Bill's extreme leadership. He owned everything; he blamed no one. And he did it out of a passion to take care of his people. Everything about Bill hovered around treating people with dignity and respect. He wanted to build a successful business, yes. But, like the very best owners and CEOs, he saw that business as part of the vast biosphere that nurtured those who showed up at his place every day.

Boat Behaviors

Over the years I've learned that if there are 10 employees in a boat, three will be happy, intent, eagerly rowing, and in sync. Gallup calls those employees the engaged. Five in the middle will be happy. The two in the back of the boat will be drilling a hole through the bottom of the boat. This is the norm.

The five in the middle are happy because they are along for the ride. They will do a good job if you tell them what to do and how to do it, troubleshoot when they get stuck, and follow up to make sure they did it. I call them "the managed." They are the ones who eat up the day for managers; they are the reason managers feel stuck, powerless, and ineffective. This is also the group that derives the most from a well-designed culture. They are usually good people who follow. A well-designed culture answers most of their questions, the ones they currently take to management:

- What is expected of me?
- How do we get things done around here?

Figure 15.2   Ten employees in a boat will all feel differently about the ride.

- How do we treat one another?
- Who do I go to if I get stuck?
- What does success look like?

A poorly defined culture, culture by default, also comes up with answers to those questions, answers that take the form of workarounds, politics, turf protection, informal alliances, whispers, insiders, outsiders, and referees (managers). Poorly defined culture is incredibly wasteful. It not only wastes most of a manager's day, but it also slows and impedes actual work.

> *Poorly defined culture is incredibly wasteful. It not only wastes most of a manager's day, but it also slows and impedes actual work.*

Using culture to nudge the middle of the boat riders toward the front is the most effective and the most sustainable lever. It is the difference between farming in rich topsoil or using fertilizers and chemicals to force the soil to produce.

Once that middle group shifts forward, it becomes much easier to deal with the toxic 20% in the back of the boat. They have no place to hide. Often, they see how out of step they have become and just choose to move on.

What Did We See, What Did We Learn?

Through our work together, MeTEOR identified some natural behaviors, strengths, that shined when they were at their best:

- Going the extra mile
- Giving people a voice
- Constantly learning and getting better
- Looking to continually innovative
- We travel in one boat

Bill and his team began to see that those descriptions formed guiding values for MeTEOR. They recognized that "we are in one boat together. We must become a company of we, not me." Suddenly, everyone could clearly see what those values looked like. They saw people who consistently modeled the values.

They also identified and called out the behaviors that had the largest adverse effect on the company. The examples helped to explain why. Leadership also explained how the compensation system, the way of keeping score, and overlooking bad behavior produced the harmful effects.

MeTEOR saw how people respond when the values of the company are simple, clear, and healthy—not just in posters, but throughout the company culture. There was nothing to fabricate in order to appear as something they were not. As Bill pointed out, "We can now work on becoming a better version of who we are." In the past, the MeTEOR culture existed by default. Today, it permeates by design. It is clear, tangible, natural, and extreme. Those in the middle of the boat have naturally begun to shift to the front. Culture now provides the answers to the five guiding questions. Managers can now plan and coach more.

In the past, the MeTEOR culture existed by default. Today, it permeates by design. It is clear, tangible, natural, and extreme.

Pressing into Well-Being

After partnering with us on our *Humanizing Education* MindShift, Bill and his team also joined us in our work on health and well-being. Chelsea Poulin, MeTEOR's new director of well-being, represented the company in our MindShift. I could see that Chelsea had been taught by Bill; she too is extreme in her pursuit of excellence and care. Our summits and our community helped Chelsea to see how many and very diverse companies approached wellness. As a result, Chelsea went back to MeTEOR and helped move them toward a culture of health.

Chelsea also invited Mim Senft to consult with them on the broad dynamics of change. Seeing MeTEOR through Mim's eyes confirmed what I saw and knew of Bill's leadership. That was especially helpful as MeTEOR built a new culture of health.

Mim saw the company change through a major leadership commitment to wellness. She clearly saw that "Bill Latham is a leader that cares. Naturally, he wants to see his company succeed, but he also cares about creating thriving teams.

Figure 15.3   Mim Senft.

"The MeTEOR team's goal was clear: 'We want to make sure that what we do is effective and leads to better lives for those on the team.' They believed that had to be a behavioral change, not simply throwing

> *The MeTEOR team's goal was clear: "We want to make sure that what we do is effective and leads to better lives for those on the team."*

some dollars or checking a box that they are supporting wellness.

Mim helped the company adjust to a new platform of health and well-being: "When we talked about the basics, benefits, pay, diversity, and demographics, that's where change really started. Bill was even fully supportive of employees' right to unfettered access and conversation with me. If they had a complaint, they were free to divulge it to me. Through all that, I saw that one of the core values at MeTEOR is the use of Co-Creative Voice. They believe it is the right and responsibility of their employees to use their voice in shaping the future.

"We've had deep conversations about paid time off (PTO). I pushed MeTEOR about creating a culture where people can take real vacations. Wellness also means that employees are encouraged to take time with their family, or friends in a personal retreat. They need to know they can go and totally recharge, knowing their team is strong enough to handle the work when they are out. And I emphasized that it starts with leadership giving the permission by example.

"So, Bill took his wife of 22 years to Scotland. He had not taken a personal vacation in the 17 years of leading Contrax and MeTEOR. But, to my surprise, he did not even take his phone or computer. His final instruction to his team was they were to only contact him if there was a "school furniture emergency." And then he reminded them there is no such thing as a school furniture emergency. *That* is what leadership does: set the example and create the tone. They demonstrate trust in everyone to take care of business. Most leaders simply don't trust their own companies. And it leads them to a belief that the place will burn down if they aren't there. That kind of attitude waterfalls down throughout the organization.

"MeTEOR is now fully committed to the quantity and the quality of the time their employees need to take to recover and renew. But they are going even further than PTO. They are exploring ways for their people to take deeply discounted vacations with their families. That's a great message for the employees: We're going to give you the opportunity to take less expensive vacations around the world.

"They are also getting a handle on e-mail. When we talk about people having a day of rest, what does that really mean? Does it mean you're resting, recovering, and taking time with family and friends? Or, are you answering work e-mails? So, MeTEOR now nudges employees away from company e-mails for the weekend!"

When we talk about people having a day of rest, what does that really mean? Does it mean you're resting, recovering, and taking time with family and friends? Or, are you answering work e-mails? So, MeTEOR now nudges employees away from company e-mails for the weekend!

Extreme Ownership: "What Gets Done"

Over the past two decades, MeTEOR has developed a culture of getting things done. It is built on a fanatical adherence to seven habits Bill and John developed over the past decade. Bill jokingly jabs, "Let's not talk about your idea unless we plan to do something about it." I've picked up their habits and they have helped me with several clients break the meeting trap of what I call "deciding to decide" but in the end not doing anything. The language of MeTEOR's "Habits of What Gets Done" produces clarity, alignment, and commitment and should permeate every company meeting.

1. What gets **PICTURED** gets done.
   - *Leader Question:* How consistently am I doing this?
   - *Idea:* People forget the vision within four weeks, so paint the picture constantly.
   - *Action:* Find ways to continuously reinforce the vision. Print it. Hang it on the wall. Sing it. Make movies about it. Slap it on the side of city busses. Use it to kick off meetings. And then close meetings with it.
2. What gets **MODELED** gets done.
   - *Leader Question:* What kind of example am I setting?
   - *Idea:* People determine what is important by what their leaders do.
   - *Action:* Model action. Don't talk. Act. Let action draw attention, generate conversation, and provide context.
3. What gets **PRAISED** gets done.
   - *Leader Question:* Do I acknowledge and thank others? Consistently and sufficiently? Is it systemized throughout our workplace?
   - *Idea:* Reinforced and honored behavior is repeated behavior.
   - *Action:* Celebrate successes in visible ways. If your team has a good existing system for recognizing success, use it. If you don't or if that system has grown sterile, create a new one. Give credit to others consistently and publicly.
4. What gets **TRAINED** gets done.
   - *Leader Question:* Is this on the calendar and is it meaningful?
   - *Idea:* A person performs up to the level of training.
   - *Action:* New skills require new experience. Evaluate the awareness, knowledge, and readiness of your organization to take on new responsibilities. Look for people in your organization who have interest and skill in teaching. Place personal growth and leadership skills at the top of your priorities.
5. What gets **MEASURED** gets done.
   - *Leader Question:* Do we measure the quantity and quality of our work?
   - *Idea:* Measurable goals get done.
   - *Action:* All goals need time-bound metrics. Identify ways to quantify your effort: participation rates, projects initiated, satisfaction scores, sick days, revenue, profit, results. Metrics incentivize team performance and allow you to determine the scope of your impact.

6. What gets **FINANCED** gets done.
   - *Leader Question:* Am I pretending some of my initiatives will get done without resources?
   - *Idea:* Budgets must reflect our plan and priorities.
   - *Action:* Strategic initiatives demand resources—time, people, capital, etc. If your initiative doesn't have dedicated resources, it's time to identify what you need and begin asking for it. Leverage your coalition to secure funding. Consider starting with a prototype and scaling accordingly.
7. What gets **SCHEDULED** gets done.
   - *Leader Question:* Are my most important activities on the calendar? Do I respect that time?
   - *Idea:* If it is not on the calendar we are not committed to it.
   - *Action:* Create an action plan and schedule accordingly. Use the Priority Matrix to focus calendar time on important priorities and weed out distractions. Set target dates for key deliverables and clearly communicate progress.

Hope, axioms, confidence, and theory only go so far. At some point, everyone needs a model of what they believe or assume. MeTEOR Education is one company that models care for employees and community. Bill's personal example of living out his convictions about responsibility makes him a lighthouse on a rocky coast.

Leadership Nudge

Take a look at your policies and wellness package and ask if these effectively support and lead to better lives for those in your organization. Look for the low-hanging fruit better clarifying, aligning, and connecting the dots between policies, programs, and the goals of better health and happier lives.

Personal Nudge

What personal practices and boundaries do you have that allow you to be present with your family, present with friends, and allow yourself true recovery time?

CHAPTER 16

Starting a Movement

How Second-Chair Leadership Can Change a Company

Are you paralyzed with fear? That's a good sign. Fear is good. Like self-doubt, fear is an indicator. Fear tells us what we have to do. Remember one rule of thumb: the more scared we are of a work or calling, the more sure we can be that we have to do it.

—Steven Pressfield

Most of us sit in "second chairs." We're not in control, not looking for trouble, and don't want to create waves. Most second chairs just want to do a good job and make a living. Second chairs provide safety and predictability. But, when circumstances disrupt that predictability, they often have the best vantage point for viewing the grand adventure coming down the road.

Some who sit in second chairs often imagine, *what if?* They watch, wait, pay attention, and listen. And we've all seen it happen: at the right time, in the right place, the known world (or an unknown one) will call him or her to a first chair. If she has not been paying attention, she'll miss the call. If he has not been dreaming, he won't see the opportunity.

How to Start a Movement Without Permission

The hashtag #MeToo disrupted the social universe on October 15, 2017, when actress Alyssa Milano posted this request on Twitter: "If all the women who have been sexually harassed or assaulted wrote 'Me too.' as a status, we might give people a sense of the magnitude of the problem."

New technology, an army of volunteers, and the historic moment created a spark that started a social forest fire. At this writing, over 200 high-tech executives, celebrities, executives, and politicians have been named and shamed and have watched their careers caught in the path of the rapidly moving flames. Ms. Milano did not have permission to do any of that. She didn't walk through the main gate.

Seeking permission is rooted in the typical and roaring need for approval. Everyone feels that; it was built into our minds as children. Asking permission was a primary pillar in gaining approval from parents, teachers, neighbors, cops, and others in our expanding network of relationships. And it continued to be part of our survival and success strategies through adolescence, college, marriage, family, etc. So, very naturally, we bring the same attitude to entrepreneurial ventures and career advancement strategies.

But those attitudes don't work like they once did. Today's success stories feature intruders, insurrectionists, and pirates. They've mastered the art of walking in like they own the place and quickly setting up shop. They've also learned the beauty of the old dictum that it's better to ask forgiveness than permission. You will find true magic in the ability and courage to just say, "Oh! Wow; I'm sorry. I'm too [old, young, new to this company, new to this country, ADD] to have seen that. But, you're right. And, since you know this stuff, can you help me?"

That approach certainly characterized the beginnings of MindShift. For example, on this Well MindShift project, we found a couple of unlocked doors around in back of the wellness industry. We quickly motioned others to come on in. More than 100 leaders and specialists—a superb mix of first and second chair leaders—streamed through the open doors to tackle an unhealthy wellness system. We all saw that wellness needed a humanizing revolution, a new story told in new language. And, like Alyssa Milano and other barbarians at the gate, we didn't have permission. Our idea was also sparked by technology, volunteers, and a significant historical moment. Because those factors aligned, we collectively challenged assumptions, disputed

> *We all saw that wellness needed a humanizing revolution, a new story told in new language.*

conventional wisdom, broke some rules, learned together, and built a new framework for change.

So, what about you? What have you seen, what do you live with, that is broken? Can you seed and feed your movement? If you can identify with any of the following conditions and dynamics, you should pay close attention to the clues in your environment:

- Dissatisfaction with the status quo
- An unrelenting personal quest for answers
- Doubt, fear, and second thoughts over doing something
- Recognizing the need for help from a guide or champion
- Starting to attract a collection of the curious . . .
- . . . while watching them become a cohort of the committed
- Asking hidden or unthinkable questions
- Inspired by a grand challenge
- A deep desire to travel into the future
- Reconciled that it means breaking barriers and absorbing repercussions

Read on; this chapter could be your GPS.

First, stir the pot; you really don't need permission. We didn't. Although our team gave serious and generous lift to the load, we received no major league grant money and no star endorsements. Our personal quest for an answer was simple: "Why did an office renovation, designed around wellness, bring such a profound effect and generate so much interest?" The genuine curiosity and interest of a dozen leaders galvanized us into action. From that point, our journey took on a life of its own. Watch for that to happen in your environment too.

Looking back now over two years of collaborative work, we see a massive national pendulum swinging back toward a humanizing and caring mindset in the workplace. The voluminous research says we must find that new pattern. That same evidence points to the promise and potential of creating virtuous cycles of happy and healthy employees performing at their best.

Why First Chair Leaders Need Second Chairs

First chair leaders often become trapped in a vortex of quarterly earnings, balance sheets, and market pressures. Most operate in a trance, with a locked gaze on outcomes. The logic or persuasion of treating people well has a hard time breaking the spread-

Second chair leaders work as artisans, crafting social capital in ways that first chair leaders cannot.

sheet spell. First chair leaders have little time or use for artisan tools. They depend on technical tools. There are no measures for the tone of culture, the rhythm of collaborating, or the relationship between belief and the balance sheet.

That is, often by default, the role of second chair leaders. They work as artisans, crafting social capital in ways that most first chair leaders cannot. Second chair leaders work inside the ecosystem, while first chair leaders often disrupt the natural attitudes and behaviors in the habitat. Second chair leaders know their own toolbox; some of their favorite tools are enthusiasm, good reports, and great stories. And those goodies and gems refuse to submit to spreadsheets.

When it comes to wellness, second chair leaders have to confront the old order's false choice between the health and well-being of employees or profits. In fact, we know that happiness and health lead to improved engagement, greater performance, strong resiliency, and sustained profits. If you start a movement toward a healthy culture, you will tilt the axis and perhaps find a new orbit for your company. You may discover that it no longer leans toward spreadsheets and revolves around short-term results. Instead, you may find it shifting toward more care, intentional design, and development of culture.

Emily's Journey: A Call to Action

The members of our MindShift projects must come through an invitation from me, sometimes based on a recommendation from one of our primary partners. Yet, somehow, Emily, a Millennial on a mission, found her way into our Well MindShift summits without that.

The first time I met her I noticed the puzzling amalgamation of her easy smile and sad eyes. Her quick verbal bio, spoken over breakfast, only told me that her interest in wellness began as a passion to see the building industry move toward greater environmental sustainability. While studying urban planning in college, she saw a deeper connection of the impact of buildings on people. Emily's path took a major turn when a global Fortune 10 organization recruited her to work in environmental sustainability.

Emily is a thoughtful connector. Her Clifton Strengths profile reveals someone who is a natural team builder. She intuitively sees the world through the eyes of others. She also believes, really believes, in a better tomorrow. Yet her eyes seem to suspect that tomorrow may not arrive.

As it often does, the universe tapped Emily on her shoulder. But she didn't recognize it. So, I told her, "Emily, this may be your time; you're ideally positioned and perfectly wired to transform your world." Although she was respectful of my perspective, she remained unclear in her own mind. I slowly began to realize that she was listening to a song I couldn't hear. But, still, I told her that day (as I tell you now): "Keep an eye out for other interested people. A collection of the curious. There are others like you, respected and interested in improving the workplace." She seemed to hear that, but I wasn't sure what she would do.

Start Easy—Get the Lay of the Land

We must be willing to get rid of the life we've planned, so as to have the life that is waiting for us.

—Joseph Campbell

Emily's story is a guide for almost anyone who finds themselves in a second chair leadership role. The MindShift process is designed for those who want to influence change but do not necessarily have the position, title, budget, or authority to launch an initiative. That requires a "pull" strategy, attracting others who identify with your journey and your conviction.

> *The MindShift process is designed for those who want to influence change but do not necessarily have the position, title, budget, or authority to launch an initiative.*

I recommended that Emily take a field trip through her headquarters. "Go and meet some of the people in HR, safety, corporate real estate, field operations, training, marketing, and wellness. Introduce yourself and let them know your interests and belief about the change you hope to see. Watch for eyes that light up when you talk. Go find your tribe."

And she did.

Not only did she make several vital connections, but she also learned a lot about the shadow culture of her company. She saw it as a wolf, coming out only at night when no one was around. She learned the identities of the entitled untouchables, the areas to avoid, how to pick up the latest news on the grapevine, and some of the grave markers of the human sacrifices to the shadow culture. Emily also met the salt-of-the-earth people, the go-to ones for help and advice. The field trips produced several dividends.

A month later, Emily reported back to me; she was surprised that she found so many, so eager to meet. She set a time and place for an initial meeting.

No Turning Back—A Collection of the Curious

Twenty-two people showed up; they packed the conference room. To her concern, about a third were not even on the invite list. Emily wondered what she had gotten herself into. One of the uninvited ones was Jerry, the vice president of finance. He seemed uncomfortable, perhaps suspicious. Emily already felt tight and scared. The group was already much larger than she had anticipated, and Jerry, of the walrus mustache, just stood in the back with arms folded.

Emily controlled her anxiety well. "Thank you for coming. Wow, I wasn't expecting so many people. What a great start. Today is simple. I want us to get to know each other a bit. Let's break into small groups of three or four. I'd like you to start by introducing yourself and where you work in the company. Then, using these questions on the flipchart, share with your group."

She flipped the blank page back to reveal the questions:

• Where did you grow up?
• Where did you go to school?
• Share one thing you accomplished or overcame as a kid.
• Do you have a personal or family health story?
• What do you hope we might accomplish together?

From that moment, the meeting took on a life of its own. Each group was buzzing with conversation and laughter. Later, when Emily gathered everyone's attention and asked what they learned about one another, the room crackled with stories of "small world" connections, shared interests, common life and health journeys, and struggles. Emily wrote many of the

People were proud that they worked for the organization, but also disconnected, stressed, and unable to do their best work.

comments and aspirations on a flip chart. In general, people were proud that they worked for the organization, but also disconnected, stressed, and unable to do their best work. Emily heard a lot of confusion about the corporate wellness program and a general feeling that it brought no value beyond the health insurance discount.

Following the meeting, Emily walked back to her office drained but so happy. She had watched Jerry; even though he participated, she really couldn't tell what he was thinking. He stayed in the back, listened, and kept his arms folded. He never introduced himself to her. But, at the end of the day, Emily was informed that Jerry wanted to meet with her the next morning. That call drained all of the happy out of her system and replaced it with fear and second-guessing. *He showed no expression the entire time. He wasn't invited. I am toast.*

When Emily arrived at Jerry's office, he started with, "So, who are you?"

"I'm Emily Longmire, I work in corporate real estate on sustainability."

"I know that, but tell me why you're interested in this stuff and how did you get so many people to show up? You've only been here six months." His bloodshot eyes seemed accusing.

Emily took a deep breath and rolled with it. She dispassionately shared her career journey over the last few years, including some of her personal health saga and why she felt so committed this project. She told Jerry about a sixth-grade teacher who recognized her interest in pulling people together for different causes. She just wanted to find others in this company with similar interests.

As she spoke, Jerry's leaned further back in his chair. He seemed increasingly interested in the ceiling tile patterns. When she stopped talking, he sighed. Emily saw that his eyes were closed.

"Do you have any advice or warning for me," she asked.

After what seemed like a full minute of silence, she wondered if he heard her question. But he leaned forward into eye contact. Emily saw that he looked older than when she arrived 15 minutes earlier. His eyes were heavy and sad.

"You Millennials. So idealistic and noble and, don't take it personally, but so damned insufferable. You know the way; no one else does. And think you can manage change. So much energy in that room . . ." he just shook his head before continuing. "I'm sorry. You asked for help. I guess, you know, just be careful. You're all young and you think it'll be easy. But this company doesn't change. I know."

She saw a cloud pass over his face. Emily could see that his thoughts were breaking him down. He reminded her of her father, squeezed in the pliers of changing times and a broken body. Her father died of, essentially, exhaustion. This beefy vice president looked like he was on the same conveyer belt.

Jerry never felt safe about expressing company concerns or personal challenges. But, as he sat alone after Emily left, he saw, for the first time, that his job was slowly killing him. Stress had added a slow but irrevocable 50 pounds to his frame. He no longer took the stairs to his second-floor office. And he had no friends, no one he could really talk to. And, since he and Hazel divorced and Josh had gone off to Texas A&M, no one would even notice if he failed to arrive home after work. Most evenings, he sat on the patio, smoking cigars and drinking Jack Daniels on the rocks. God, he wished he had the youth, the energy, the friendships that he saw in Emily's meeting. Those kids may be pains in the company butt, but they sure had passion for something better.

He also saw the company, feeling pressure from the growing cultural chorus of wellness worry, throwing money at various vendor health programs for several years. Despite the expense and coercion, no one had stopped smoking, quit drinking, or lost weight. A quick cloud of cigar smoke exhaled at the sudden recognition that he was the ideal poster child for that failure.

Emily also caught a glimpse of the corporate concerns about the nominal benefits and the meager wellness program. As VP of finance, Jerry certainly knew that none of it was making a dent in lowering costs. Emily saw that Jerry owned the numbers, but HR owned the wellness program. And the numbers were all going in the wrong direction. And, worse, no one on the executive team really had the time to dig deeply into why the program wasn't working.

Having survived her first adventure, Emily began planning the next meeting.

"Who Owns Employee Health or Happiness?"

Emily sent invitations to the second meeting. She brought 20 copies each of pivotal books, Jeffrey Pfeffer's *Dying for a Paycheck* and Bob Chapman and Raj Sisodia's *Everybody Matters*.[1] Emily lined the wall ahead of time with several sticky back poster pages; each one had a heading: Human Resources, Wellness, Safety, Training, Marketing, Facilities, Corporate Real Estate, Finance, etc. She was really on a roll. But only seven people showed up. Jerry was one of them. Although Emily was generally disappointed, she pressed on.

After greeting the seven, she asked, "From where you sit, what do you think is our biggest wellness challenge?" The responses flowed more naturally this time.

"A lack of leadership support," "insufficient training," "poor incentives," "no participation," "no funding," "communication problems," "policy problems." Emily saw a lot of polite finger pointing at deficiencies in someone else's area of responsibility. Some people began defending their work. Tension increased. Emily called for a break.

Emily was nervous. The tension and finger pointing were not at all what she had expected or prepared for. Jerry walked up and asked how she felt about the meeting. Emily shrugged. But as she looked at the wall and chatted with the others, a question began to form in her mind: "Who owns employee health or happiness?" And she carried the question back into the meeting after the break.

The discussion was like a Magic Eye poster. The 3-dimensional picture slowly emerged: "No one." The earlier tension and division in the room explained why: employees felt disconnected and disengaged. As that picture came into focus, it shifted the energy in the room. The silos explained why no one felt inspired by their piece of the wellness pie. It also exposed some overlapping and confusing initiatives. In some cases, they were competing against one another for budget dollars and scope. It was *Murder on the Orient Express*: connecting the dots began to reframe the entire conversation.

The energy shifted toward a positive curiosity; people began mixing. An eager and friendly curiosity drove them into questions like, "Just what

The problem was structural, but Emily was learning that the solutions to complexity are found in the social capital of relationships.

is it you do?" The room became a more extensive and exciting conversation about how each person's role helped or hindered how others pursued their jobs. Emily couldn't map all the links, disconnects, and overlaps, but she had unknowingly altered the system. The relationships in the room shifted. The problem was structural, but Emily was learning that the solutions to complexity are found in the social capital of relationships.

Emily found her tribe, her first followers. By mapping "the system" each experienced how their narrow roles created unintended collisions with their peers and how those collisions spread through the organization.

Standing in that moment of clarity, some felt an urge to "fix it." But Emily deflected that premature thought by giving everyone a few assignments. She first handed out copies of the books. With the extra books from the no-shows, she gave each person two additional copies and asked that they recruit two more people as part of their team, preferably from different departments.

Emily already knew the location of the low-hanging fruit for improving wellness throughout the organization. She thought field trips through the company, like the ones she took, would make a good next step in discovery.

Emily discovered an essential lesson to cracking complex problems. Answers hinge on the quality of relationships among stakeholders. Many corporate wellness efforts stumble at this starting gate. They begin with a

Answers hinge on the quality of relationships among stakeholders.

problem to solve, but then fail to consider the very real people who live with a system that keeps everyone locked into recurring patterns.

Emily solved the first grand challenge, identifying key stakeholders who were willing to come together to address a common challenge. From that, and as the group grew to about two dozen members, Emily discovered the power of small teams engaged in a quest for a new future. She assigned small groups of three to four people to scour the company for positive outliers who were influencing their immediate surroundings.

When a group found someone doing something winning and effective, they interviewed and photographed those involved. A couple

Figure 16.1 Small groups hold great power for change.

weeks later, each team recapped what they saw, along with the significant artifacts observed. The room was covered with photos of the many creative approaches. Emily remembered a presentation at one of the Well MindShift summits about the power of finding and expanding solutions already living inside a community or organization. So, she scheduled a follow-up meeting to invite some of the outliers to come share their idea and how they worked to get others to adopt the new approaches.

The meeting of positive outliers produced a watershed moment for the group. The variety of improvements were no longer just ideas; they saw at least a dozen prototypes already alive and well throughout the organization. And Emily's cohort of second chair leaders had doubled.

The Grand Challenge

When Emily stopped by Jerry's office to report the progress, she saw a tint of personal warmth, maybe even respect, in his eyes. At least his sense of despair and vexation was not as visible. Was his face a little slimmer? It didn't seem as puffy and red. Her anxiety subsided.

Jerry knew she had cracked through a barrier. He also knew that the shadow culture saw and would resist the intrusion. The supervisors for

Emily's team members would soon be questioned. Success brings higher visibility and a need for more time and eventually budget dollars. That would typically lead to very innocent-looking shifts in responsibility, stripping away time and starving resources. Jerry mentally walked through the political terrain and some of the cultural issues she and her team would need to navigate.

He could not admit his slight paternal attitude toward her; he wanted to help. He assumed he knew things she and her group would need. But Jerry was also surprised at Emily's ability to get past the guards. Her project had already penetrated further than the efforts of the past. Still, for Emily's grand challenge to have a chance, she needed a formal executive champion. Sure, he'd do that for her. That meant Jerry needed to talk to his peers who managed members of Emily's team and persuade them to not only allow but support this joint effort. He would minimize concerns and lower some of the exposure by framing the effort, first as a fact-finding mission. Jerry recruited two of his peers, who were already interested in health and well-being, to form an oversight committee.

Jerry was impressed that Emily had attracted most of the key stake-holders. But he suggested some additional participants, including a union representative, a call center manager, and a retail rep. She would also need some subject experts, some who had achieved success at implementing comprehensive wellness initiatives and someone with a strong back-ground in analytics.

The Ladder of Engagement

A few more attendees joined the next meeting. The stakes were getting higher. It was time to turn the grand challenge into a tangible goal. When she invited comments about goals, ideas flew like buckshot. When the group returned from a break, Emily had drawn a ladder on a flip chart with three major rungs and smaller rungs in between.

Emily continued, "Before we aim for transforming our business and industry, let's step back and talk about where we are starting from. The idea behind this ladder is to help us to identify our 'why' and where we think we are starting. This creates a floor and a ceiling. The first rung, clearly where we are now, takes a tactical approach to wellness. The focus is to lower costs and risk. And that leaves us with an insurance company that provides a generic package, and we have little say or involvement in what they do. Even our leadership admits they hate it." (Refer to Figure 16.2.)

"The second rung takes a strategic approach, focusing on attracting and retaining talent. The companies I saw in this category at the MindShift project pay a premium for talent and provide a lot of amenities and options. These companies partner with benefits providers to tailor benefits and provide a broader range of options. Companies that take this approach typically have executive-level ownership, a chief people or talent officer, and look more holistically at employee experience, including the design of the workplace, training and mentoring, work opportunities, and work/life considerations.

"The top rung considers happiness and health a core value. It sits as a transformational driver for growth and the deepening of culture. The by-product is innovation and market leadership. Companies that adopt this approach are motivated by vision and values and the desire to be market leaders. They are culture driven. They may partner with outside suppliers, but their strategy and programs are internally developed."

Everyone saw that their company lived on the bottom of the tactical rung. No one was proud of the offering, and it lacked any intentionality or coordination. A hand went up: "So, what would it take to make it to the top of the tactical rung and maybe break into the strategic?"

Silver Lining

When Emily's team measured and mapped their current state, they identified large areas of improvement by eliminating overlaps and the waste of competing agendas, simplifying and clarifying to remove confusion, expanding the work of positive outliers, and several low-cost and no-cost improvements.

That effort connected them to the deeper inner workings and culture of the company. They created an employee experience map which identified overstressed as well as underutilized positions. It also helped to determine what employees valued most from the benefits packages and programs.

The team conducted an asset scavenger hunt and mapped what they found, including employees with unique skills, local health resources, underutilized spaces, and a cafeteria that was only used during breakfast and lunch. They found an idea called "microenvironments" used in

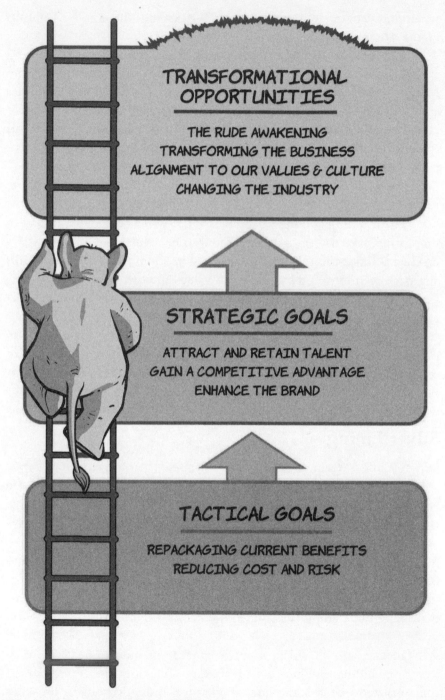

Figure 16.2   The Ladder to Wellness.

school renovations and found ways to turn underutilized areas into quiet nooks or connecting spaces. All this research was funneled through a list of questions:

- What is working well?
- What and where are the challenges?
- What can we improve through better alignment?
- What is missing that might improve or become a catalyst?
- Where and who are leverage points we can influence?

The Network Effect

When I interviewed Dr. Nicholas Christakis, coauthor of *Connected: The Surprising Power of Our Social Networks and How They Shape Our Lives*,[2] he described the power of networks on behavior and health. According to his research, health is profoundly impacted by where we are in our networks and who is immediately nearby.

> *Change your friends and change your happiness and health.*

For example, if you smoke, struggle with weight, or feel depressed you likely live and work inside a network of similar people. Christakis said that is why change is so hard. Change your friends and change your happiness and health. Emily's team learned that first hand. They began to see the company as networks—a network of communication, a network of commitments, a network of relationships, and a network of beliefs. With the aid of some new tools, they were able to visualize and map some of these networks.[3]

Mapping the networks identified several key leverage opportunities:

- People who were either communication hubs or key influencers.
- People who were viewed as the "go to" ones.
- People who were considered mentors or wise advisors.
- Groups that had very different beliefs, mindsets, and outlooks. Some were naturally resistant and others more open and easier bridge builders.

As second-chair leaders, Emily's team not only discovered how the different networks functioned but how influencing a few key or receptive people inside these networks had a greater effect than trying to roll out new programs.

Future Travelers

The future is already here. It's just not very evenly distributed.

—William Gibson

The progress that Emily's team made in 18 months brought noticeable changes in the workplace: a simpler and more accessed benefits program and a much different conversation among managers and leaders.

Because of Emily's team, the conversations in the C-suite also shifted from a focus on cost to a deeper and genuine awareness of the value of good health and the benefits of healthy employees. Her team had earned the credibility to be given a budget for visiting companies known for their new thinking on relating to employees as family. Her team began to see how to help the company rise above the tactical rung.

At the outset, Emily faced strong turf protection, but a larger number saw the inadequacy of the status quo and why their silos created those conditions. And mutual awareness led to information sharing and improved coordination. That immediately showed up in lower cost, higher participation, and improved satisfaction. Coordination soon evolved into cooperation and the willingness to share resources and budget dollars. The effort transitioned from turf to trust. Cooperation grew into collaboration around common goals. More importantly, it shifted norms. A pay-it-forward mindset emerged. After about 18 months, the work and positive results expanded. The team was ready to find ways to improve upon a tactical foundation. They might even help the company to see and treat employees as strategic members.

Kyle Majchrowski and Seek Change

Emily met Kyle at the Denver summit. He is the senior director for construction at Banner Health. Dissatisfied with the adversarial construction culture and the constant battles over missed schedules and budget overruns of one of his projects, Kyle had started a movement six years earlier in Portland. He and some of his more open-minded suppliers created an event, the Capital Projects Symposium.

His initial goal was to start a new conversation around trust-based collaborative projects, invite other owners and suppliers, and just see who showed up. It quickly became an annual event and grew larger every year. When Kyle left Portland and joined Banner in Denver, he launched a similar event. The Portland event continued because Kyle deliberately shifted responsibility and ownership to a few second chair leaders. He created a sustainable ecosystem and flipped the behaviors in the marketplace.

Both Kyle and Emily learned that the solution to a complex, dysfunctional system is to first shift the nature of the relationships in that system. The successes in Portland and Denver moved to Phoenix and are now incubating in Houston. Kyle created a nonprofit, Seek Change, to help grassroots efforts to bring change, primarily to the local construction community.

> *The solution to a complex, dysfunctional system is to first shift the nature of the relationships in that system*

Emily set a new goal for next year, to enlist the help of Seek Change and bring local owners, wellness providers, architects, furniture manufacturers, contractors, and real estate firms together and create a local movement for change. She is experiencing, first hand, the secrets of grassroots change and second chair leadership. If she can recruit other local stakeholders for a symposium, she knows it will make it easier to continue to push the boundaries.

Second chair leaders are also first-hand leaders. They work in the trenches. Emily's credibility derives from her dissatisfaction, curiosity, transparency, and conviction. Only one qualification is needed: "This really bugs me and I've got to find an answer. Does it bug you too?"

You won't find that statement in a leadership book. It's too human for that.

At the end of the day, a second chair leader isn't looking for heroics. They know or soon discover that if you answer the call, it will change you. It changed Emily. It changed Kyle. It changed me. It can change you.

Leadership Nudge

Who is trying to bring positive change to the organization but needs coaching and some political cover?

Personal Nudge

What is the question or issue that won't go away for you? Who else has similar interests and wants to make positive change instead of simply complaining?

CHAPTER 17

Haven in a Heartless World

The Promise of a Good Workplace

Jack Hess, the executive director for CivicLab in Columbus, Indiana, works with communities across the country to tackle complex topics like improving education or revitalizing communities. But Jack knows what most leaders know: integrating the needs and preferences of multiple stakeholders is a minefield. Everyone at that table carries agendas, assumptions, hot buttons, pet programs, and grievances that compete against all the others.

That's why Jack's work provides a framework for creating collective success. Part of his secret is a simple exercise of overlapping circles called "The Acorn and the Oak." We used this exercise in our first summit at the Mayo Clinic to arrive at a common understanding of where to begin.

The acorn is crucial. It is the seed; without it, oaks would have no future. Therefore, the acorn lies in the center circle; it is the one thing that is essential. The second ring includes necessary ingredients to the growth of the acorn: air, water, soil, and sunlight. The third ring includes supporting factors: fertilizer, pruning, etc. In other words, this exercise

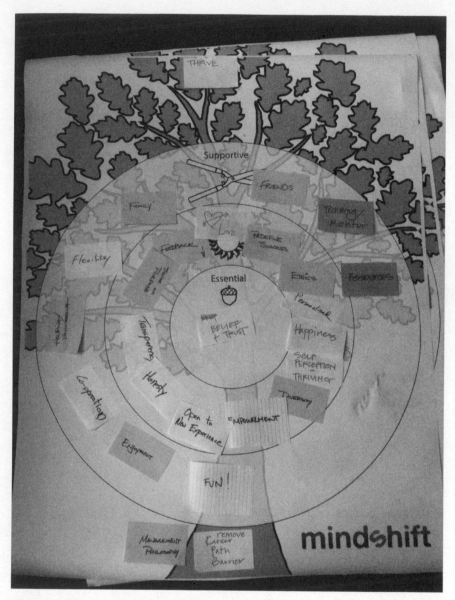

Figure 17.1 Acorn and Oak Exercise.

finds agreement on the one essential thing. Everything else must exist in support of the "acorn."

So, for the purpose of this book, the "acorn" of the workplace is the happy and healthy employee. He or she is the future. Every other issue and factor must find purpose and harmony around that. Just as a natural acorn requires a complex ecosystem, a happy and healthy human at work requires a safe, nurturing, and supportive haven. In the same way that healthy acorns are certifiably, inalterably, and thoroughly essential, flourishing and fully engaged employees are indispensable.

That is not debatable.

This final chapter examines the haven of the good workplace. If Paul Batalden is correct that "Every system is perfectly designed to get the results it gets," then acorns are perfectly designed to grow oak trees. And our eighteenth-century-designed workplaces are perfectly designed to produce disengagement, stress, toxicity, and chronic disease in our twenty-first-century work. The existential crisis described in Chapter 1 confirms that we face this crisis because we designed it that way.

But now: Time is running out. We have no other choice. We must design a better way. I close this book with good news. The convergence of new tools, new language, and new thinking makes a new world possible. I think many years from now, we will all look back on the present as the historic period that brought us to a new platform for change. All the ingredients for creating havens in a heartless world exist now. Today probably represents an unprecedented opportunity to live and work together in a better way.

> *The convergence of new tools, new language, and new thinking make a new world possible. History brings us to a new moment and a new platform for change. All the ingredients for creating havens in a heartless world exist now.*

Let's look at some of the details of this historic moment.

From Complicated to Intuitive

For example, think of what has happened to computing over the past 50 years. From the late 1960s on through the 1970s, computers represented an arcane, nerdy world of *Popular Electronics*, tubes, circuits, FORTRAN, COBOL, Bell Labs, and computers as big as boxcars. The UNIVAC computer contained more than 5,000 vacuum tubes, weighed about 30,000 pounds, and cost a million dollars. As strange as it may seem to younger readers, in those days computing was *supposed to be* hard. And only the acne-faced, too-weird-for-daylight, cultic, basement dwellers could lead the way.

But a revolution led by Steve Jobs, Steve Wozniak, Bill Gates, and many others toppled the titans of that weird world. To their horror, computers became innate, fun, creative, and cool. The whole earth passed from seeing computers as "wonky technical" to "easy intuitive."

That revolution, which was largely led by Apple, allowed me and millions like me to start new businesses. We did not need full-time or expensive accounting services, tech support, administrative help, expensive web designers, e-commerce specialists, a graphics department, PR, etc. All those special disciplines have become easy and intuitive. We may still need such experts and specialties from time to time, but we're not as dependent on them as we were in the old days. That interdependent ecosystem was designed to let the individual call the shots.

I see a comparable vision for the future of workplace health, happiness, and high performance. For example, after a long history of distrust, proprietary dominions, and silos, in 2013 medical science and building science worked together, in side-by-side collaboration to create something new. Corporate real estate and human resources discovered they had a common mission. They could build an idea, a whole environment, that released humans to flourish in safe and healthy buildings and furnishings. We are still in the exciting early days of watching the workplace health and well-being ecosystem take shape, become more human, and increasingly allow individuals to manage their own time, space, tools, and preferences. It also allows them to integrate their working roles with their real-life needs and constraints.

The outside world continues to be hostile. Think about it: Atlanta, Houston, Phoenix, and other cities along the lower band of America became business centers because of air conditioning. In other words, American ingenuity and business momentum subdued the natural hostility of climate. In the very same way, we no longer have to submit to the status quo. Good work and a good workplace have become a haven for many. The workplace is the one social invention with the resources, reach, and reasons to make those havens in a heartless world a reality. The outliers we have highlighted throughout this book have made employee happiness and health a centerpiece of their culture and business strategies. They have not only broken through old barriers, but demolished our old paradigms about the value of workplace health and well-being. For some, cost was the final threshold guardian. After too long of mumbling "too expensive," even that has been overthrown as a barrier to worker health and happiness.

The Collapse of the Cost Barrier

Throughout the 1990s and early 2000s, to build a highly sustainable building meant paying a steep premium of between 10% and 30%. Today that cost is negligible. When CBRE opened their new office in 2013, they were pioneers in the field of creating a healthy workplace by design. Even at that birthing moment, the additional cost was 1.73%. Today, the cost hovers around 1% over conventional construction.

> *Throughout the 1990s and early 2000s, to build a highly sustainable building meant paying a steep premium of between 10% and 30%. Today that cost is negligible.*

CBRE blazed a trail that became a road, that became an interstate highway. And in just four years. So much progress in such a short time; today WELL design[1] is quickly becoming the starting point. No one has a reason to not build that way.

DPR Construction, one of the nation's premiere builders of technically-challenging and sustainable projects, is one of the latest examples of that new reality. The very culture of DPR brings high expectations to every project, especially their company offices. Each office construction tries to outdo the last project.

Chris Gorthy, one of DPR's project executives and a core member of our Well MindShift team, explained why the DC/Reston project was important to DPR: "We've always been a highly collaborative culture. It's in our roots. Our old office just didn't support the culture. That all came back to life in our new office."

> *A high-performing workplace could return productivity agreement figures of 90%+, while poorly performing space might languish around 20–30%.[2]*

"One of the best improvements was a new sense of community. We now find people eating lunch together, interacting more, getting up and moving around. Knowing that five minutes of walking is enough to stimulate blood flow, we worked with our design partners to create opportunities for movement within the office. It was simple concepts; putting the kitchen at the far end of the workstations, allowing employees to engage in ping ping, shuffleboard, or take a walk while on a call. All of those changes were brought in to assist our employees with being healthier while creating opportunities for casual encounters of communication and sharing.

That's a completely different shift from our old office. People came in. They did their job. They went home. There was little dialogue outside of getting stuff done.

"If you walk into our 'living room' right now, you may find very diverse conversations among employees, contractors, vendors, and visitors. That kind of interaction and community exchange was limited in our old office. Our environment makes it easy to meet new people, to learn from each other—it's just so natural. It's hard to describe, but powerful. It is one of those unintended consequences of creating an environment flexible enough for people to just act natural.

"Our challenge was balancing elements of our project goals. We did not want the design for sustainability, health, and well-being, energy, and a productive workplace to keep us from achieving any of the others. We wanted to provide 100% natural air, and that pushed against our goal for targeting Net Zero (an annual Net Zero certification within the International Living Future Institute Certification program). We also found that natural circadian lighting throughout the space did not work with the varied schedules of our employees. So, we adapted by providing task-adjustable lighting to allow each person to control their light. In the end, our investment to apply for and submit for WELL certification was less than 1% of our total costs for the project. We were already doing so many of the right things. The biggest lesson was, you don't have to choose between cost, wellness, sustainability, and creating an incredible workplace. With the right team, engaged early, you can maximize the benefits of all four goals."

. . . we don't have to make a choice among cost, wellness, or creating a great place for people to work.

Chris expressed a core truth about commercial construction. Culture is like Bigfoot to management. It's out there, and we fear it even though no one has ever gotten a good look at it. When you begin planning to move people to new space, all of a sudden all of those once-hidden attitudes and behaviors come out of the woods to protect their turf. With proper leadership, creating new space can expose Bigfoot and also release the positive potential that too many environments keep caged. Chris already knew DPR had a very collaborative organization, but did not see how much their old space was constraining—and damaging—that natural inclination.

Planning how you will work and live together provides the single most effective tool to understand what your organization is today, and what it could be tomorrow. To those who know how to hear it, the workplace speaks. It says, "We'd like to be a little more like this and less like that." That is why traditional expert-directed approaches too often fail to deliver improvement.

> *Planning how you will work and live together provides the single most effective tool to understand what your organization is today, and what it could be tomorrow.*

In Chapter 2, we described the CBRE project as a journey. We describe it (and other projects) that way because the outcome was not predetermined. Traveling with purposeful ignorance and curiosity will lead people to unexpected destinations. The difference between the CBRE's journey and DPR's is that better maps guided DPR. And, as we suggested earlier, in time the trail became a well-traveled highway. And, that is why DPR's new building project is a very big deal. It confirms the timeless pattern of how civilization unfurls. It's how things never imagined a short time ago so quickly become routine.

Seven Golden Nuggets

We all know that new eras do not leave the patterns of the past intact. Everything changes when the future comes into view. Most institutions just instinctively fight that process. The coming storm demands we not yield to that impulse. We should do all we can to hasten that transition.

I see seven mind shifts (paradigms, patterns, assumptions, and structures) that are essential to a new era of business. They all confirm a transition from complicated to simple, from wonky to common sense, from siloed to connected, and from bureaucratic to human. I believe they are all inevitable. But those who see and adopt them early will find better positions in the marketplace.

1. **Change the environment:** Trying to shift human behavior through rational approaches turns out to be expensive and futile. We will all

save time and money when we see humans as they really are, *irrational*, but *predictably irrational*. If people naturally take the path of least resistance, it is infinitely better to design environments that make healthy and wise choices as natural and easy as possible.

2. **Well-being comes before wellness:** The corporate focus on physical health is pointless if employees hate their job, fear their boss, or feel isolated and lonely. As Sylvia's story affirmed in Chapter 4, leaders and managers must reduce friction, provide competent and caring supervisors, and make work meaningful. Happiness and health follow. Naturally.

3. **We must care for people before we can help them:** And we can't care for those we don't know. Some things just take time; like wine, diamonds, and pearls. And knowing and caring for people. Wise leaders and managers know you can't delegate or organize care. Leaders must be willing to be themselves and take the time to discover the gifts and life experiences the employees bring with them. That human touch will create a positive domino effect that radiates beyond the workplace, on out to the family and rolling right on into the community.

4. **Build a healthy building:** After reminding us how much of life is lived inside of four walls and a roof, Paul Scialla asked, "What if we could activate that space to provide a passive and constant delivery of preventative medical benefits that wouldn't require the occupant to do a thing? An individual, *just by being in the space*, whether at home, office, or school . . . could have positive exposure to cardiovascular health, respiratory health, immune health, sleep health, cognitive health. This is a slam dunk!" That is one of the largest pillars of this book.

5. **Design work for a person's natural strengths:** Perhaps the most compelling motivation behind this book is the need to allow people to work at what they do best and enjoy most. So many stories in this book examine the wisdom of releasing people to work in their strengths. The hardest leadership, management, or parenting habit we face is the twitch to fix what's wrong instead of patiently building on what is already strong.

6. **Build social capital:** Civilization has always required trust, reliability, connection, collaboration, and reciprocity. When those features are active in human relationships, they build hothouses of social networks,

entrepreneurialism, barn raising, and devotion to the common good. That's why human resources, corporate real estate, organizational development, facilities, occupational safety, and procurement function best when they work in harmony. Social capital is the least expensive and most effective asset an organization owns.

7. **The age of balancing cost and wellness has ended:** Investing in people is exactly that, an investment. Like good seed sown in good soil, that investment produces an exponential harvest. That may be the core insight shared by Apple, Google, and many of the companies we have profiled in this book; they see *human* resources as an asset to leverage, not a cost to contain.

The Power of a Psychologically Safe Workplace

> *In an ordinary organization, most people are doing a second job no one is paying them for . . . most people are spending time and energy covering up their weaknesses, managing other people's impressions of them, showing themselves to their best advantage, playing politics, hiding their inadequacies, hiding their uncertainties, hiding their limitations.*
>
> —Robert Kegan & Lisa Lahey[3]

DaVerse Lounge, located in Dallas, works with severely traumatized kids. Most are deeply hurt, damaged, shamed, and angry. Will Richey, cofounder of DaVerse Lounge, found a key to making it safe for those kids to finally embrace relationships with others. He uses their story as their road to identity, confidence, inclusion, and community.

In that new zone of safety, Will and his team show them how to draw strength from the pain. Imagine skilled lion tamers who enter a cage with abused and starved lions, and then slowly turn them into a healthy, playful, and loving pride. That is what DaVerse Lounge does kid after kid, year after year.

He encourages participating with a rhythmic and appealing promise:

> *"When I share my joy,*
> *I multiply my happiness.*
> *When I share my pain,*
> *I divide my sadness.*
> *And when I embrace the two,*

I become whole . . .
WE become . . . Whole."

— Norman Bouffard and Will Richey

Many workplaces could benefit from their own DaVerse Lounge, a safe place and a way to embrace community.

Will's poem sets the tone for a friendly and safe time together.

Many workplaces could benefit from their own DaVerse Lounge, a safe place and a way to embrace community. I've found Will's approach—a simple template that makes it easy to create an engaging personal story—with kids in that early stage of fear and shame also works for people in any organization. Step 1 follows the template as a way to write a short personal story. Step 2 is to share those stories. I like to start in small groups and let each cluster group report a summary to the larger group. The stories create immediate interest and emotional resonance. They shine a positive spotlight on everyone. You can find a sample of the template in Appendix C.

The Story of a Good Workplace: The Promise of the Future

What leaders do: they give people stories they can tell themselves. Stories about the future and about change.

— Seth Godin

The wellness ship is turning. But it is a big ship. We see firms, like DPR and others in this book, turning their own ships and discovering the old barriers simply don't exist anymore. The better workplaces they create, in fact, gives a measurable boost in employee engagement and productivity. Ryan Picarella, president of the Wellness Coalition of America, believes this is no longer a perk for companies, "it's a business imperative."[4] That's why we must bring clearer definition to how organizations get beyond the focus on programs and deliver on the promises of health and happiness.

Until 2013 we were stuck in a story on workplace wellness that had a tragic ending. However, one small project created a "disturbance in the force." That became a beacon that invited thousands. I was one of them.

Although I missed some of the ramifications, I did see the possibility of a new story for American business. We have done our best to tell you that story. The artifacts we leave to you include some secrets, maps, experiences, and a few warnings to prepare you as you explore the safe haven your organization can build. Our mission was to find a new narrative with hope, humanity, and high performance as a testimony to a new order. A new future begins with a new and believable story, and once that story takes hold it will also guide our imaginations, our conversations, our decisions, and will create new ways of working and living.

APPENDIX A
THE WELL MINDSHIFT CORE TEAM

I would like to thank our core Well MindShift team. These members participated in our summits, provided ongoing advice, and were invaluable resources. This group of highly diverse experts and business leaders quickly developed a trusted and safe environment to wrestle with hard issues.

In addition to listing them I have also provided their Clifton Strengthsfinder results. This was an invaluable tool to get to know one another faster and deeper. It allowed us to discover the diverse talents we brought together and to free people to function in areas they naturally enjoy and excel at. We also took time to teach and practice how using this knowledge can improve our happiness and performance in life and work.

Bryan Berthold
Cushman & Wakefield
Managing Director Workplace
    Strategy, Global Business
    Consulting
Bryan.Berthold@cushwake.com
1. Futuristic
2. Strategic
3. Relator
4. Learner
5. Ideation

Rich Blakeman
Four Winds Interactive
VP, Alliances & Partnerships

rich.blakeman@
    fourwindsinteractive
    .com
1. Strategic
2. Relator
3. Belief
4. Self-Assurance
5. Woo

Steven Carter
Carter Group, Inc.
Principal Owner
scarter@thecartergroupinc.com
1. Input
2. Strategic

3. Strategic
4. Ideation
5. Connectedness

Mabel Casey
Haworth
Vice President, Global Marketing
    and Sales Support
mabel.casey@charter.net
1. Strategic
2. Responsibility
3. Relator
4. Input
5. Arranger

Ed Chinn
Cool River Pub, Inc.
Brewmeister
edchinn@me.com
1. Adaptability
2. Intellection
3. Developer
4. Positivity
5. Activator

Emma Cox
McDonalds
emma.cox@us.mcd.com
1. Empathy
2. Individualization
3. Relator
4. Futuristic
5. Activator

Calvin Crowder
GoDaddy
Director of Real Estate and
    Facilities

calvin@godaddy.com
1. Belief
2. Analytical
3. Significance
4. Learner
5. Achiever

Patrick Donnelly
BHDP
Principal
tdonnelly@bhdp.com
1. Strategic
2. Adaptability
3. Connectedness
4. Activator
5. Ideation

Rachel Druckenmiller
SIG
Director of Wellbeing
rachel@silbs.com
1. Strategic
2. Achiever
3. Ideation
4. Significance
5. Activator

Ted Eytan
Kaiser Center for Total
    Health
Director in the Permanente
    Federation
Ted.a.Eytan@kp.org
1. Strategic
2. Learner
3. Individualization
4. Futuristic
5. Relator

Mike Ford
DPR
Management Committee
    Member
MikeF@dpr.com
1. Strategic
2. Ideation
3. Communication
4. Activator
5. Individualization

Bob Fox
FOX Architects
Principal
bfox@fox-architects.com
1. Self-Assurance
2. Activator
3. Futuristic
4. Command
5. Arranger

Josh Glynn
Google
Director of Health and
    Performance
jglynn@google.com
1. Ideation
2. Analytical
3. Arranger
4. Strategic
5. Relator

Christopher Gorthy
DPR
Strategic preconstruction services
    leader and expert in building
    sciences

ChristopherG@dpr.com
1. Woo
2. Positivity
3. Developer
4. Communication
5. Empathy

Charlie Grantham
Future of Work
Owner
cegrantham@gmail.com
1. Connectedness
2. Strategic
3. Ideation
4. Woo
5. Maximizer

Whitney Gray
Delos
Executive Director, Research
    and Innovation
whitney.gray@delos.com
1. Activator
2. Communication
3. Strategic
4. Achiever
5. Woo

Chuck Hardy
GSA
Chief Workplace Officer
charles.hardy@gsa.gov
1. Strategic
2. Self-Assurance
3. Relator
4. Command
5. Activator

Jack Hess
Institute for Coalition
    Building
Executive Director
jhess@coalitionbuilding.org
1. Learner
2. Achiever
3. Futuristic
4. Strategic
5. Maximizer

Lew Horne
CBRE
Executive Managing Director
lew.horne@cbre.com
1. Achiever
2. Relator
3. Activator
4. Strategic
5. Belief

Mike Humphrey
DPR
Management Team
MikeH@dpr.com
1. Achiever
2. Belief
3. Positivity
4. Woo
5. Communication

Craig Janssen
Idibri
Principal
cjanssen@idibri.com
1. Ideation
2. Strategic
3. Achiever

4. Command
5. Input

Michelle Kleyla
Haworth
Marketing Manager
michelle.kleyla@haworth.com
1. Strategic
2. Individualization
3. Arranger
4. Connectedness
5. Ideation

Michael Lagocki
Art Love Magic
Scribe/Live Artist
mike@artlovemagic.com
1. Strategic
2. Connectedness
3. Ideation
4. Activator
5. Adaptability

Bill Latham
MeTEOR
Principal
BLatham@meteoreducation.com
1. Strategic
2. Ideation
3. Command
4. Communication
5. Belief

Wade Lewis
ISS
Vice President of Business Services
wade.lewis@us.issworld.com
1. Communication
2. Strategic

3. Woo
4. Futuristic
5. Positivity

Kate Lister
Global Workplace Analytics
President
kate@globalworkplaceanalytics
.com
1. Strategic
2. Relator
3. Focus
4. Achiever
5. Analytical

Kyle Majchrowski
Banner Health
Construction Project Executive,
Senior Director
kyle.majchrowski@bannerhealth
.com
1. Achiever
2. Learner
3. Self-Assurance
4. Intellection
5. Deliberative

Clayton Mitchell
Kaiser Permanente
Executive Director
Clayton.O.Mitchell@kp.org
1. Positivity
2. Connectedness
3. Arranger
4. Woo
5. Responsibility

Jamie Moore
DPR
Business Consultant
jamiem@dpr.com
1. Arranger
2. Individaulization
3. Relator
4. Focus
5. Signifiance

Scott Muldavin
The Muldavin Company
President
Smuldavin@muldavin.com
1. Achiever
2. Learner
3. Positivity
4. Individualization
5. Developer

Irene Nigaglioni
PBK Architects Inc.
Partner
irene.nigaglioni@pbk.com
1. Achiever
2. Learner
3. Maximizer
4. Responsibility
5. Command

Mike O'Neill
Haworth
Lead Global Research, Workplace
Strategy and Market Analytics
michael.oneill@haworth.com
1. Restorative
2. Command

3. Harmony
4. Focus
5. Significance

Chelsea Poulin
MetEOR
Marketing Director
cpoulin@meteoreducation.com
1. Individualization
2. Achiever
3. Input
4. Relator
5. Restorative

Paul Scialla
Delos Living LLC
Founder
pscialla@delosliving.com
1. Futuristic
2. Ideation
3. Competition
4. Positivity
5. Self-Assurance

Miriam Senft
Motivity
President, CEO
mim.senft@motivitypartnerships
    .com
1. Learner
2. Achiever
3. Positivity
4. Strategic
5. Responsibility

Linda Sorrento
Sorrento Consulting LLC
Founder

Lsorrento2@gmail.com
1. Connectedness
2. Learner
3. Maximizer
4. Responsibility
5. Relator

Dean Stanberry
Abraxas Energy
Client Services
dean.stanberry@abraxasenergy
    .com
1. Analytical
2. Learner
3. Responsibility
4. Input
5. Achiever

Jonathan Stanley
Tarkett
National Vice President Education
    Sales
jonathan.stanley@tarkett.com
1. Maximizer
2. Individualization
3. Belief
4. Responsibility
5. Arranger

Dean Strombom
Gensler Architects
Principal
dean_strombom@gensler.com
1. Adaptability
2. Maximizer
3. Relator
4. Ideation
5. Focus

Drew Suszko
BHDP
Lead Strategist/Architect
andrew.suszko@gmail.com
1. Achiever
2. Competition
3. Futuristic
4. Focus
5. Learner

Randy Thompson
Cushman & Wakefield
Managing Director & Senior
    Project Manager
randy.thompson@cushwake.com
1. Maximizer

2. Learner
3. Strategic
4. Achiever
5. Empathy

Phil Williams
Delos
Executive Director Project
    Delivery
phil.williams@delos.com
1. Strategic
2. Learner
3. Ideation
4. Input
5. Developer

APPENDIX B
WELL MINDSHIFT PARTICIPANTS

The following list is a thank you to the experts we interviewed, participants in our virtual dialogues, and contributors in a variety of ways. Without this group of people we could not have gathered the stories, raised the issues, or challenged our thinking to dig deep to find out what really works.

Shari Barkin
Vanderbilt University School of
    Medicine
Director, Pediatric Obesity
    Research DRTC

Robin Bass
Google
Real Estate and Work Strategy

Mark Benden
Texas A&M University
Department Chair, EOH;
    Director, Ergonomics Center

Thom Browne
Voice is Power
Writer, Educator, Advocate

Carrie Burke
PARABOLA
Principal

Kevin Burke
PARABOLA
Principal

Ian Cameron
EyeCameron.com
President

Tom Carmazzi
Tuthill
CEO

Ben Cating
Idibri
Senior Consultant–VP

Robert Chapman
Barry-Wehmiller
CEO

Nicholas Christakis
Yale University
Director, Human Nature Lab

Andrew Cohen
Gensler
CEO

Chris Cox
Newmont Mining
Corporate Real Estate & Facilities
    Professional

Mark Cunningham-Hill
World Wide Health
Principal

Kyle Davy
Kyle V. Davy Consulting
Owner & President

Steven Elliott
MIRA/Black Creek Group
Investor–Consultant

Tom Emerick
Emerick Consulting
Owner

Laurie Ferrendelli
Barry-Wehmiller
Director of Organizational
    Development

Ron Goetzel
IBM Watson Health
Senior Scientist

Mark Gorman
Ciena
Vice President, Corporate Real
    Estate & Facilities

Jessica Grossmeier
HERO
Vice President of Research

Greg Haldeman
DPR
Management Committee
    Member

Chris Hoffman
Jacobs Corporation
Purchasing Manager

Kristen Holmes-Winn
WHOOP
Vice President, Performance
    Optimization

Cathy Hutchison
Idibri
Marketing Director–VP

Barbara Jackson
University of Denver
Director, Burns School of Real
    Estate

Edward Jackson
DPR Construction
Project Engineer

Rebecca Johnson
Haworth
Senior Research Specialist

Lea Kaltenbach
Carter Group, Inc.
Director, Strategic Alliances

Michelle Kinder
Momentous Institute
Executive Director

Greg Kunkel
NextJump
President

Al Lewis
What They Said
Owner

Mike Lewis
Fidelity
Corporate Real Estate & Facilities
    Professional

Ray Lucchesi
Regenisis
Principal

Cynthia McBride
Interactive Health, Inc.
Regional Market Leader

Clayton Mitchell
Kaiser Permanente
Vice President of Facilities
    Operations

John Montgomery
Threshold Interactive
President

Steven Orfield
Orfield Laboratories, Inc.
President

Ray Pentecost
Texas A&M
Director, Center for Health
    Systems & Design

Jeffrey Pfeffer
Thomas D. Dee II Professor
    of Organizational
    Behavior
Stanford University

Ryan Picarella
Welcoa
President

Dana Pillai
Well Living Lab
CEO

Betsy Price
City of Fort Worth
Mayor

Anthony Ravitz
Google
Real Estate and Work
    Strategy

Will Richey
Journeyman Ink
Founder, DaVerse Lounge

Michael Roizen
Cleveland Clinic
Chief Wellness Officer

Veronica Schreibeis Smith
Vera Iconica Architecture
Principal Architect

Steve Selkowitz
Lawrence Berkeley National Labs
Senior Advisor, Building Science

Dexter Shurney
Zipango, Inc.
Senior Vice President of Clinical
    Affairs

Amit Sood
Mayo Clinic College of Medicine
Consultant, Division of General
    Internal Medicine,
    Department of Internal
    Medicine

Vincent Sorrento
Engineer and Drone Pilot

Rhonda Spencer
Barry-Wehmiller
Chief People Officer

Barbara Spurrier
Well Living Lab
Chief Strategy Officer

Shaun Stewart
Delos
Vice President

Joe Stiefel
National University of Health
    Sciences
President

Leigh Stringer
EYP
Workplace Research and Strategy

Ed Strouth
Barry-Wehmiller
Director, Health & Wellbeing

Andrew Sykes
Habits at Work
President

David Thurm
Lehrer, LLC
Executive Vice President

Alan Vanderberg
Ottawa County
COO

Rosie Ward
Salveo Partners
CEO

Gigi Westerman
S&G Group: Blue Zones Fort
    Worth
Partner

Jay Wilkinson
Fire Spring
President

APPENDIX C
PERSONAL STORY TEMPLATE

My name is _____

I was born in _____

I speak _____

My ancestors come from: _____

I grew up in _____

I went to grade school at: _____

What are things you overcame growing up you are proud about? _____

My job is: _____

What I really do is: _____

My hero is: _____ because _____

I experience pain when: _____

In my life I'm planting seeds of: _____

I am searching for: _____

NOTES

Introduction

1. Jonathan Haidt, The Righteous Mind: Why Good People Are Divided by Politics and Religion (New York: Pantheon, 2012)
2. Nitin Nohria and Michael Beer, "Cracking the Code of Change," Harvard Business Review, 13 July 2015, hbr.org/2000/05/cracking-the-code-of-change.
3. Amadeo, Kimberly. "The Rising Cost of Health Care by Year and Its Causes." The Balance, 26 Oct. 2017, www.thebalance.com/causes-of-rising-healthcare-costs-4064878.
4. Gallup, Inc. "Employee Engagement in U.S. Stagnant in 2015." Gallup.com, 13 Jan. 2016, news.gallup.com/poll/188144/employee-engagement-stagnant-2015.aspx.
5. Miller, Stephen. "Study: Wellness Programs Saved $1 to $3 per Dollar Spent." SHRM, 12 Sept. 2012, www.shrm.org/resourcesandtools/hr-topics/benefits/pages/wellness-dollars-saved.aspx.
6. Roizen, Michael. YouTube, YouTube, 31 Oct. 2017, www.youtube.com/watch?v=ix_PRutK6E0.
7. "EPA." EPA, Environmental Protection Agency, cfpub.epa.gov/roe/chapter/air/indoorair.cfm. Accessed 18 Aug. 2017.

Chapter 1

1. Cormac McCarthy, All the Pretty Horses (New York: Vintage House, 1992).
2. George Beahm, I, Steve: Steve Jobs in His Own Words (Evanston, IL: Agate, 2011).
3. Ibid.
4. "RealAge" is Dr. Roizen's test that brings lifestyle into the equation for a person's virtual age. He is also the author of RealAge: Are You as Young as You Can Be? (New York: William Morrow, 1999) and the subsequent series of "RealAge" branded books. https://www.sharecare.com/static/realage-oz (accessed 4 October 2017).
5. Henry J. Kaiser Family Foundation, "2015 Employer Health Benefits Survey," 22 September 2015, https://www.kff.org/health-costs/report/2015-employer-health-benefits-survey/.

6. Sin-Ye Wu and Anthony Green, *Projection of Chronic Illness Prevalence and Cost Inflation*. Report. RAND Corporation, 2000.

7. Centers for Disease Control and Prevention, "Chronic Disease Prevention and Health Promotion," 28 June 2017, https://www.cdc.gov/chronicdisease/overview/index.htm (accessed 27 July 2017).

8. Roizen, Michael. YouTube, YouTube, 31 Oct. 2017, www.youtube.com/watch?v=ix_PRutK6E0.

9. The massive US effort to rebuild Western Europe after World War II.

10. Please view Dr. Roizen's presentation, "6 Processes to Slow Down Your Own Aging," January, 2017. Visit https://www.whacc.org to see our list of upcoming events: https://www.youtube.com/watch?v=SzSaI73NKaw&t=57s.11.

11. https://www.kff.org/report-section/health-care-costs-a-primer-2012-report/

Chapter 2

1. Rex Miller, Mabel Casey, and Mark Konchar, Change Your Space, Change Your Culture (Hoboken, NJ: Wiley, 2014).

2. Delos, http://delos.com/project/cbre-headquarters (accessed 31 August 2017).

3. The other leaders included Parabola Architects' Kevin and Carrie Burke, Mabel Casey and Steve Kooy from Haworth, Balfour Beatty's Eric Stenman, Andy Cohen from Gensler, Kate Lister from Global Workplace Analytics, and Michael Lagocki, our facilitator and live scribe.

4. World Health Organization, "Healthy Workplaces: A WHO Global Model for Action," http://www.who.int/occupational_health/healthy_workplaces/en/ (accessed 12 August 2017).

Chapter 3

1. Scale of Student Engagement and Disengagement (SOS ED), studentengagement.net/.

2. Rex Miller, *Humanizing the Education Machine: How to Create Schools That Turn Disengaged Kids into Inspired Learners* (Hoboken, NJ: Wiley, 2017).

3. Quizzify, "6 Shocking Facts About Employee Opioid Abuse You Need to Know," 12 September 2017, http://www.quizzify.com/single-post/2017/09/12/6-Shocking-Facts-About-Employee-Opioid-Abuse-Which-Cost-You-Money.

4. Matthew A. Stults-Kolehmainen and Rajita Sinha, "The Effects of Stress on Physical Activity and Exercise." *Sports Medicine* 44, no. 1 (Jan. 2014): 81–121, https://www.ncbi.nlm.nih.gov/pmc/articles/PMC3894304/.

5. Pew Charitable Trusts, "Americans' Financial Security: Perception and Reality," 5 March 2015, http://www.pewtrusts.org/en/research-and-analysis/issue-briefs/

2015/02/americans-financial-security-perceptions-and-reality (accessed 26 August 2017).

6. Jean Houston, *Myths for The Future* (Boulder, CO: Sounds True Audio, 1995).

7. M. Rex Miller, *Millennium Matrix: Reclaiming the Past, Reframing the Future of the Church* (San Francisco: Jossey-Bass, 2004).

8. Becker's Hospital Review, "Hospitals Face Unprecedented Turnover, Attrition Rates: 4 Survey Findings," 11 May 2017, https://www.beckershospitalreview .com/human-capital-and-risk/hospitals-face-unprecedented-turnover-attrition-rates-4-survey-findings.html.

9. Compdata Surveys, "Rising Turnover Rates in Healthcare and How Employers Are Recruiting to Fill Openings," 17 September 2015, http://www. compdatasurveys.com/2015/09/17/rising-turnover-rates-in-healthcare-and-how-employers-are-recruiting-to-fill-openings-2/ (accessed 26 August 2017).

10. Kate Lister and Tom Harnish, *Work on the Move 2* (Houston: IFMA Foundation, 2016).

Chapter 4

1. Mark Shwartz, "Robert Sapolsky Discusses Physiological Effects of Stress," *Stanford Report*, 7 March 2007, https://news.stanford.edu/news/2007/march7/sapolskysr-030707.html (accessed 16 September 2017).

2. John Heminway, dir., *Stress: Portrait of a Killer* (Washington, DC: National Geographic, 2008), DVD.

3. M.G. Marmot, G. Rose, M. Shipley, and P.J. Hamilton, "Employment Grade and Coronary Heart Disease in British Civil Servants," *Journal of Epidemiology and Community Health* 32, no. 4 (December 1978): 244–249, https://www.ncbi.nlm. nih.gov/pmc/articles/PMC1060958/.

4. "Pub Chain Watami, Founder Settle Suit over Suicide of Overworked Staffer," *Japan Times of News*, 10 December 2015, http://japan.timesofnews.com/pub-chain-watami-founder-settle-suit-over-suicide-of-overworked-staffer.html.

5. Jeffrey Pfeffer, *Dying for a Paycheck: How Modern Management Harms Employee Health and Company Performance—and What We Can Do About It* (New York: Harper-Collins, 2018).

6. Jeffrey Pfeffer, "Is Your Employer Killing You?" *Fortune*, 13 April 2015, http:// fortune.com/2015/04/13/is-your-employer-killing-you/.

7. Paul Hjemdahl, "Stress and the Metabolic Syndrome: An Interesting but Enigmatic Association." *Circulation* 106 (2002): 2634–2636, circ.ahajournals.org/content/ 106/21/2634 (accessed 13 September 2017).

8. Emma Seppala and Marissa King, "Burnout at Work Isn't Just About Exhaustion. It's Also About Loneliness," *Harvard Business Review*, 11 July 2017, hbr.org/2017/ 06/burnout-at-work-isnt-just-about-exhaustion-its-also-about-loneliness.

9. Diane, Coles Levine, and Nancy Johnson Sanquist. *Work on the move 2: how social, leadership and technology innovations are transforming the workplace in the digital economy.* IFMA Foundation, 2016.

10. Employers Take Wellness to a Higher Level." *SHRM*, 28 Aug. 2017, www.shrm.org/ hr-today/news/hr-magazine/0917/Pages/employers-take-wellness-to-a-higher-level .aspx. Accessed 16 Sept. 2017.11. Travis Bradberry, "Why Leaders Lack Emotional Intelligence," *Inc.com*, 15 March 2015, https://www.inc.com/travis-bradberry/why-leaders-lack-emotional-intelligence.html.

Chapter 5

1. Kate Lister and Tom Harnish, *Work on the Move 2* (Houston: IFMA Foundation, 2016).

2. Rex Miller, Mabel Casey, and Mark Konchar, *Change Your Space, Change Your Culture: How Engaging Workplaces Lead to Transformation and Growth* (Hoboken, NJ: Wiley, 2014).

3. Diane, Coles Levine, and Nancy Johnson Sanquist. *Work on the move 2: how social, leadership and technology innovations are transforming the workplace in the digital economy.* IFMA Foundation, 2016.

4. Ben Zimmer, "Wellness." *New York Times*, 17 April 2010, http://www.nytimes .com/2010/04/18/magazine/18FOB-onlanguage-t.html (accessed 2 October 2017).

5. "Wellness Programs," HealthCare.gov, https://www.healthcare.gov/glossary/ wellness-programs/.

6. "What Is a Wellness Program?" 25 March 2015, https://www.shrm.org/ resourcesandtools/tools-and-samples/hr-qa/pages/whatarewellnessbenefits.aspx.

7. John Naisbitt, *Megatrends* (New York: Warner Books, 1982).

8. Martin E.P. Seligman, *Flourish: A Visionary New Understanding of Health and Well-Being* (New York: Free Press, 2011).

9. You can take the PERMA assessment at: https://www.authentichappiness.sas .upenn.edu/testcenter.

Chapter 6

1. Leo Widrich, "The Origin of the 8-Hour Work Day and Why We Should Rethink It," *Buffer Social* (blog), Buffer, 11 June 2013, https://blog.bufferapp.com/optimal-work-time-how-long-should-we-work-every-day-the-science-of-mental-strength.

2. Tony Schwartz and Catherine McCarthy "Manage Your Energy, Not Your Time." Harvard Business Review, October 2007. https://hbr.org/2007/10/manage-your-energy-not-your-time.

3. David Zax, "Track Your Happiness iPhone Study Finds That Your Mind Is Wandering Too Much," Fast Company, 30 July 2012, https://www.

fastcompany.com/1702117/track-your-happiness-iphone-study-finds-your-mind-wandering-too-much.

4. Amy Novotney, "Strong in Mind and Body," *Monitor on Psychology* 40, no. 11 (December 2009): 40. www.apa.org/monitor/2009/12/army-program.aspx.

5. Paul Petrone, "How to Calculate the Cost of Employee Disengagement," *The Learning Blog*, LinkedIn, 24 March 2017, https://learning.linkedin.com/blog/engaging-your-workforce/how-to-calculate-the-cost-of-employee-disengagement.

6. Even though the Momentous Institute's kids funnel back into the public-school system at sixth grade, more than 85% graduate from high school and go to college. That incredible number is a testament to the power of a well-designed and congruent system.

Chapter 7

1. Michael Lewis, *The Big Short: Inside the Doomsday Machine* (New York: W.W. Norton, 2010).

2. Al Lewis, *Why Nobody Believes the Numbers: Distinguishing Fact from Fiction in Population Health Management* (Hoboken, NJ: Wiley, 2012).

3. Lewis, *The Big Short*.

4. "Statistics & Facts," Global Wellness Institute, https://www.globalwellnessinstitute.org/press-room/statistics-and-facts/ (accessed 17 July 2017).

5. Soeren Mattke, Christopher Schnyer, and Kristin R. Van Busum, "A Review of the U.S. Workplace Wellness Market," *RAND Health Quarterly* 2, no. 4 (Winter 2013): 7. https://www.ncbi.nlm.nih.gov/pmc/articles/PMC5052082/ (accessed 23 September 2017).

6. Bruce Japsen, "Employers Boost Wellness Spending 17% from Yoga to Risk Assessments," *Forbes*, 26 March 2015, https://www.forbes.com/sites/brucejapsen/2015/03/26/employers-boost-wellness-spending-17-from-yoga-to-risk-assessments/#2803b46c6d0f (accessed 23 September 2017).

7. Self-insured employers and third-party insurers in the United States spend about 2% of total company health-care costs on wellness (source: http://www.shrm.org/hrdiscipline.... 2010). Total company healthcare costs = $700 billion. Taking these figures, the total market = $14 billion. https://www.shrm.org/resourcesandtools/hr-topics/benefits/pages/wellnessbudgets.aspx

8. "Remarks by the President on the Affordable Care Act," White House, Office of the Press Secretary, 26 September 2013, https://obamawhitehouse.archives.gov/the-press-office/2013/09/26/remarks-president-affordable-care-act (accessed 23 September 2017).

9. David S. Hilzenrath, "Misleading Claims about Safeway Wellness Incentives Shape Health-Care Bill," *Washington Post*, 17 January 2010.

10. RAND Corporation, *Do Workplace Wellness Programs Save Employers Money?* (Santa Monica, CA: RAND, 2014). https://www.rand.org/content/dam/rand/pubs/research_briefs/RB9700/RB9744/RAND_RB9744.pdf.

11. Soeren Mattke et al., "Workplace Wellness Programs Study," *RAND Health Quarterly* 3, no. 2 (2013): 7. https://www.rand.org/pubs/periodicals/health-quarterly/issues/v3/n2/07.html (accessed 23 September 2017).

12. Beverly Beyette, "Author Lamott Addresses Humanity with Humor," *Los Angeles Times*, 6 October 2002.

13. Alterity is a joint venture of management consultants with expertise across benefits, HR, and finance for the private equity sector.

14. Alan Deutschman, "Change or Die," *Fast Company*, 1 May 2005, https://www.fastcompany.com/52717/change-or-die (accessed 23 September 2017).

15. Jones, Damon, et al. "What Do Workplace Wellness Programs Do? Evidence from the Illinois Workplace Wellness Study." University of Chicago and the University of Illinois, The Illinois Workplace Wellness Study, Jan. 2018, www.nber.org/workplacewellness/s/IL_Wellness_Study_1.pdf.

Chapter 8

1. "What Is Truly Human Leadership?" Bob Chapman's Truly Human Leadership, https://www.trulyhumanleadership.com?page_id=36.

2. T. Ore and V. Casini, "Electrical Fatalities among U.S. Construction Workers," *Journal of Occupational and Environmental Medicine* 38, no. 6 (June 1996): 587–592. https://www.ncbi.nlm.nih.gov/pubmed/8794957.

3. Rachel Druckenmiller, "Be. Belong. Become: A New Vision for the Workplace," LinkedIn, 7 September 2017, https://www.linkedin.com/pulse/belong-become-new-vision-workplace-rachel-druckenmiller-ms-cne/.

4. Dr. Anderson passed away in 2014 at the age of 68.

5. Hebrews 13:2, New International Version®, NIV®. Copyright © 1973, 1978, 1984, 2011 by Biblica, Inc.™ Used by permission of Zondervan. All rights reserved worldwide. www.zondervan.com. The "NIV" and "New International Version" are trademarks registered in the United States Patent and Trademark Office by Biblica, Inc.

6. Druckenmiller, "Be. Belong. Become."

7. *Joseph Campbell and the Power of Myth*, episode 1, "The Hero's Adventure," aired 21 June 1988, on PBS, http://billmoyers.com/content/ep-1-joseph-campbell-and-the-power-of-myth-the-hero%E2%80%99s-adventure-audio/.

8. "Remarks at the National Defense Executive Reserve Conference, November 14, 1957," *American Presidency Project*, http://www.presidency.ucsb.edu/ws/?pid=10951.

9. Conscious business.https://www.consciouscapitalism.org/

10. Benefit corporation. http://benefitcorp.net/

11. Servant leadership. . https://www.greenleaf.org/what-is-servant-leadership/

12. David Slocum, "5 Questions with Robert Kegan, Lisa Lahey and Andy Fleming on 'An Everyone Culture.'" *Forbes*, 23 April 2016, https://www.forbes.com/sites/

berlinschoolofcreativeleadership/2016/04/23/5-questions-with-robert-kegan-lisa-lahey-and-andy-fleming-on-ddos/#8b627b57eedb.

13. Bob Chapman and Raj Sisodia, *Everybody Matters: The Extraordinary Power of Caring for Your People Like Family* (New York: Portfolio Penguin, 2015).

Chapter 9

1. Salynn Boyles, "An Apple a Day May Really Keep the Doctor Away," WebMD, 21 June 2000, https://www.webmd.com/food-recipes/news/20000621/benefits-of-eating-fruit#1.

2. Stephen J. Dubner, "How to Launch a Behavior-Change Revolution," Freakonomics, 29 October 2017, freakonomics.com/podcast/launch-behavior-change-revolution/.

3. Lee Breslouer, "All 110 times Homer Simpson says, 'Mmm ...'" Thrillist, 13 November 2014, https://www.thrillist.com/eat/nation/every-time-homer-simpson-says-mmm-in-the-simpsons.

4. Dan Ariely, *Predictably Irrational: The Hidden Forces That Shape Our Decisions* (New York: Harper Perennial, 2010).

5. Behavioraleconomics.com, "Framing Effect," https://www.behavioraleconomics.com/mini-encyclopedia-of-be/framing-effect/.

6. James Nye, "Google Applies Data Wizards to Solve the Problem of Their Staff Eating Too Many Free M&Ms." *Daily Mail Online*, 3 September 2013, http://www.dailymail.co.uk/news/article-2410555/Googles-Project-M-M-applies-data-wizards-problem-staff-eating-free-sweets.html.

7. Stephen Morris, "Domino Chain Reaction," 4 October 2009, https://www.youtube.com/watch?v=y97rBdSYbkg.

8. Nadia Arumugam, "How Size and Color of Plates and Tablecloths Trick Us into Eating Too Much," *Forbes*, 26 January 2012, https://www.forbes.com/sites/nadiaarumugam/2012/01/26/how-size-and-color-of-plates-and-tablecloths-trick-us-into-eating-too-much/#3aeac0532fcf.

Chapter 10

1. Charles Montgomery, *Happy City: Transforming Our Lives Through Urban Design* (New York: Farrar, Straus and Giroux, 2013).

2. Tom Emerick; Rosie Ward, cofounder of Salveo Partners; Soeren Mattke with RAND; and Ryan Picarella, president of WELCOA, agree with him.

3. "Explore the Standard," International WELL Building Institute, 2 October 2017, https://www.wellcertified.com/en/explore-standard.

4. Fitwel, https://fitwel.org/system.

5. Living Building Challenge, https://living-future.org/lbc/

6. Blue Zones, https://bluezones.com/

7. *The Next Industrial Revolution*, directed by Christopher Bedford and Shelley Morhaim, Bullfrog Films, 2002. http://123movie.fm/watch/0v8137xw-the-next-industrial-revolution.html.

8. DPR recently completed their new Northern Virginia offices with WELL upgrades of less than 1%.

9. Rex Miller, Mabel Casey, and Mark Konchar. *Change Your Space, Change Your Culture: How Engaging Workspaces Lead to Transformation and Growth* (Hoboken, NJ: Wiley, 2014).

10. "The Well Building Standard," Delos, https://delos.com/services/programs/well-building-standard.

11. "Daylighting the New York Times Building," Lawrence Berkeley National Laboratory, facades.lbl.gov/newyorktimes/nyt_overview.html.

12. "Daylighting the New York Times Building.

Chapter 11

1. You can get a copy of the Team Health process and instructions to create your own dashboard at https://www.slideshare.net/mrexmiller/team-health-dashboard-sample.

2. James Gleick, "What Defines a Meme?" *Smithsonian Magazine*, May 2011, https://www.smithsonianmag.com/arts-culture/what-defines-a-meme-1904778/.

3. Richard Dawkins, *The Selfish Gene* (Oxford: Oxford University Press, 1976).

4. "Meme," Merriam-Webster Dictionary, https://www.merriam-webster.com/dictionary/meme.

5. The Bureau of Labor Statistics reports that cost of benefits for middle-income employees is approximately 31%. In the 1980s it was 3%. https://www.bls.gov/news.release/ecec.nr0.htm.

6. Kate Lister and Tom Harnish, *Work on the Move 2* (Houston: IFMA Foundation, 2016).

7. Rex Miller, Dean Strombom, Mark Lammarino, and Bill Black, *The Commercial Real Estate Revolution* (Hoboken, NJ: Wiley, 2009).

8. That is how we came up with the name of our process, MindShift. Although our group had dedicated two years to exploring alternatives to the old system, we had to walk through our own mind shift.

9. Lister and Harnish, *Work on the Move 2*.

10. The benefits described are part of The Cleveland Clinic's Tier 1 program. The entire benefit program is available at this link: https://clevelandclinic.org/total-rewards/mybenefits.clevelandclinic/documents/2018/2018-OH-Employee-Benefits-Summary.pdf

11. Scott Muldavin, Chris R. Miers, and Ken McMackin, "Buildings Emerge as Drivers of Health and Profits," *Corporate Real Estate Journal* 7, no. 2 (Winter 2017): 177–193.

Chapter 12

1. Drake Baer, "Why You Need to Unplug Every 90 Minutes," Fast Company, 28 May 2016, https://www.fastcompany.com/3013188/why-you-need-to-unplug-every-90-minutes.

2. "13 Essential 21st Century Skills for Todays Students," Envision, https://www.envisionexperience.com/blog/13-essential-21st-century-skills-for-todays-students.

3. Cal Newport, *Deep Work: Rules for Focused Success in a Distracted World* (New York: Grand Central, 2016).

4. Ibid.

5. Ibid.

Chapter 13

1. Roger L. Martin, "M&A: The One Thing You Need to Get Right." *Harvard Business Review*, June 2016, https://hbr.org/2016/06/ma-the-one-thing-you-need-to-get-right.

2. Bob Chapman and Raj Sisodia, *Everybody Matters: The Extraordinary Power of Caring for Your People Like Family* (New York: Portfolio-Penguin, 2015).

3. Peter Drucker, *The Effective Executive: The Definitive Guide to Getting the Right Things Done* (New York: Harper-Collins, 2006).

Chapter 14

1. Rex Miller, Bill Latham, and Brian Cahill, Humanizing the Education Machine: How to Create Schools That Turn Disengaged Kids into Inspired Learners (Hoboken, NJ: Wiley, 2017).

2. Tom Peters, Thriving on Chaos: Handbook for a Management Revolution (New York: Alfred A. Knopf, 1987).

3. Nohria, Nitin, and Michael Beer. "Cracking the Code of Change." Harvard Business Review, 13 July 2015, hbr.org/2000/05/cracking-the-code-of-change.

4. E.H. Schein, Organizational Culture and Leadership: A Dynamic View, 2nd ed. (San Francisco: Jossey-Bass, 1992).

5. ISS is a facility management service. As such it provides the full menu of facility support to clients: security, food services, cleaning, reception, guest services, etc.

6. Robert Kegan and Lisa Laskow Lahey, An Everyone Culture: Becoming a Deliberately Developmental Organization (Boston: Harvard Business Review Press, 2016).

7. Kim Cameron and Robert Quinn, Diagnosing and Changing Organizational Culture: Based on the Competing Values Framework, 3rd ed. (San Francisco: Jossey-Bass, 2011).

Chapter 15

1. Jocko Willink and Leif Babin, *Extreme Ownership: How U.S. Navy SEALS Lead and Win* (New York: St. Martin's, 2015).
2. Rex Miller, Mabel Casey, and Mark Konchar, *Change Your Space, Change Your Culture: How Engaging Workspaces Lead to Transformation and Growth* (Hoboken, NJ: Wiley, 2014).
3. Rex Miller, Bill Latham, and Brian Cahill, *Humanizing the Education Machine: How to Create Schools That Turn Disengaged Kids into Inspired Learners* (Hoboken, NJ: Wiley, 2017).

Chapter 16

1. Jeffrey Pfeffer, Dying for a Paycheck: How Modern Management Harms Employee Health and Company Performance—and What We Can Do About It (New York: HarperCollins, 2018); Bob Chapman and Raj Sisodia, Everybody Matters: The Extraordinary Power of Caring for Your People Like Family (New York: Portfolio-Penguin, 2015).
2. Nicholas A. Christakis and James H. Fowler, Connected: The Surprising Power of Our Social Networks and How They Shape Our Lives (New York: Little, Brown, 2009).
3. Rex Miller, Mabel Casey, and Mark Konchar, Change Your Space, Change Your Culture: How Engaging Workspaces Lead to Transformation and Growth (Hoboken, NJ: Wiley, 2014).

Chapter 17

1. The WELL Building Standard and Fitwel each provide clear roadmaps to evaluate your current space and plan a healthy design.
2. "The Next 250K Report," Leesman Index 2017, http://www.leesmanindex.com/250k_Report.pdf
3. Robert Kegan and Lisa Laskow Lahey, *An Everyone Culture: Becoming a Deliberately Developmental Organization* (Boston: Harvard Business Review Press, 2016).
4. Jen Arnold, "Your Wellness Questions Answered by Ryan Picarella, President of WELCOA." November 15, 2017, http://redesigningwellness.com/2017/11/070-wellness-questions-answered-ryan-picarella-president-welcoa/

INDEX